AMERICAN
— CAR —
SPOTTER'S GUIDE
1981 - 1990

Tad Burness

Motorbooks International
Publishers & Wholesalers ®

First published in 1990 by Motorbooks International Publishers & Wholesalers, P O Box 2, 729 Prospect Avenue, Osceola, WI 54020 USA

Motorbooks International books are also available at discounts in bulk quantity for industrial or sales-promotional use. For details write to Special Sales Manager at the Publisher's address

Library of Congress Cataloging-in-Publication Data
Burness, Tad.
    American car spotter's guide, 1981-90 / Tad Burness.
        p.   cm.
    ISBN 0-87938-428-X
    1. Automobiles—United States.   2. Automobiles—United States—Pictorial works.   3. Automobiles—United States—Identification.   I. Title.
TL23.B78 1990   90-5646
629.222'0973—dc20   CIP

On the cover: The 1988 Corvette convertible in traditional red with white softtop owned by Jess D. Price of Gladstone, Missouri. *Jerry Heasley*

Printed and bound in the United States of America

Contents

AMC
(pages 7-15)
Alliance (1983-87)
pages 7-9

Concord (1982-83)
page 11

Eagle (1981-88)
pages 12-13

Spirit (1981-83)
pages 14-15

Acknowledgments

For many years, I've collected ads and brochures for both new and old motor vehicles; but no accumulation is ever complete! Graciously, several individuals and organizations provided additional pictures and details which were helpful for this new book.

First of all, I'd like to thank my wife, Sandy, and daughter, Tammy, for their patience and encouragement while I was engrossed in the preparation of this project! And I'm grateful to my mother, Wallea B. Draper, and to my sister, Nina Taylor, for their kindness in providing some much-needed brochures and pictures.

Special thanks, also, to Elliott Kahn, Alden C. Jewell and Bruce Gilbert for items they generously shared from their collections! They managed to find certain hard-to-get pieces which helped make this book more complete.

Also, I'm grateful to the following, for additional details:

American Motors Corporation
Jeff Anderson
Automotive Fleet
Avanti Automotive Corporation
Jack "Curly" Baker
Rob Bilott
Bremen Motor Corporation
Buick Club of America
California Vehicle Foundation
Chrysler Corporation (Chrysler-Plymouth Division; Dodge Divison; Jeep-Eagle Division)
Classic Motor Carriages
Grant A. Cole
Elegant Motors, Inc.
Fiberfab
Ford Motor Company (Ford Division, Lincoln-Mercury Division)
General Motors Corporation (Buick, Cadillac, Chevrolet, Oldsmobile and Pontiac Divisions)
Allan Gutcher
Arthur and Martha Herring
Larry Hill
Lawrence C. Holian
John Lloyd
Alberto and Daisy Lowenstein
Model A & Model T Motor Car Reproduction Corporation (SHAY)
Plaza Chrysler-Plymouth
Marjorie Reither
Renault/Jeep Corporation
Don Snyder
Bryon Stappler
Calvin Steimetz
Jim and Wanda Van Nortwick
R. A. Wawrzyniak
Ken Wilson
W.P.C. Club (Chrysler Product Restorers)

Introduction

Thank you for your interest! I hope you'll enjoy browsing through *American Car Spotter's Guide 1981-1990* again and again . . . and that it will help to familiarize you with these recent models.

Cars, trucks and buses from the 1920s to the early 1980s are covered in other Spotter's Guides in this series. And if you have the giant-sized, 1,075 page *Monstrous American Car Spotter's Guide 1920-1980* you've probably been waiting for a new volume to pick up where that one left off. Now it's here, for you!

This new book covers American cars and "captive imports" (foreign-made with American brand names) from 1981 to 1990 inclusive. You'll notice a growing foreign influence in American car design, between the early 1980s and 1990, as reflected in the illustrations. Some may complain that "all cars look alike these days," but if you study this book you'll see *many* differences! This book will help to clarify those differences, and the various features that distinguish one model from another.

Shopping for a used American car? This handy volume can be of great help, as you put it to use! And in a few years, these pictures and specifications will be helpful still, as the cars of 1981 to 1990 gain new interest and status as "collectibles."

In past decades—especially before the 1960s—it was much easier to identify cars. There were fewer variations. A Ford was a Ford, a Chevy a Chevy, and there were no great proliferations of "sub-makes" as there are now. For example, the Chevrolet Beretta, Camaro, Cavalier, Corsica, Corvette and so forth . . . each with its own particular purpose and style!

Moreover, there used to be distinct annual model changes. In late September or early October, the following year's models would be ready. At that time, local car dealerships would be dazzlingly illuminated on new-model night. In a yearly ritual, the spectacular new models were unveiled to eager crowds!

Lately, there's been less and less of the annual hoopla, as each company seeks to slip a new model into one of its many series, every few months or weeks—to keep abreast of the competition.

The addition of new or extra models, at odd times of the year, makes it more difficult to pinpoint annual changes. Example: Is a certain model, introduced in early 1987, to be considered a "1987," "1987½" or "1988" model? That depends on what its manufacturer designates. And sometimes the manufacturer doesn't clearly specify the year model!

American Car Spotter's Guide 1981-1990 helps you to visually pinpoint the various clues to model years and model changes. And in most cases, VINs (vehicle identification numbers) are also listed; in certain instances, they may be the only positive way to identify a specific year model of car that didn't change for two, three or more years!

The cars of the 1980s are more interesting than you may have previously thought! "Muscle cars" have made a comeback, since the early 1980s, and so have convertibles. And luxury cars have abounded. You'll find "delectable collectibles" on many pages, and these cars should be in ever-growing demand as time moves on.

For those who may not be familiar with every automotive term used on these pages, may I quickly explain that WB (wheelbase) is the distance (length) between the center of the front axle and the center of the rear axle. MPG means miles per gallon of fuel (and figures quoted are, for the most part, official EPA ratings. In some cases, differing California figures are also listed.)

HP (horsepower) is the actual brake or net horsepower of a car (with engine and transmission connected.) CID stands for cubic inch displacement of the engine, and L stands for liters. MPH equals miles per hour (top speed).

What about the prices listed? These are West Coast prices. In some advertisements, lower prices were sometimes quoted; either for the Midwest or for special sales which lasted for a limited time only. The actual prices paid for cars could vary, depending on region of the country, and the dealer's individual markup. But I've attempted to record the price that the coast-to-coast majority of buyers would pay—without optional "extras," or added taxes, license fees, delivery charges and so on, which could often add an extra ten to twenty-five percent, or even more!

Space limits here prevent the inclusion of kit cars, custom applications, limousine conversions and "stretch" models, oddballs, neo-classics, replicars and other limited-production "specials" of the 1980s. Likewise, the European and Asian cars (assembled either abroad or within the United States of America).

You'll notice a growing influence of foreign design, as you compare the cars of the early 1980s with the more recent models: more "blackout trim" instead of brightwork, more bare wheels of odd designs, and less of the prosperous-appearing, typical "American look" as found on most pre–1980 cars.

Dull colors can be boring. Flat-finish black plastic can never equal the bright beauty of chrome trim and decorative woodgrain. And brutish-looking wedge-shaped bombers can't compare to the "classic" American look, as far as this writer is concerned.

Designs tend to run in cycles. What's "out" today should be back "in," eventually. Take wristwatches, for example: just a few years ago, everything was going "digital" (including *car clocks* of the early 1980s.) But now the analog dial has made a comeback.

Traveling with others who like cars? You might bring this handy book along so they can "check out" a few models they may "spot" along the way.

And, as mentioned earlier, when you shop the classifieds for a late-model American car, this book will *show* you what's listed in those columns. In a short time, most of these models will be advertised as "collector's cars."

I hope this guide will be a continuing source of interest and information!

Tad Burness
Pacific Grove, California

American Motors / ◆ RENAULT

ALLIANCE.

(AVAIL. 1983 TO 1987)

Built in America. **NEW**

SPECIAL ADV. PRICE = **$5595***

ALLIANCE

96-0 STD. 2 DR. (REG. $6409.)

52 est. hwy.* / **37** est. EPA MPG

83

56 HP 4 CYL. 85.3 CID 97.8" WB

155/80GR13 TIRES (175/70SR x 13 ON DL, MT, LTD.)

Alliance DL 4-door

95-6

Motor Trend experts name Alliance 1983 Car of the Year.

AVAIL. IN THE FOLLOWING MODEL SERIES = (9TD.) ABOVE, RT. L — $6834. UP DL — 7469. UP LTD. 4 DR.= $8284. MT — $8087 UP

ELECTRONIC FUEL INJECTION, TWIN AXIAL REAR TORSION BARS, FOUR-WHEEL INDEPENDENT SUSPENSION

Alliance DL

DL 4 DR. ↑ $7719.

ALLIANCE SIMILAR TO RENAULT "9"

Designed in Europe, built in America. To last.

V.I.N. START WITH 1AMAC 9

REAR QUARTER CLOSE-UP

2.97 GR (MANUAL TR.)

3.27 GR (AUTO. TR.)

12½ GAL. FUEL TANK

$5,959† (REG. $6826.)

Alliance 2-door

V.I.N. START WITH 1XMDC 9 — XEX

DL 4-DR. $8051.

↙ 95-6

84

OTHER MODELS = L 2 DR.-$7248. L 4 DR.- 7498. DL 2 DR.- 7751. LTD. 4 DR.- $8713. (new)

new DECK-LID LUGGAGE-RACK; IMPROVED RADIO. 3 new COLORS. ADDITIONAL LEATHER SEAT COLOR.

(MT NO LONGER LISTED)

ENCORE S $7126. UP " LS 7659. UP " GS 8211.

New

52 EST HWY, **38** EPA EST MPG**

American Motors *and*

RENAULT
THE ONE TO WATCH ◆

↑ new HATCHBACK VERSION IS KNOWN AS THE

$6600. 930 (STD.)

ENCORE

5-DR. ALSO, IN S AND LS ENCORE SER.

7

Alliance DL.
4-DR. 956
$8067.

American Motors ALLIANCE

Renault Alliance. Born in Europe... Raised in America.

NEW
Convertible

The Convertible Alliance — The First AMC Soft-top since the 1968 Rambler Rebel.

4 CYL. ENGINE

AS BEFORE, THE DIAMOND-SHAPED RENAULT EMBLEM APPEARS ON GRILLE.

V.I.N. = 1XMDC9 — XFX #

85

CVT. IS new, AVAIL. IN 2 SERIES:
973 L = $11,001.
976 DL = 12,001.

"DL" has 5-SP. TRANS. and FUEL INJECTED 1.4-LIT. 4 CYL. ENG.

Renault Alliance Limited fully adjustable rocker/recliner bucket seats are trimmed in luxury Pin Dot fabric in Almond or Garnet. Honey leather trim is available.

105 CID 4 has 77 HP @ 5000 RPM

3.56 GEAR RATIO

INTERIOR (LTD.)

"L" 2 DR.
$7317.
963

(ENCORE HATCHBACKS ALSO AVAIL.
$6386. 8293.)

LTD.
$8567.
958

STD. WHEEL

LIMITED (LTD.) ONLY AVAILABLE AS A 4 DR. SEDAN.

The new more powerful 1.7L engine, standard on Alliance Limited and Convertibles and available on all other models, except base, utilizes closed loop, electronic fuel injection

Renault Alliance Limited. The Most Elegant Alliance.

8

Alliance

Fog lamps are available on all Alliance models.

SUNROOF (OPT.)

DC956

DL 4 DR.
$7360. →

('86 ½)

SPEC. PRICE, 7-86
(REG. $7927 ~ 8645.)

IMPROVED MPG IN 1986
41 MPG HWY 35 CITY
12½ GALLON FUEL TANK

3 SPEED AUTO. TRANS. AVAIL.
(W. 3.56 TO 1 GEAR RATIO)

ENCORE
DISCONTINUED
DURING
1986
MODEL
YEAR.
(REPLACED BY
1987 GTA
2 DR. SED.
$9364.
CONVERTIBLE
$13264.)

RPM X100

TACH.
STD. ON DL
and LTD.
OPTIONAL ON
L SERIES.

A Keyless Entry System uses coded infrared lightwaves to remotely operate door lock mechanisms. It's available on Alliance L, DL and Limited models.

86-

CHRYSLER CORP.
BUYS CONTROLLING
INTEREST IN AMC
FROM RENAULT,
AS OF MARCH,
1987.

87

5/50 PROTECTION

1987
ALLIANCE MPG
(W. AUTO. TRANS.):
27/31 (85 CID 4)
24/29 (105 CID 4)

ALLIANCE PRICE RANGES:
7058.-12001. ('85)
6759.-12284.
('86)
7219.-
12844.
('87)

Encore

3 DR. or
5 DR.
AVAIL.

V.I.N. ══
1XM (DC 930) - F - # (1985)
1XM (DC 933) - G - # (1986)
1XM (DC 960) H # (1987)
GTA, ALLIANCE
BOTH DISCONT'D.
DURING
1987.

BLACK
LEATHER WRAP.
STEERING WHEEL
(OPT.; STD. ON DL CVT.)

('86)

$7377-8535.
(FINAL 1986
ENCORE)

Electronic DASH WITH
LCD (LIQUID CRYSTAL DISPLAY) INSTRUMENTATION

Power door locks and windows (front windows only on sedans) may be ordered on Alliance DL, Limited and Convertibles.

ALLIANCE DL ↗

By the autumn of 1987, the entire AMC car line was renamed Eagle, and American Motors itself became the Jeep/Eagle division of Chrysler Corporation.

Concord

EPA MILEAGE VARIES FROM 19 CITY, 26 HWY.
TO 23 CITY, 34 HWY., DEPENDING ON ENG.
AND TRANS.
USED.

(SINCE 1978)

VEHICLE I.D. NUMBERS START WITH
STD. = 1AMBM 060 —
DL = 1AMBA 0650B —
LTD. = 1AMBA 0670B —

Custom wheel cover
standard base

Full styled wheel cover
(stainless steel)
standard Concord DL

INTERIOR

81
new GRILLE

Turbocast II
aluminum wheels
optional all models

Wire wheel cover
standard Concord Limited

06-7

LTD. 2 DR. **8347.**
(LIMITED)

WITH
**Ziebart Factory Rust Protection and Full Five (5) Year
Perforation from Corrosion Warranty**

151 CID 4
OR 258 CID 6

108" WB

3.08 GR
w. 4 CYL.;
2.37, 2.53
OR 2.73
w. 6.
CYL.
22-G.
FUEL
TANK

**CONCORD
SEDAN**

05-5

DL
4 DR.
$ **8025.**

DL

(LOWEST-PRICED MODEL IS
STD. 2-DR. CONCORD, AT $7501.)

REAR HATCH OF
WAGON

P195/75R14
TIRES

08-5

WAGON
INTERIOR

DL
WAGON $**8242.**

10

In June 1981, it was announced that Renault would now handle all car design for
American Motors. AMC engineers would work only on Jeep and Eagle designs.

Concord

24 MPG (EPA) WAGON

DL WAGONS FROM $9466. (GRAINED AVAIL. ALSO)

25 MPG (EPA) SEDAN

22 GAL. FUEL TANK

LTD. 2-DR. $9217. 06-7

STARTING V.I.N.
STD. -0 IACBM060-
DL. -5 IAMBM065-
LTD. -7 IAMBM067-

82

DL

TILT STEERING WHEEL

AVAIL. WHEEL and COVER STYLES

Custom Wheel Cover — Std. Spirit/ Concord Base.

Full Styled Wheel Cover — Std. Concord DL. Opt. Concord Base.

Styled Wheel Cover (Noryl) — Opt. Spirit/Concord Base; Concord DL.

Spoke Style Wheels — Std. Spirit G.T. Pkg. Opt. other Spirit/ Concord.

Turbocast II Aluminum Wheels — Opt. all Spirit/Concord.

Wire Wheel Cover — Std. Concord Limited. Opt. all other Spirit/ Concord.

FULL VINYL ROOF	STANDARD
4.2-LITER 6-CYLINDER ENGINE	STANDARD
INDIVIDUAL RECLINING SEATS	STANDARD
QUARTZ DIGITAL CLOCK	STANDARD
DELUXE BODYSIDE MOLDING	STANDARD
WHITE SIDEWALL RADIAL TIRES	STANDARD
WIRE WHEELCOVERS	STANDARD
DELUXE EXTERIOR TRIM	STANDARD
FRONT AND REAR BUMPER GUARDS	STANDARD
REMOTE CONTROL EXTERIOR MIRROR	STANDARD
EXTRA-QUIET SOUND INSULATION PACKAGE	STANDARD
WOODGRAIN INSTRUMENT PANEL	STANDARD
EXCLUSIVE BUYER PROTECTION PLAN®	STANDARD
FULL 5-YEAR NO RUST-THRU WARRANTY™	STANDARD
ZIEBART® FACTORY RUST PROTECTION	STANDARD
PRICE	$6995

AVAILABLE AT OVER 1500 AMERICAN MOTORS DEALERS NATIONWIDE.

*LIST PRICE EXCLUDING TAX, LICENSE, DESTINATION CHARGES, AND OTHER OPTIONAL OR REGIONAL EQUIPMENT EXTRA. SEE YOUR DEALER FOR WARRANTY AND RUST PROGRAM DETAILS.
Ziebart is a registered trademark of Ziebart International Corporation.

258 CID 6 CYL. IS ONLY ENGINE AVAILABLE IN 1983 CONCORDS. NO 2-DR. MODELS.

TRUST THE TOUGH AMERICANS TO BUILD IN VALUE. AMERICAN MOTORS

CONCORD DL
$6995.*
(REG $8823.)
*=SPECIAL PRICE

83

FINAL CONCORD MODELS (WAGON IS ONLY LTD MODEL FOR 1983.)

(1983 V.I.N. START W. IAMCA)

11

SAFETY IS A SNAP

AMERICAN MOTORS CORPORATION
EAGLE
SINCE 1980

Eagle SX/4 NEW
(97.2" WB)

81 new GRILLE
53-0 or 53-5 (50) (DL)

56-5 DL
New Kammback
$7997.

50, DL, 30 OR LTD MODELS, WITH PRICES RANGING FROM $7477. TO $10,330.

LTD 2-DR. $9780.

151 CID 4 or 258 CID 6

P195/75R 15 TIRES

Sedans
(109.3" WB)

30 4 DR. STD. $9633.

(97.2" WB)

CAN BE OPERATED ON 2 OR 4 WHEEL DRIVE.

V.I.N.= IAMBC — (B) (—) 000001 UP

2 WD   4 WD
STOP VEHICLE — PULL — ENGAGE

INTRODUCING SELECT DRIVE. THE MOST ADVANCED DRIVETRAIN SYSTEM IN THE WORLD.

WAGON 109.3" WB

OPT. GAUGE PACKAGE AND T-BAR AUTOMATIC SHIFT LEVER

MPG (4 CYL.)
22 / 29
EST MPG   EST HWY

Eagle Wagon

(30 WAGON AVAIL. W. BLACK GRILLE, SPORT TRIM)

American Motors

Experience driving in the 4th Dimension.
12

Handwritten left margin: After being on the market since 1980 with a body style that dated back to the autumn of 1969, production of the Eagle station wagon, last of the cars that can be considered AMC models, ended on December 14th 1987. It was the last model of the last series of the last independent.

Handwritten bottom: The Eagle was the first major four-wheel-drive passenger car produced in America in modern times. It was also the first 4WD model to be built in volume with independent front suspension.

AMC

EAGLE
FROM AMERICAN MOTORS

$10388.
UP
'82
4
DR.

1982 V.I.N. = 1AMBH (360) (-) CK000001 UP

22 GAL. GAS TANK

4-DR.
(AVAIL.
UNTIL
1987)
FINAL USE OF GM-BLT.
2.5L 4 IN 1983

2-DR. SEDAN DISCONTINUED
AFTER 1982; SX/4 D/SC. AFTER '83.

(1982 EXAMPLES ILLUSTRATED)

1982 SX/4
FR. $9030.

21 GAL.
GAS TANK
(SX/4 OR
KAMMBACK)

SX/4

1983
V.I.N. = 1AMCA (350) XD (-) 000001
UP

82-84

4 OR 6 CYL.
new AMC-BLT. 2.5L 4

1984 V.I.N. = 1ACCK
(355) XEX
000001 UP

INTERIOR

KAMMBACK (ABOVE) DISCONTINUED
AFTER 1982.   FROM **$8378.**

32	(23)

(ALL EAGLES)
2.73 GEAR RATIO
('85)

2-WHEEL/4-WHEEL DRIVE

WAGON ADOPTS THE
STRAIGHT-ACROSS GRILLE
(AS ILLUSTRATED BELOW)

1982
WAG.
FROM
$11235.

22 GAL. GAS
TANK

23 MPG (EPA)

258 CID 6 IS ONLY
AVAIL. ENGINE
(115 HP @ 3200 RPM)

EARLY

85-88

1985 WAGON
$12,872.

EARLY '88 WAGON
$13,417.

V.I.N. INCLUDES   F (1985)
G (1986)
H (1987)
J (EARLY '88)

P195/
75 R15
TIRES

22 GAL.
FUEL TK.   ('85)

WAGON IS THE ONLY MODEL IN
EARLY '88 LINE. CHRYSLER CORP.
BUYS AMC FROM RENAULT. FOR
'88-90 CHRYSLER BLT. MODELS,
SEE "EAGLE."

13

AMC nameplate de-emphasized in 1985.

In 1984 a deal was finally agreed on whereby the Republic of China and AMC would jointly build Jeeps for the Chinese market and eventually for export to other Asian markets, including Japan. The new company, named Beijing Jeep would build the new Cherokee from kits, taking advantage of China's 60 cents per low wages.

AMERICAN MOTORS

SPIRIT

(1979 TO 1983)

REPLACES GREMLIN

V.I.N.
STD.= I (A)M (B) M 4 (5) 0 (-) B (-) —
DL = I AMBM 455 XB (-) 000001 UP

DASH (WITH OPTIONAL EQUIPMENT)

23/33 EPA EST MPG / EST HWY*

DL LIFTBACK $6079.

43-5

Standard

43-0

81

new GRILLE

Full styled wheel cover (Noryl) standard Spirit DL

"DELUXE GRAIN" VINYL SEAT (DL)

Spoke styled wheels standard Spirit G.T.

STD. SPIRIT LIFTBACK $5772.

COVENTRY CHECK VINYL-AND-FABRIC UPHOLST. PATTERN

ONLY CAR BUILT IN AMERICA WITH 100% EXTERIOR BODY PANELS OF GALVANIZED STEEL.

96" WB 151 CID 4 OR 258 CID 6

G.T. LIFTBACK (WITH BLACKED-OUT CENTER PILLARS, ETC.)

21-GALLON FUEL TANK

P185/75 R14 TIRES

Inside Spirit

STD. DASH

DL SEDAN $5979.

GREMLIN ANCESTRY EVIDENT, IN THIS BODY TYPE.

46-5

BUILT TO LAST

14

$6648.
DL
43-5

AMERICAN MOTORS SPIRIT

SPIRIT LIFTBACK

note "SPOILER" with GT PACKAGE (new)

46-0

STD. SPIRIT SEDAN
$6165.

82

V.I.N. STARTS WITH 1ACBM

GRILLE CLOSE-UP →

37 HWY EST. | 25 EPA EST. MPG

5-SP. TRANS., GAUGE PACKAGE OPTION ←

POP-UP SUNROOF (OPT.)

21 MPG EPA

DL LIFTBACK IS ONLY OTHER 1983 MODEL ($6765.)
43-5

AND STANDARD FEATURES.

4.2-LITER 6-CYLINDER ENGINE	STANDARD
HALOGEN FOG LAMPS	STANDARD
TURBOCAST II ALUMINUM WHEELS	STANDARD
ARRIVA STEEL BELTED RADIALS	STANDARD
TACHOMETER	STANDARD
RALLY GAUGES—OIL PRESSURE, AMPERE, VACUUM	STANDARD
LEFT AND RIGHT REMOTE SPORT MIRRORS	STANDARD
FRONT AND REAR SWAY BARS	STANDARD
SPORT LEATHER-WRAPPED STEERING WHEEL	STANDARD
ELECTRIC CLOCK	STANDARD
FULL CENTER SHIFT CONSOLE WITH ARMREST	STANDARD
RECLINING BUCKET SEATS	STANDARD
SPLIT FOLDING REAR SEAT	STANDARD
FRONT AND REAR BUMPER GUARDS AND NERF STRIPS	STANDARD
BLACKOUT G.T. APPEARANCE PACKAGE	STANDARD
EXCLUSIVE BUYER PROTECTION PLAN®	STANDARD
FULL 5-YEAR NO RUST-THRU WARRANTY**	STANDARD
ZIEBART® FACTORY RUST PROTECTION	STANDARD
PRICE	$6495

AVAILABLE AT OVER 1500 AMERICAN MOTORS DEALERS NATIONWIDE.

*LIST PRICE EXCLUDING TAX, LICENSE, DESTINATION CHARGES, AND OTHER OPTIONAL OR REGIONAL EQUIPMENT EXTRA. SEE YOUR DEALER FOR WARRANTY AND RUST PROGRAM DETAILS.
Ziebart is a registered trademark of Ziebart International Corporation.

GT DASH (GT NOW A SERIES)

V.I.N. STARTS WITH 1AMCA ENDS WITH XD (-) 000001 UP

83 NEW

GT IS

TRUST THE TOUGH AMERICANS TO BUILD IN VALUE.

AMERICAN MOTORS

258 CID 6 IS ONLY ENGINE OFFERED IN 1983.

(SPIRIT DISCONTINUED 1983) 15

43-9 LIFTBACK

SPIRIT G.T.

$6495.* | *REG. $7347.

(SINCE 1903)
A GM PRODUCT SINCE 1908

GM MARK OF EXCELLENCE

BUICK

WOULDN'T YOU REALLY RATHER HAVE A BUICK?

(SKYHAWK NOT AVAIL. 1981)
SKYLARK SEDANS
$7958. UP

SKYLARK CPES. $7812. UP

SKYLARK

SPORT COUPE
4D37
$8446.

SKYLARK HAS
104.9" WB,
FRONT-WHEEL
DRIVE,
151 CID 4
(90 HP)
OR
173 CID V6
(115 HP)
P185/80R13 TIRES
(P205/70R13 ON
SPT.)

V.I.N. STARTS WITH 1G4(-) —
ENDS WITH -B- #

81

↑ note SPORT MODEL HAS DIFFERENT GRILLE.

REAR DOOR POWER VENT WINDOW OPT.

SPT. SEDAN ALSO AVAIL.

CENTURY DASH

CENTURY HAS
231 CID V6 (110 HP)
OR 265 CID V8
(119 HP)

108.1" WB CENTURY

CENTURY LIMITED

AVAIL. IN RIVIERA = TRIP MONITOR

CENTURY WAGONS AVAIL.

4L69 $9037.

16

BUICK

Wouldn't you really rather have a Buick?

T-BAR ROOF OPTION

VOLTMETER OPT.

108.1" WB **REGAL** (COUPES ONLY)
231 CID V6 (110 HP) OR 265 CID V8 (119 HP)

REGAL DASH

4J47 REGAL CPE. $8593.
4M47 LTD. CPE. 9062.
4K47 TURBO SPT. COUPE 9565.

81

3.8 L (231 CID) TURBO V6 (170 HP) AVAIL. IN REGAL SPT. CPE.

REGAL

AVAILABLE COACH LAMPS AND LANDAU TOP

REGAL LTD.

LE SABRE 4N37 CPE. $8864.

LE SABRE

231 CID V6 (110 HP) 28/19 MPG
252 " (125 HP, NEW AUTO. O.D. TRANS.) 29/18 MPG

4N69 SEDAN $8954.

4P37 LTD CPE. $9115.
4P69 LTD. SED. $9250.

IN BACKGROUND = 1878 VICTORIAN GREENHOUSES IN GOLDEN GATE PARK, SAN FRANCISCO

115.9" WB (AL90 307 CID V8, 150 HP) OR 350 CID DIESEL V8 (105 HP)

LE SABRE DASH

The 1981 Buick LeSabre.

P205/75R15 TIRES (LE SABRE)

ELECTRA

4W69 ELECT. PARK AVENUE SEDAN $12,203.

4X69 ELECTRA LTD. $11,353.

ELECTRA

118.9" WB

105 HP, 350 CID DIESEL V8 AVAIL.; STD. 307 CID V8 (150 HP)

Electra

LTD. and PK. AVE. COUPES AVAILABLE

17

P225/75R x15 TIRES

BUICK 81

WAGON HAS OWN 116" WB

$12,441. UP

4V35
ELECTRA ESTATE WAGON

TAIL-GATE SWINGS SIDE-WAYS OR DOWN.

ELECTRA WAGON V.I.N. = 1G4A V35 Y0B (-) 10001 UP

Electra

RIVIERA

V.I.N. = 1G4AZ5730 B (-) 10001 UP

RIVIERA ROOFLINES

T TYPE ROOF

114" WB
105-180 HP

LANDAU ROOF OPTION FORMAL

RIVIERA DASH

Engine Riviera: • Standard 4.1 liter V-6 • Available 3.8 liter turbocharged V-6 (N.A. California) • Available 5.0 liter V-8 • Available 5.7 liter diesel V-8   T TYPE: • Standard 3.8 liter turbocharged V-6 (N.A. California) • Available 4.1 liter V-6 • Available 5.0 liter V-8 (Buicks are equipped with GM-built engines supplied by various divisions. See your dealer for details.) • **Chassis** Standard: • Front-wheel drive • Power steering • Power front disc/rear drum brakes • Four-wheel independent suspension • Front torsion bars, rear coil springs • Automatic level control • Gran Touring suspension (T TYPE) Available: • Four-wheel disc brakes • Firm ride-and-handling (Riviera) • Gran Touring suspension (Riviera) • **Comfort and Convenience** Standard: • 45/45 notchback seats with fold-down center armrest on driver's side (Riviera) • Cloth bucket seats (T TYPE) • 6-way power seat, driver's side • Door courtesy and warning lights • Storage console (T TYPE) • Side-window defroster outlets • Quartz-crystal-controlled digital clock • Soft-Ray tinted glass • Power windows • AM-FM stereo radio (delete radio option available) • Lights: front ashtray, under-dash, courtesy, glove compartment, engine compartment, luggage compartment • Electric door locks • Automatic power antenna • Air conditioner • Trip odometer • Remote-control, outside left- and right-hand rearview mirrors • Headlamps "on" indicator • Cornering lights • Tungsten-halogen, high-beam headlights (T TYPE)   Available: • Luggage compartment protective floor mat • Front and rear carpet savers with inserts • Exterior coach lamps (included with vinyl tops) • Door-edge guards • Color-coordinated, protective body-side moldings • Sunroof—electric operation • Astroroof—electric sliding glass (Headroom is reduced slightly with either option) • Heavily padded Landau top with coach lamps • Electric fuel cap lock (not available with diesel engine) • Custom locking wire wheel covers • Chrome-plated road wheels (4) • Theft-deterrent system with starter interrupt • Leather-trimmed seats (in seatbacks and seating areas) • 6-way power seat, passenger side • Reclining electric seatback, passenger side • Reclining electric seatback, driver's side • Reclining manual seatback, passenger side (T TYPE) • Tilt steering column • Tilt and telescoping steering column (Riviera) • Automatic electric door locks • Electric trunk lock release • Electric trunk lock • Front and rear light monitors • Lighted visor vanity mirrors • Rear quarter courtesy and reading lamps • Two-speed wiper with low-speed delay feature • Tungsten-halogen, high-beam headlights (Riviera) • Extended-range speakers • Concert Sound speaker system • ETR AM-FM stereo radio • 8-track tape player with AM-FM stereo radio • 8-track tape player with ETR AM-FM stereo radio • Cassette tape player and ETR AM-FM stereo radio • Cassette tape player with AM-FM stereo radio • CB and AM-FM stereo radio with Triband power antenna • CB, 8-track tape player and ETR AM-FM stereo radio with Triband power antenna • Full-feature AM-FM stereo radio • Cassette tape player and Full-feature AM-FM stereo radio • 8-track tape player and Full-feature AM-FM stereo radio • Electronic Touch Climate Control air conditioner • Electric rear-window defogger • Cruise-Master speed control with resume-speed feature • Fuel usage light • Low fuel indicator • Trip monitor • Illuminated door lock and interior light control • Twilight Sentinel headlamp control • Electrically operated, outside rearview mirrors • ... ...-fluid indicator • **Appearance and Protection** Standard: • A... ... T TYPE) • Front and rear bumper guards • Bumper-prote... ...ld wipers • Sport steering wheel (T TYPE) • ... ... "Designers' Sport wh... ... belts • Dual ... ...ont and re... ...xe wheel ... ...el (Rivie...

RIVIERA FEATURES AND OPTIONS LISTED ABOVE.
T TYPE V.I.N. = 1G4A Y5730 B (-) 10001 UP

$12,821.   **The 1981 Riviera.**

T TYPE = $13,765.

$8817. UP

New
SKYHAWK
RETURNS.
(PREVIOUSLY
AVAILABLE
1975 — 1980.)

SKYHAWK DASH

101.2" WB
112, 122
CID 4

CUSTOM
or LTD
CPE9.,
SEDANS

AVAILABLE
SUNROOF

23 MPG
(EPA)

CENTER BACK-UP LTS.   P175/80R13 TIRES
13.6 GAL.
FUEL TK.

82

V.I.N. =
1G4A1 (   )
- C - 000001
UP

T27 SKYHAWK LTD. CPE.

$9259.

173 CID V6 (115 HP)

SKYLARK

(ALSO
A
151 CID
4 (90 HP)
14½ GALLON
FUEL TANK

41 EST. HWY.	26 EPA EST. MPG

2.8 liter High Output V-6.

104.9" WB

SKYLARK,
SPT., LTD.
COUPES and
SEDANS,
FROM
$9028.
TO 9769.

Skylark Limited notchback seat.

VXG 185

Buick Skylark.

Buick

2.5 Liter L4
40 Hwy. Est. / **25** EPA Est. mpg

New CENTURY CUSTOM COUPE 4H27

CENTURY

$10054.

V6 (3.8L)

15½ GAL. FUEL TK. 25 MPG (EPA)

82

new OPT.

4.3 liter diesel V-6.

REGAL DASH

Regal Estate Wagon instrument panel with available equipment.

1982 Regal Sedan
HAS OWN GRILLE

18.1 GAL. FUEL TK.

NEW

REGAL FROM $9885.

108.1" WB

30 EST. HWY. / **21** EPA EST. MPG

4P37 LE SABRE LIMITED CPE. $10431.

(REGAL ESTATE WAGON AVAIL., AT $10,231. 4J35)

LeSabre Limited Coupe

LE SABRE

115.9" WB

ELEC. LTD. $12,738.

$14,044.
4W69

25 GAL. FUEL TANK

ELECTRA
118.9" WB

4N69

CUSTOM SED. $10,130.

28 EST. HWY. / **19** EPA EST. MPG

ELECT. PK. AVE. CPE $13,893. 4W37

ELECTRA PARK AVE. SEDAN

RIVIERA (new CVT. ALSO)

Coupe.

Electra Estate Wagon

ELECTRA DASH (LESAB. SIMILAR, BUT WITH BOOMERANG-SHAPED STEERING-WHEEL HUB.)

16 MPG (EPA) 22 GAL. FUEL TK. (WAGON)

(GRILLE SIMILAR TO THAT OF 1981 MODEL)

21 GAL. FUEL TANK

20

RIVIERA
15,868. UP

Z67 RIVIERA CVT. $25590. ←

BUICK
Wouldn't you really rather have a Buick?

ELECTRA
$13,973. UP
18/29 MPG (V6)

LESABRE
$10,604. UP

		EST. HWY. MPG	EPA EST. MPG	EST. HWY RANGE	EST. DRIVING RANGE	FUEL TANK CAPACITY
BUICK SKYHAWK	1.8 Liter L-4#	46	28	625	380	13.6
BUICK SKYLARK	2.5 Liter L-4	42	27	613	394	14.6
BUICK CENTURY	2.5 Liter L-4	39	24	612	377	15.7
	4.3 Liter Diesel V-6#†*	44	27	730	448	16.6
BUICK REGAL	3.8 Liter V-6*	30	21	543	380	18.1
	3.8 Liter Turbo V-6	29	18	525	326	18.1
	4.3 Liter Diesel V-6#†*	36	25	712	495	19.8
BUICK LESABRE	3.8 Liter V-6*	27	19	675	475	25.0
	5.7 Liter Diesel V-8#†*	34	23	884	598	26.0
BUICK ELECTRA	4.1 Liter V-6*	29	18	725	450	25.0
	5.7 Liter Diesel V-8#†*	36	22	936	572	26.0
RIVIERA	4.1 Liter V-6*	29	17	612	359	21.1
	3.8 Liter Turbo V-6†*	27	16	569	337	21.1
	5.7 Liter Diesel V-8#†*	36	21	821	479	22.8

REGAL
$10,351. UP
21/30 MPG

1983 BUICK
V.I.N.
1G4A
(S69P)
-D-#

CENTURY
$9980. UP
24/39 MPG

83

SKYLARK T TYPE DASH

27/42 MPG
SKYLARK
$9068. UP

SKYLARK T TYPE

28/46 MPG
SKYHAWK
$8547. UP

TAIL-LIGHT DETAIL

FOR 1983, RIVIERA T TYPE IS JOINED BY HIGH-PEFORM. T TYPE MODELS IN REGAL, CENTURY, SKYLARK (ILLUSTR.) AND SKYHAWK LINES.

note THE DIFFERENCE FROM REGULAR SKLK. GRILLE.

MORE T-TYPE DETAILS ON NEXT PAGE.

THE SKYLARK TYPE. *new*

D372 $10,857.

21

new SKYHAWK WAGON T35 LTD. (LEFT FOREGROUND) $9523.

BUICK
Wouldn't you really rather have a Buick?

T-TYPES

RIV. · REGAL · SKYLARK

NEW

SKYHAWK

CENTURY T Type

$10,564.

83

CENTURY T-TYPE INTER.

CENTURY T Type

SKYHAWK TYPE
DASH

103 MPH (RIVIERA T-TYPE)

THE T TYPE POWERTEAMS.

	Horsepower @ RPM	Torque @ RPM	5-speed Manual Overdrive Transmission (standard)	4-speed Manual Transmission (standard)	Automatic Transmission (standard)	Automatic Transmission (available)	Automatic Transmission with Overdrive (standard)
Skyhawk T TYPE Powerteam							
1.8 liter (112 CID) OHC L-4 (LH8) [0] (Standard)	84@ 5200	102@ 2800	3.83			3.18 (3.33)	
Skylark T TYPE Powerteam							
2.8 liter (173 CID) H.O. 2-bbl. V-6 (LH7) [Z] (Standard)	135@ 5400	145@ 2400		3.65		3.06	
Century T TYPE Powerteam							
3.0 liter (181 CID) 2-bbl. V-6 (LK9) [E] (Standard)	110@ 4800	145@ 2000			2.97		
Regal T TYPE Powerteam							
3.8 liter (231 CID) 4-bbl. Turbocharged V-6 (LC8) [8] (Standard)	180@ 4000	290@ 2400					3.42
Riviera T TYPE Powerteam							
3.8 liter (231 CID) 4-bbl. Turbocharged V-6 (LC8) [8] (Standard)	180@ 4000	290@ 2400					3.36

[0]—Produced by GM-Brazil [Z]—Produced by GM-Chevrolet [E]—Produced by GM-Buick [8]—Produced by GM-Buick

22

MODELS AVAIL.

Skyhawk Custom Coupe
Skyhawk Custom Sedan
Skyhawk T TYPE Coupe
Skyhawk Limited Coupe
Skyhawk Limited Sedan
Skyhawk Custom Wagon
Skyhawk Limited Wagon

SKYHAWK

Skylark Custom Coupe
Skylark Custom Sedan
Skylark T TYPE Coupe
Skylark Limited Coupe
Skylark Limited Sedan

SKYLARK

FROM $ **9079.**

84

CENTURY

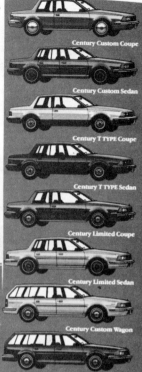

Century Custom Coupe
Century Custom Sedan
Century T TYPE Coupe
Century T TYPE Sedan
Century Limited Coupe
Century Limited Sedan
Century Custom Wagon
Century Estate Wagon

SKYHAWK DASH   SKYLARK DASH

SKYHAWK DASH and REAR $8964. UP

Selected 1984 Features
1. The 1984 Buick Century Olympia Sedan. A limited number of these specially equipped and appointed Century Sedans are being produced to commemorate Buick's sponsorship of both the 1984 Olympics and the 1984 U.S. Olympic Team.

The Century Olympia is well-equipped for its assignment. Beyond its gleaming white exterior, gold accented aluminum wheels, deck lid luggage rack, gold accent striping, and special ornamentation is an interior that's pure Century, but with plenty of its own commemorative touches. Like rich brown interior trim with handsome tan cloth covering either the standard 55/45 notchback seating or the available 45/45 seating with console. And front seat headrests we embroidered with official U.S. Olympic Team symbols.
2. Tilt steering column. Facilitates driver entry and exit while offering a wide range of driving positions

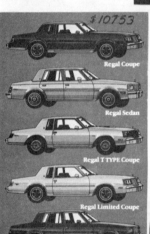

$10753

Regal Coupe
Regal Sedan
Regal T TYPE Coupe
Regal Limited Coupe
Regal Limited Sedan

REGAL (116 MPH (T-TYPE))

new

CENTURY OLYMPIA   CENTURY DASH

CENTURY T-TYPE HAS OWN GRILLE

1984 V.I.N.
IGA4 (569 P)
- E - #

REGAL DASH

OFF AUTO LIGHTS MAX DELAY

LE SABRE

LeSabre Custom Coupe
LeSabre Custom Sedan
LeSabre Limited Coupe
LeSabre Limited Sedan

"TWILIGHT SENTINEL" (OPT.) LEAVES HEADLTS. ON UNTIL DRIVER IS INDOORS.

Electra Limited Coupe
Electra Limited Sedan
Park Avenue Coupe
Park Avenue Sedan

LE SABRE / ELECTRA DASH

ELECTRA

FROM $14952.

(AT LEFT) V 35 ESTATE WAGON $15633. UP

Riviera Coupe
Riviera T TYPE
Riviera Convertible

RIVIERA

RIVIERA DASH

23

Skyhawk Limited Sedan.   JT69P $9682.   121 CID 4 (86 HP @ 4900 RPM) (110 CID + TURBO 4 AVAIL.)

BUICK
Wouldn't you really rather have a Buick?

Skyhawk Wagon

P175/80R13 TIRES
3.65 GEAR RATIO

13.6 GAL. FUEL TANK

JE270 T-TYPE
$9961.

Skyhawk Custom Wagon.

Skyhawk Limited Wagon interior.

Skyhawk Custom Wagon cargo area.

SKYHAWK   101.2" WB

1985 BUICK V.I.N. = 1G4 (J869P) - F - #

85

SKYLARK
104.9"   151 CID 4
2.53 GEAR RATIO   or 173 CID V6
(112 HP @ 5100 RPM)

15.1 GAL. FUEL TK. $9667.

XB69R
SKYLARK CUSTOM SED.
(XC69R LTD. " $10,243.)

J935P CUSTOM = $9518.
JT35P LIMITED = 9978.
(SKYHAWK WAGONS)

note MEDALLION ON CENTURY T-TYPE GRILLE VARIATION

Century   AL273

High-mounted center stop lamp

Deck lid luggage rack

AL 353

CENTURY LIMITED COUPE
$11580.

231 CID V6 (125 HP @ 4400 RPM)
181 CID V6 AVAIL.

2.84 GEAR RATIO
P195/70R14 TIRES

Rear facing third seat

AH 353

Century Custom Wagon.

SEDAN (AH193) $11,284. (CUSTOM)   15.1 GAL. FUEL TK. $11,680.

(IN UPPER VIEW, WITH BOY ON BIKE = CENTURY EST. WAGON: $12,118.)

24

P185/80R13 TIRES
13.6 GAL. FUEL TK.

INSTR. PANEL

SOMERSET
2.84 GEAR RATIO

4 CYL. OR 181 CID V6 (125 HP @ 4900 RPM)

Buick

$10,252.
NJ27U SOMERSET REGAL

N M27U SOMERSET LIMITED $10,861.

103.4" WB

(V6 FOR $485. EXTRA)

New SOMERSET

(ALSO KNOWN AS "SOMERSET REGAL" IN 1985.)
COUPES ONLY

REAR DECK SPOILER ON REGAL T-TYPE

GM47A

Buick Regal Limited.
$10,861.

REGAL

BUICK REGAL

Regal Grand National.

121 MPH

85 NEW

REGAL GRAND NATIONAL
231 CID V6
(200 HP @ 4000 RPM)
4-SP. TRANS.

Cast aluminum wheel

LE SABRE COLLECTORS EDITION INTERIOR

LeSabre Estate Wagon
BR35Y

LE SABRE

$13179.

$13121.

$11658.

LE SABRE CUSTOM CPE.
BN37A

Buick LeSabre Collectors Edition.

SED.

BP69A

25

Park Avenue Sedan.

231 CID V6 (125 HP @ 4400 RPM) (V6 DIESEL ALSO AVAIL.) 2.84 GEAR RATIO

Electra 380 Coupe.

18 - GAL. FUEL TANK

307 CID V8 IN WAGON, WITH DIESEL V8 ALSO AVAIL.

P205/75R x 14 TIRES

Buick

Electra Estate Wagon interior.

CW693

$16,740.

PARK AVE. INT.

ELECTRA

SEDANS AND COUPES TOTALLY RESTYLED **NEW** 110.8" WB

Electra Estate Wagon cargo area.

Electra Estate Wagon (WAGON NOT RESTYLED)

CF693
ELECTRA T-TYPE SED.
$16,528. **NEW**

108 MPH

BV35Y

$16,078. 2 SEAT
16,298. 3 SEAT
WAGON RETAINS 115.9" WB

RIVIERA **85**

307 CID V8 (140 HP)
350 CID DIESEL V8 (105 HP)

$27,297.

Z57 COUPE
17,210.

114" WB

Riviera Coupe interior.

ASTROROOF (OPT.)

Riviera Convertible.

Leather-wrapped sport steering wheel (T Type)

Z67

TURBO 231 CID V6 (200 HP) IN T-TYPE

Y57
T-TYPE V6
TURBO CPE.

$18,154.

BUICK **SKYLARK**
FR. $11100.

4 OR V6

SOMERSET DASH

SKYHAWK
4 OR TURBO 4
101.2" WB
FR. $9539.

T-TYPE $10591.
JE270
SKYHAWK

SKYHAWK DASH

Somerset S/E.

4 OR V6

SOMERSET

$10905. UP

SKYHAWK LTD.
$10293.
JT69P

V6 OR 4

CENTURY
$12136. UP

$14128.
REGAL T TYPE

86

V.I.N. =
1G4 ( )
-C-#

GK477

REGAL DASH

new 110.8" WB
FRONT WH. DRIVE
LE SABRE

V6
(V8 WAGON)

V6 TURBO,
V6, OR
V8

REGAL FROM

(STD. GRILLE) $11818.

124 MPH
(REGAL GR.
NATIONAL)

(LE SABRE DASH SIMILAR)

RIVIERA ELECTRONIC DASH (BELOW) (V6)

ELECTRA
DASH

T TYPE
SEDAN
CF69B

V6 **ELECTRA**

$16316. UP

(V8 WAGON AVAIL.)

COUPE

110 MPH
(RIVIERA
T-TYPE)

55 MPH
UNLEADED FUEL ONLY
022.0

RIVIERA
Touch the screen of the Graphic Control Center to tell it what you want and it responds with information, it provides control of audio and climate control systems, it even tells you specifically about systems that need your attention. And tells

Riviera T type.

Buick

SKYHAWK CPES.
FROM $10,282. →

25/31 MPG w. 122 CID 4
21/27 " w.
121 CID TURBO 4

"J" BODY

SKYHAWK

INT.

87

JS811
CUSTOM
WAGON
$11,009.

JT 811 LTD. WAGON
$11,601.

SKYHAWK
WAGON MPG:
24/31 (121 CID 4)

1987 BUICK V.I.N.
1G4 (JS51K) - H - #

AVAIL. ON SKYLK.

OR SOMRST.

SKYLARK
$11,450. UP

SKYHAWK WHEEL CHOICES
"N" BODY

SKYLARK

(SEDANS ONLY)

SKYLARK DASH

SOMERSET DASH

MPG:
22/32 (151 CID 4 SKYLK. and SOMRST.)

AVAIL. ON SKYLARK
OR SOMERSET
WITH
DECK
RACK

NM 14 U SOMERSET LTD.
$12,538.

INTERIOR

(THE FINAL
SOMERSET)
"N" BODY

SOMERSET

(COUPES ONLY)

NJ14U SOMERSET
CUSTOM
$11,492.

TAXI

WITH BLACKOUT "T"
PKG. ↑

W. EXTERIOR SPORT PKG.

PRICED FROM
$12,643.

22/32 MPG
w. 151 CID
4;
20/26
w. 173 CID
V6

"A" BODY
CENTURY
V6 OR 4

CENTURY DASH

CENT. LTD. INTERIOR

AL51W LIMITED SEDAN
$13,392.

CENTURY WAGON

AL81W

(UNGRAINED AH81W
CENTURY CUSTOM WAG.
$13,277.)

CENTURY
WAGON MPG:
21/28 (151 CID 4)

ESTATE WAGON
$13,797.

87
"G" BODY
REGAL
V6 OR V8
OR V6 TURBO

(FINAL) GRAND NATIONAL

REGAL MPG:
19/24 (231 CID V6)
17/23 (307 CID V8)

REGAL DASH

$13,492.

GM11A LIMITED COUPE
115 MPH

"T" PKG. (w. TURBO)

29

Buick

BR8IY

LeSabre

new GRILLE

FROM $13,913.

"H" BODY

3.8 L V6

LeSabre ESTATE WAGON
"B" BODY

$15,199.

W. T-TYPE PKG. 117 MPH
(new for Le S.)

87

"C" BODY

ELECTRA

PRICED FROM
$18,269.

CW 513
$19,641.

BV8IY

ELECTRA ESTATE WAGON

$18,744.   "B" BODY
ELECTRA DASH

WAGON
MPG:
16/24
(307 CID V8, IN
LE SAB. OR ELECT.)

WHEEL CHOICES

ELECTRA/PARK AVENUE

"E" BODY

RIVIERA

EZ113

RIVIERA DASH (new OIL PRESSURE GA.)

30

IMPROVED
3.8 L V6

$21,229.

JS511 SEDAN
$10,800.

26/36 MPG (5 SP. MAN.)
25/32 MPG (AUTO. TR.)

JS 811 WAGON
$11,745.

FRONT DETAIL

POWER STEERING, POWER FRONT DISC BRAKES, AM/FM STEREO RADIO, CLOCK ARE STD. EQUIPMENT.
MPG: 36 HWY, 26 CITY (5-SP.)

2.0 L 4 (90 HP @ 5600 RPM)

SKYHAWK
(LEFT, and ABOVE)

25/36 MPG

(THE FINAL SKYHAWK)

89

1989 BUICK
V.I.N. =
1G4 (JS511)
-K-#

JS111 SKYHAWK CPE.
$10,800.

SKYLARK INTERIOR

Skylark

REAR QUARTER VIEW OF SKYLARK SEDAN

(SKYLARK COUPE ON NEXT PAGE)

NC54U CUSTOM SEDAN
$12,116.
ND 54U LIMITED SEDAN $13,376.

23/32 MPG (4 CYL.)
20/27 MPG (V6)

32

BUICK

3300 MFI V6 27/20
(160 HP @ MPG
5200 RPM)

NJ14U CUSTOM $12,116.
COUPE

SKYLARK
(CONT'D.)

2.5 L TECH 4
(115 HP @
5200 RPM)

DOHC 2.3 L
QUAD 4
(150 HP @
5200)

NM14U
LIMITED COUPE
$13,376.

MPG
(SKYLARK)
32/23 2.3 4
30/23 2.5 4

89

AL8IN
CENTURY
ESTATE
WAGON

$14,406.

19/30
MPG

AH8IN
CENTURY
CUSTOM
WAGON

$13,606.

Century offers a wealth of premium features: New
optional 160-horsepower 3300 V-6 engine Automatic transmission, power steering and power front disc brakes
6-passenger roominess and 16.2-cubic-foot trunk AM-FM
stereo radio and clock, and extended-range speakers White-
wall tires with deluxe wheelcovers And more.

Century.

2.5 L TECH 4
(98 HP @
4800 RPM)

AHIIN
CUSTOM COUPE $12,649.

MPG:
30 HWY,
23 CITY
(4 CYL.)

$12,879.

AH5IN
CUSTOM
SEDAN

20/29 MPG
(6 CYL.)

CENTURY
RESTYLED

AL5IN LIMITED
SEDAN

$13,806.

33

WB14W CUSTOM CP.
$14,669.

BUICK

Regal.

20/29 MPG

Regal features: a 2.8-litre V-6 engine 4-wheel independent DynaRide suspension 4-wheel power disc brakes Front-wheel drive Air conditioning Automatic transmission with overdrive Reclining front seats AM-FM stereo with seek and scan.

The Great American Road belongs to
BUICK

BUICK LeSABRE

WD14W LIMITED COUPE
$15,194.

FINAL LE SABRE T-TYPE in 1989

(UNGRAINED)

17/24 MPG

LeSabre Estate Wagon.

T-TYPE COUPE 3800 V6 (165 HP @ 4800 RPM) MPG: 28/19

89

19/28 MPG (LE SAB.)

HR14C LIMITED CPE.
$17,135.

BUICK

BR81Y LE SABRE ESTATE WAG. (GRAINED)

LE SABRE ESTATE WAGON

$17,275.

LE SABRE
HP54C CUSTOM SEDAN $15,835.
HR54C LIMITED " 17,235.

Electra and LeSabre Estate Wagons
RETAIN OLD STYLING, V8s

FINAL YR. FOR SEPARATE LESABRE and ELECTRA ESTATE WAGONS.

WAGON MPG: 24 HWY., 17 CITY

WAGON 5.0 L V8 has 140 HP @ 3200

$21,440.
BV81Y ELECTRA ESTATE WAGON

ELECTRA

ELECTRA ESTATE WAGON

34

Buick CF54C T TYPE

$22597.

ELECTRA

Electra/Park Avenue. $21142.

(SAME V6, MPG AS LeS.)

CU54C

new Buick Ultra.

Riviera

$23,525 EZ11C

RIVIERA GRILLE

RIVIERA

RIVIERA FRONT END CLOSE-UP

19/28 MPG

REATTA INT.

89

The distinctive Reatta combines the exhilaration of a sports car with the luxury of a Buick.
Crafted in limited numbers to exacting quality standards, its long list of premium features includes: 165-horsepower 3800 V-6 · 4-wheel anti-lock disc braking system · 4-wheel independent suspension · 6-way power seats · Hand-buffed finish.

Reatta

EC11C
$27,250.

19/28 MPG

35

BUICK

(SKYHAWK MODELS DISCONTINUED)

SKYLARKS FROM $11811.

13.6 GAL. FUEL TANK 20/31 MPG

NJ14U

SKYLARK 4 or V6 (110 or 160 HP)

$13063.

SKYLARK CUSTOM COUPE

New DASH and INTERIOR (SKYLARK)

New GRILLE

new SKYLARK LUXURY EDIT. SEDAN HAS UNIQUE REAR DOOR and REAR QUARTER PANELS →

103.4" WB

ND54U SKYLARK LUXURY EDITION $14585.

$16615.

90

V.I.N. = 1G4 (NV54U) — L-#

$15730. CENTURY CUSTOM WAG.

CENTURY LIMITED WAGON

AL84N

CENTURY A SERIES 104.8" WB HAS 2.5 L 4 (110 HP) OR 3.3 L V6 (160 HP)

CENTURY SED. REAR QUARTERS

REGAL HAS 3.1 L, 191 cid V6 OR 3.8 L, 231 cid V6 (135 or 170 HP)

W SERIES V6 REGAL

new REGAL SEDAN HAS ITS OWN GRILLE DESIGN ←

NEW

REGAL COUPE $15655. UP

REGAL CUSTOM OR LIMITED SEDANS

16.5 GALLON FUEL TANK 19/30 MPG

REGAL   BUICK   REGAL

107½" WB

36

BUICK

LE SABRE SEDAN $16555. and up

CUSTOM OR LIMITED TYPES IN MOST BUICK MODEL SERIES.

COUPE

LeSABRE V6

H SERIES

LE SABRE GRILLE

110.8" WB ON LE SABRE OR ELECTRA

90

ELECTRA/PARK AVENUE

← ULTRA CU54C

C SERIES

ELECTRA/ CF54C T TYPE

3.8L V6 231 CID (165 HP @ 4800 RPM) 19/28 MPG 18 GAL. FUEL TK.

$21784. UP (LTD. SEDAN)

PARK AVE CW54C $23125.

ELECTRA PARK AVENUE FRONT END

2 DIFF. RIVIERA ROOFS

108" WB

ULTRA WHEEL DESIGN

$28375.

$24455.

new RIVIERA DASH LIKE REATTA's BUT GRAINED.

RIVIERA V6

RIVIERA GRILLE

EC14C

$28885.

REATTA V6 LIKE ELECT.

NEW

REATTA CONV'T. EC34C

18/27 MPG (EPA)

REATTA FRONT END

DASH (REATTA)

98½" WB

WAGON INT.

$18445.

WITH 307CID 5.0L V8 (140 HP @ 3200 RPM) 17/24 MPG

BR84Y ESTATE WAGON (1 TYPE ONLY) REPLACES SEPARATE LE SABRE/ELECTRA WAGONS

37

22 GAL. FUEL TK.

115.9" WB

FR. END

$14,999.

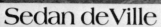

Cadillac

Trust Cadillac to lead the way.

Sedan deVille

Coupe deVille

81
121.4" WB

Cabriolet

The Cabriolet roof treatment shown is available for Coupe deVille with gleaming crossover roof molding. A similar treatment is standard with Fleetwood Brougham Coupe.

$14,997.

GM Cadillac

New for 1981... V8-6-4 Fuel Injection is standard equipment.

V8 (GAS) 368 CID

V.I.N. = 1G6A( )B(-) 000001 UP

252 CID V6

NEW GRILLE

New 24.6 Gallon Fuel Tank. Standard with V8-6-4 engine. 25 gallon fuel tank standard with V6. 27 gallon fuel tank standard with Diesel.

New Underhood Light. Provides nighttime illumination of oil dipstick, belts and other engine components.

Available V6 engine. (With overdrive for Fleetwood Broughams and DeVilles.)

1981 Cadillac Radios
including new Symphonic Sound System.

New Symphonic Sound System with Cassette Player and Electronically Tuned AM/FM Stereo Radio

Diesel Power available across the line.

Cadillac announces V8-6-4 Fuel Injection

New
As you drive, the 1981 Cadillac automatically goes from 8 to 6 to 4 cylinders.

350 CID 105 HP

Fleetwood Brougham

(4 OTHER RADIO/TAPE SETS SHOWN W. 1981 SEVILLE.)

$16,552.

1981 only → (though limousines kept it several years longer). The Buick V-6 continued as underbonnet alternate.

Is V8-6-4 Fuel Injection standard equipment?
Yes, the V8-6-4 fuel-injected engine is the standard gasoline engine for all 1981 Cadillacs.

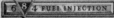 6 8 4 FUEL INJECTION

How does it operate?
As you leave your driveway, all 8 cylinders in your gasoline-powered 1981 Cadillac are in operation. Then, as you reach intermediate speeds on a street or avenue and your power requirements lessen, the car automatically switches to 6 cylinders. And then, when you reach cruising speeds and your power needs decrease further, the car automatically switches to 4-cylinder operation.

Active cylinder display shown left ... one function of new MPG Sentinel

Can I tell how many cylinders are active at any given time?
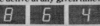 8 6 4
Yes. Push a button and Cadillac's MPG Sentinel on the instrument panel shows a digital display of the number of cylinders active at that moment. The MPG Sentinel will also show instantaneous mpg and average mpg.

38

SPECIAL 144.5" WB
$25,933.

Cadillac Limousine

new FUEL DATA PANEL

new DEVILLE WHEEL COVER

New GRILLE

Cadillac
It's a new power system

CABRIOLET. The Cabriolet roof treatment shown left is available for Coupe deVille. It features a gleaming crossover roof molding. A similar treatment is standard with the Fleetwood Brougham Coupe.

FUEL DATA
INSTANT AVERAGE · RESET · RANGE FUEL USED
New Fuel Data Panel

# 82
V.I.N.=IG6A( )
(-)C(-) 000001 UP
ENGINES

252 CID BUICK V6

4.1 LITER V8 ("HT 4100 DFI")

6.0 LITER V8-6-4 OR DIESEL V8 (350 CID OLDSMOBILE)

New DeVille Wheel Cover.

WARMER COOLER · ELECTRONIC CLIMATE CONTROL · OUTSIDE TEMP · AUTO · OFF ECON LO HI
New Outside Temperature Display.

new OUTSIDE TEMPERATURE DISPLAY

Coupe DeVille $16,491.

25 GAL. FUEL TK. 17 MPG (EPA)

"BEST OF ALL, IT'S A CADILLAC."

$19,227.

Fleetwood Brougham Sedan

Tilt and Telescope Steering Wheel, Fleetwood Broughams.

for Fleetwood Broughams.

New TAIL LIGHTS

25 GAL. FUEL TK. 10 MPG (EPA)

P R N 321
New Automatic Overdrive.

new AUTOMATIC OVERDRIVE

New "Fuel Used" readout to help you pick the most fuel-efficient route.

New Fleetwood Brougham Tail Lamp.

$29,601. Fleetwood Limousine

Cadillac

THE FLEETWOOD LIMOUSINES
$32,197. (FORMAL)

LIMO. SED.
$31,323.

144 1/2" WB

PARTIAL VIEW OF DASH

17 MPG EPA 22 DIESEL

252 CID V8 (135 HP) 350 CID DIES. V8 (105 HP) OR 368 CID V8-6-4 (140 HP) '83
SEDAN DE VILLE $18,494.

"Cadillac" NAME MOVED DOWN ONTO GRILLE, 1983.

new 1983 HT 4100 ALUMINUM-BLOCK EFI ENG. STD. IN ALL BUT CIMARRON + FLEETWD. LIMO.

83-84

(DETAIL AT LOWER LEFT OF DIFFERENCE BETW. 1983 and 1984.)

$18,009.

DE VILLES

COUPE DE VL.

Standard De Ville Wheel Disc.

note new 1984 WINGED EMBLEM ON TURN SIGNAL GLASS.

V.I.N. INCLUDES
– XD (1983)
– XE (1984)

Front Cornering Lights and Lamp Monitors

WINGED EMBLEM NOT ON 1983 GLASS.

105 MPH

1984 EXAMPS. ILLUSTR.

FLEETWOOD BROUGHAM

CPE. $20,811.

REAR QUARTER EMBLEM ON FLTWD. BR. 4-DR.

Standard Fleetwood Brougham Wheel Disc.

40

New 1985 Coupe de Ville $16,999**

Cadillac

TOTALLY RESTYLED DE VILLE and STD. FLEETWOOD NOW WITH FRONT-WHEEL-DRIVE **New** →

* REGULARLY $18,859.

SEDAN DE VILLE

FRONT-WH-DR. FLEETWOOD $21,909.

10.5 MPH

249 CID V8 (135 HP @ 4400 RPM) 2.97 GEAR RATIO P205/75R14 TIRES 18-GAL. FUEL TK. $19,440.

FLEETWOOD BROUGHAM

FRONT DETAILS OF FRONT-WHEEL-DRIVE FLEETWOOD

V.I.N.= 1G6 ( ) XF (-) #   **85**   SOME MODELS DOWNSIZED TO 110.8" WB, WITH FRONT-WHEEL-DRIVE

Some Cadillacs are equipped with engines produced by other GM divisions, subsidiaries or affiliated companies worldwide.

(REAR WHEEL DR.) 121½" WB

HIGH MOUNTED CENTER STOP LAMP BECOMES MANDATORY ON ALL NEW CARS SOLD IN U.S.A. STARTING FALL, 1985.

New

"STRETCH LIMOUSINE" (BY MOLONEY) CHICAGO

(NEW 134.4" WB LIMO. ALSO AVAIL. IN FRONT-WH-DR. FLEETWOOD SER.)

Cadillac Fleetwood with center high-mounted stop lamp.

41

CADILLAC'S NEW 4-YEAR/50,000-MILE LIMITED WARRANTY! The 1985 front-wheel-drive Fleetwood and De Villes are backed by Cadillac's special new limited warranty. In some cases, a deductible applies. See your dealer for details.

BEST OF ALL...IT'S A CADILLAC.

CADILLAC

FLEETWOOD BROUGHAM
CONTINUES
(w. new 5.0-litre
V8 (140 HP @
3200 RPM)
307 CID

← TOURING COUPE
← TOURING SEDAN
106 MPH

NEW
(w. 4.1 litre V8)
130 HP @ 4200 RPM
249 CID

DEVILLE PRICES START AT $**20,559**.
(new TOURING COUPE
OR TOURING SEDAN PKG. OPT.)

BACKGROUND:
SAN FRANCISCO, CA.

SEDAN DE VILLE

86 new MODELS ADDED

DIESEL ENGINES NOT LISTED IN 1986.

FLEETWOOD
(FLEETWOOD BROUGHAM
$**22,155**.
DW698)

V.I.N.=106 (DW698)
-G-#

FLEETWD. 75
NEW

Limousine

CLOSE-UP OF
FORMAL ROOFLINE
REAR QUARTERS

42   CH33B   FORMAL LIMOUSINE
134.4" WB $**36,590**.

1987 (DEVILLE) MPG:
17/25 (w. 302 CID V8)
(SAME FOR FLEETWOOD)

Cadillac

1987 (BROUGHAM)
MPG:
18/25 (w.
307 CID V8)

1987
(LIMOUSINE)
MPG: 17/24
(w. 249 CID V8)

"C" BODY

('87)

DE VILLE

(ABOVE)

1987 V.I.N. = 1G6
( )-H-#
(new COMPOSITE HDLTS.)

(DEVILLE TOURING
OPTION PACKAGE
$2880. EXTRA
IN 1987.
ALSO AVAIL. '88)

AVAILABLE 1987~1988
MODELS =   (PRICES)

MODEL ID #

DEVILLE 4-DR. — $23,138. ('87) CD518
      24,834. ('88) CD515
DEVILLE 2-DR. — 22,795. ('87) CD118
      24,479. ('88) CD115
BROUGHAM — 24,096. ('87) DW518
      25,072. ('88) DW51Y
FLEETWOOD D'ELEGANCE — 27,333. ('87) CB518
      29,454. ('88) CB515
new
FLEETWOOD 60 SPECIAL — 36,079. ('87) C9518
(115.8" WB)   36,180. ('88) C9515
FLEETWOOD 75 LIMOUSINE — 37,739. ('87) CH518
PRESIDENTIAL LIMO. (LWB) ('88)

87-88

new GRILLE
WITH "WAFFLE"
CRISS-CROSS
PCS.

1988 V.I.N. =
1G8 ( )
-J-#

INTERIOR (BR.)

CADILLAC BROUGHAM
"D" BODY

('88)

THIS
121½" WB BRGHM.
WAS AMERICA'S
LONGEST REGULAR
PRODUCTION CAR,
AT THE TIME
(EXCEPT FOR
LIMOUSINES)

Cadillac Brougham, America's
longest production car.

THE ONLY WAY TO TRAVEL IS   CADILLAC STYLE.

43

CADILLAC

DEVILLE

$26,309.

$28,446. ('90)

DEVILLE DASH

89-90

longer

WB ON SEDANS (113.8")

(2 DR., 110.8")

Sedan de Ville

17/25 MPG

4.5 LITRE, 273 CID V8 ENGINE (155 HP) (180 HP IN 1990)

CADILLAC STYLE

10/25 MPG 18 GAL. FUEL TK.

DE VILLE

(1989 EXAMPLES ILLUSTR., UNLESS OTHERWISE INDICATED)

Cadillac 4.5 LITER V8

FLTWD. SEDAN $30,850.

$33,530. ('90)

FLEETWOOD

60 S. INT.

Sixty Special

('90)

17/24 MPG ('89)

60-SPECIAL SEDAN has EXCLUSIVE 22-WAY-ADJUSTABLE POWER SEAT! →

$34,780. 37,530. ('90)

■ Standard full padded roof w Sedan and Fleetwood Sixty Special)

Standard formal cabriolet roof–Fleetw

1990 DASH W. AIR BAG IN STEER. WH. HUB

1989 DASH

■ Available painted metal roof shown with available Astroroof (reduces headroom slightly)

FLEETWOOD

44

$26,968. ('89)
28,718. ('90)

CADILLAC

CHROME PILLAR ON 1990 →

BROUGHAM

QUILTED UPHOLSTERY (PLEATED ALSO AVAIL.)
('89)

BROUGHAM MODELS WITH OWN GRILLE DESIGN.

OWN GRILLE DESIGN.

NEW

(BOLDER)

BROUGHAM
FUEL TK. 25 GAL.
17/24 MPG (307 CID)
14/21 " (350 CID)

new 175 HP
5.7 L V8 AVAIL. 1990
(350 CID) (307 CID ALSO)

1990 has COMPOSITE HDLTS. + new ORNR. LIGHTS.

89-90
S T R E T C H
LIMOUSINES

LIMOUSINE
NINETEEN HUNDRED NINETY

1989 V.I.N. =
1G6 ( ) -K- #

24K GOLD-FINISH KEYS

LIMO. INTERIOR

The only way to travel is Cadillac style.™

1990 V.I.N. =
1G6 ( ) -L- #

CADILLAC ALLANTÉ

"V" BODY

ALUMINUM OR FABRIC TOPS

ROADSTER
123 MPH ('87)
119 MPH ('88)

* V.I.N. = VR 3/8 ('87) - H - #
VR 3/7 ('88) - J - #
" " ON ('89) - K - #;
CVT. VR 338 ('90)
CVT./HT VR 338 ('90) - L - #

BUCKET RECARO LEATHER SEATS

87-90
New
FOR 1987

* ALL V.I.N.s BEGIN WITH 1G6

22 GAL. FUEL TANK
15/22 MPG (EPA)

STD. EQUIPMENT
DRIVER AIRBAG and
new ANTI-SPIN
TRACTION CONTROL
IN 1990
PININFARINA
DESIGN

PRICES =
$55,200. ('87)
56,533. ('88)
57,183. ('89)
CVT.
51,550. ('90)
1990
CVT./HT
57,183.

TRUNK

REAR

(1989 EXAMPLES ILLUSTRATED)

99.4" W.B.
V8 ENGINE
249 CID
170 HP @ 4300 RPM
(1989 = new 200 HP)
@ 4400 RPM)   273 CID ('90)

ANALOG OR DIGITAL GAUGES

15/22 MPG, 1990

DIGITAL

ANALOG

ALLANTÉ

Allanté

TRUNK LOCK DETAIL

46

THIS IS THE NEW
Cadillac Cimarron

CADILLAC'S FIRST AND ONLY COMPACT CAR! (4 DR. SEDANS ONLY)

6JG69

DASH →

P195/70R13 TIRES

REG. PRICE $12,906.

($12,131. SPECIAL PRICE)

FRONT-WHEEL-DRIVE

Quick-handling. Road-hugging. And fun to drive. This . . . is Cimarron. An efficient new kind of Cadillac. With the traction of front-wheel drive . . . MacPherson strut front suspension . . . and power-assisted rack and pinion steering with responsive 14:1 steering gear ratio. Plus, it has Cadillac refinements such as genuine leather seating areas for five, body-contoured front bucket seats, air conditioning and more. All standard. Test-drive Cimarron by Cadillac. Now available at all Cadillac dealers.

42 HWY EST / 26 EPA EST MPG *

*Use estimated mpg for comparison. Your mileage may differ depending on speed, distance, weather. Actual highway mileage lower. Some Cadillacs are equipped with engines produced by other GM divisions, subsidiaries, or affiliated companies worldwide. See your dealer for details.

A NEW KIND OF CADILLAC FOR A NEW KIND OF CADILLAC OWNER.

X-RAY VIEW BELOW

Genuine leather seating areas for five.

Leather-wrapped steering wheel.

Front-wheel drive.

Power-assisted rack and pinion steering with responsive 14:1 steering gear ratio.

Semi-independent rear suspension with variable rate springs.

Fully independent MacPherson strut front suspension.

Stabilizer bars— front and rear.

Same front legroom as some full-size cars.

42 highway estimate . . . 26 EPA estimated mpg * . . . with manual transmission.

Body-contoured front bucket seats with lumbar support.

$12,131 **

Four-speed manual overdrive transmission. (Three-speed automatic available at extra cost.)

Aluminum alloy wheels . . . with computer-matched tires.

V.I.N. = 1G6AG69G (-) C (-)

82 new

101.2" WB
4 CYLINDER, 112.4 CID ENG.
85 HP
14 GALLON FUEL TANK

	CIMARRON
EPA MILEAGE RATINGS WITH STD. TRANS. HWY. EST/ EPA EST. MPG*	42 / 26
FRONT-WHEEL DRIVE	STANDARD
POWER-ASSISTED RACK AND PINION STEERING	STANDARD
FOUR-SPEED MANUAL INCLUDING OVERDRIVE	STANDARD
TACHOMETER	STANDARD
EPA PASSENGER COMPARTMENT VOLUME	89 CU. FT
ALUMINUM ALLOY WHEELS	STANDARD
AIR CONDITIONING	STANDARD
LEATHER-WRAPPED STEERING WHEEL	STANDARD
LEATHER SEATING AREAS	STANDARD
MSRP**	$12,131 (F.O.B.)

V.I.N. 1G6A-G69 (-) XD (-) 000001 UP

new 121 CID 4
88 HP 25 MPG, EPA

$12,905.

"Cadillac" NAME IN SCRIPT, ON GRILLE

6JG69

83

new GRILLE

new HOOD MEDALLION

new FOG LAMPS (TUNGSTEN HALOGEN)

new ALUMINUM ALLOY WHEELS

CADILLAC CIMARRON

1984 DASH →

2.83 G.R. (5 SP. MANUAL TR.)
3.18 G.R. (3 SP. A/T)

"D'ORO" PKG.
BLACK w. GILT TRIM   LEATHER UPHOLSTERY

(LEATHER FACED FRONT BUCKET SEATS STD.)

84

new GRILLE IN 1984

CIMARRON '84
THIS ONE'S GOT THE TOUCH.

new TAIL LIGHTS and EXTERIOR TRIM

V.I.N. = 1G6A G69 PXE (-) 000001 UP

$13,304.

G69P (6JG69)

6JG69P

V.I.N. = 1G6A G69 PXF (-) 000001 UP

85

New SIDE TRIM and MOLDINGS

CADILLAC CIMARRON

new STEERING WHEEL WITH SQUARED CENTER PC.

$14,242.
("D'ORO" PKG. $934. EXTRA)

A NEW BREED OF AGILE, MOBILE, NEW STYLE CADILLAC
CLOSE-UP VIEW OF HOOD MEDALLION

THE LUXURY OF LEATHER IN THE CADILLAC OF SMALLER CARS

101.2" WB
3.18 GEAR RATIO
P195/70R13 TIRES
13.6 GAL. FUEL TANK

TAIL LIGHT DETAILS

new 173 CID * V6 AVAIL., IN ADDITION TO 4-CYL. 121 CID. 88 HP ENG.

110 MPH with V6
* 129 HP @ 4800 RPM

CHOOSE V6 POWER AND GAS-CHARGED SHOCKS IN CIMARRON... CADILLAC CIMARRON

1985 Cimarron
The Cadillac of smaller cars

Best of all...it's a Cadillac.

48

1986 CIMARRON
BEST OF ALL...
IT'S A CADILLAC.
Let's Get It Together... Buckle Up.

new HIGH-UP EXTRA BRAKE LIGHT IN REAR WINDOW

Cadillac **CIMARRON**

86

2.8 Liter V6

BUCKET SEATS

V.I.N. = 1G6 (JG69P)-G-#

FRONT   REAR

4 = 88 HP @ 4800 RPM
V6 = 129 " @ 4800

$15,004.

new DASH

JG69P

PERHAPS THE MOST SURPRISING NEW CAR YOU'LL DRIVE THIS YEAR.

V.I.N. (1987) = 1G6 (JG51W) -H- #

JG51W (1987-1988)

SHEDS NEW LIGHT ON LUXURY AND PERFORMANCE.

(1986½ SLOGAN)

$15,817.
($16,886. IN 1988)

THIS new FRONT STYLING FIRST AVAIL. ON SPECIAL "D'ORO" EARLY '86 MODEL.

new COMPOSITE HEADLIGHTS, WITH WRAP-AROUND TURN INDICATORS and PARKING LAMPS

CONTROL STALK OF THE IMPROVED

CUSTOM CRUISE III

(AVAIL. ON MOST GM-BLT. CARS)

(86½)

"J" BODY

('87)

(1986½ STARTS SPRING, 1986 ; SOME MAY CONSIDER IT "EARLY 1987.")

1987 MPG 23/30 (121 CID 4) 20/26 (173 CID V6)

CIMARRON DISCONTINUED 1988.

86½-88
The Sporty Spirit of Cadillac.

(1987)

49

V.I.N. (1988) = 1G6 (JG51W) -J- #

Gallons of Fuel Remaining

Miles Per Hour

Approximate Driving Range on Fuel Remaining (V8-6-4 only)

Electronically Tuned AM-FM Stereo Radio (also with time-of-day readout)

Electronic Climate Control and On-Board Computer Diagnostics

Number of Active Cylinders...8, 6 or 4

Biarritz

$20,186. (BIARRITZ)

81 "V8-6-4" ENGINE AVAIL. (368 cid)

Standard Eldorado Wheel Covers.

Cast Aluminum Wheel.

New Wire Wheel Cover. (Standard with Biarritz.)

FRONT-WHEEL-DR. (SINCE 1967) $17,249.

114" WB

V.I.N.=1G6AL5740B(-)#

CHOICE OF 5 COLORS OF LEATHER UPHOLSTERY IN BIARRITZ, $22880.

(NOT ILLUSTR.)

$19,545.

new GRILLE with ONLY 4 HORIZONTAL PCS.

8. / 1. / 9. / 12. / 5 / 7. / 2. / 14. / 4. / 15. / 6. / 13. / 3. / 10. / 11.

20.3 GAL. FUEL TK. 17 MPG (EPA)

V.I.N.=1G6AL578(-)C(-)00000I UP

TOURING COUPE HAS CAP-LIKE FLAT HOOD ORNAMENT, AS ILLUSTR.

82

Special Edition...Eldorado Touring Coupe

Touring Suspension...
Available for Eldorado and Seville.

TOURING CPE. INTERIOR

50

note GROOVED BRIGHTWORK, LOWER SIDES.

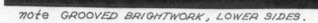

CADILLAC
ELDORADO

BIARRITZ $23,593.

Eldorado Biarritz
Outside, this Eldorado "dream machine" for 1983 features a brushed stainless steel roof cap, wire wheel covers, opera lamps and "Biarritz" script on the sail panels. Inside, tufted pillow-style seating and steering wheel are tailored in rich Sierra Grain leather. Eldorado Biarritz is shown in Cotillion White with a matching Elk Grain Cabriolet vinyl roof.

OPT. FULL CABR. ROOF

Eldorado Touring Coupe
Created for the person who loves to drive, Eldorado TC has a firm "feel the-road" responsiveness. Large diameter stabilizer bars. Reclining leather-faced bucket seats with lumbar and lateral support. Large P225/70R15 steel-belted blackwall radial tires. (Tire chains should not be used with these tires. Their use may cause damage to your car.) And more. Including a special cloisonne medallion on the hood. Available in two colors: Sonora Saddle Firemist and Sable Black, shown.

17 MPG EPA
21 MPG, DIESEL EPA

83

V.I.N. =
1G6AL578
XD (-) 00001/ UP

STD. ELDORADO FROM $20,198.

four-wheel disc brakes, Digital Fuel Injection and more. Including the available Full Cabriolet roof shown.

20.3 GAL. FUEL TANK (22.9 " " " WITH DIESEL V8)

BEST OF ALL...IT'S A CADILLAC.
Let's Get It Together...Buckle Up.

COUPE

the Eldorado Biarritz Convertible for 1984.

135 HP @ 4400 RPM (105 @ 3200 IN DIESEL V8)

$32,155. (CONVT.)

(STD. ELDORADO COUPE FROM $21,211.)

2.10 G.R. (1.95 " WITH DIESEL)

CADILLAC'S FIRST STOCK CONVERTIBLE AVAIL. SINCE '76!

84 NEW!

THE CADILLAC OF CONVERTIBLES IS BACK!

V.I.N.=1G6AL 578XE (-) 00001/ UP

51

C A D I L L A C
ELDORADO

BIARRITZ COUPE
EL 578

$25,195.

COUPE

EL 678

FINAL
BIARRITZ CVT. $32,974.

85

V.I.N. = 1G6A
L578 XF (-)
000001 UP

COUPES FROM
$21,800.

EL 578
$24,751. ('86)
$24,819. ('87)
EL 118

CONVT. NOT
LISTED 1986 ON

V.I.N. (1986) = 1G6 (EL 578)
— G — #

(CABRIOLET-STYLE ROOF OPTION
AVAIL. 1987.)

SUSPENSION
RE-TUNED 1987
FOR A SOFTER
RIDE.

STD.
EL DORADO COUPE (has CADILLAC
CREST ON REAR QUARTER PANEL)

1986 EXAMPLES
SHOWN

86-87

TOTALLY RESTYLED,
AND
WHEELBASE
SHORTENED TO
108" IN 1986.

"E" BODY

INTERIOR
(BIARRITZ)

1987 MPG: 17/25
(249 CID V8)

note "Biarritz" NAME
ON RT. SIDE OF
DECK LID
and ON
PADDED
REAR
QUARTER
PANEL.

BIARRITZ (CPE. ONLY)
$27,846. ('86) EL 578

27,664. ('87) EL 118

V.I.N. (1987) = 1G6 (EL 118)
— H — #

FRONT END
(ELDORADO)

52

CADILLAC

Eldorado

DRIVER AIRBAG STD.
IN 1990

108" WB

■ Available gold ornamentation
—rear script (shown)*

RESTYLED

88 — 90

LONGER AMBER
SIDE LIGHT,
new GRILLE

17/25 MPG
('89)

EL 115 ('88)
EL 118 ('89)
EL 133 ('90)

273 CID
new 180 HP (4.5 L) EFI V8 in 1990,
new BUMPER MOLDINGS

STD. "SNOWFLAKE LOOK" ALUMINUM
ALLOY WHEEL new IN 1988.
WIRE WHEEL DISC ON
BIARRITZ, OPT.
OTHERWISE.

DASH

RESHAPED REAR WINDOW TREATMENT, 1988

Standard painted metal roof (not available on Eldorado Biarritz)

Available full cabriolet roof for Eldorado (not available on Eldorado Biarritz)

Standard formal cabriolet padded roof with opera lamps for Eldorado Biarritz

■ Available full padded roof for Eldorado (not available on Biarritz). Shown with available Astroroof (reduces headroom slightly)

16/25
MPG,
1990
18.8
GALLON
FUEL TANK

FROM
$26,321.
('88)
$27,288.
('89)

(1989 EXAMPLES
ILLUSTRATED)

V.I.N. ENDS WITH —J—# (1988);
—K—# (1989); —L—# (1990)

Cast aluminum wheel. Available at no extra cost.

Standard cross-laced wire wheel cover.

Cadillac SEVILLE (SINCE 1976)
BRITISH-STYLE CLASSIC "KNIFE-EDGE" BODY SINCE 1980

TRUNK DETAILS

Cadillac-size trunk has over 14 cubic feet of usable space.

Seville.

$21547.

81

V.I.N. =
1G6 (-)
S69 (N)
(-) B
(-)
000001
UP

350 CID (105 HP) DIESEL V8 (CADILLAC V6 OR V8 GAS ENGINES AVAIL.) 114" WB

ELEGANTE

Seville Elegante $ **24446.**

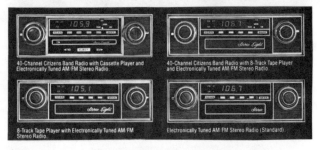

40-Channel Citizens Band Radio with Cassette Player and Electronically Tuned AM/FM Stereo Radio.

40-Channel Citizens Band Radio with 8-Track Tape Player and Electronically Tuned AM/FM Stereo Radio.

8-Track Tape Player with Electronically Tuned AM/FM Stereo Radio.

Electronically Tuned AM/FM Stereo Radio (Standard).

(ABOVE) VARIOUS RADIO/STEREO/TAPE COMBINATIONS AVAILABLE (IN ADDITION TO TYPE ILLUSTR. WITH 1981 CADILLAC DEVILLE/ FLTWD.

ELECTRONIC CLIMATE CONTROL →

ELECTRONIC CLIMATE CONTROL

54

The HT 4100 DFI Power System
...only Cadillac has it.

For 80 years, Americans have trusted Cadillac to lead the way. And their confidence has been rewarded. The first American production car with a V8 engine. The first V16. The first Diesel V8 as standard equipment. And now another first...the remarkable new

HT 4100 DIGITAL FUEL INJECTION

HT 4100 Power System. With everything from Digital Fuel Injection and automatic overdrive to a smooth new V8. From a Fuel Data Panel that can help you become a more efficient driver...to On-Board Computer Diagnostics to help take the guesswork out of servicing.

There's an HT 4100 DFI Power System standard for DeVilles, Fleetwood Broughams, Eldorado and Seville.

Cadillac
Seville
BY CADILLAC

V.I.N. 1G6A9698 (-) C (-) 000001/ UP

REAR VIEW

Four-Wheel Disc Brakes, Seville shown) and Eldorado.

("HT-4100 DFI" V8 [GAS] is std., but other engines opt.) **82**

with automatic overdrive.

Front-Wheel Drive, Seville (shown) and Eldorado.

Seville...

$24,093.

Seville Interiors

From one of the world's most advanced engine plants...

At the heart of the HT 4100 Power System is a smooth new V8. Its chrome-plated valve covers are just one indication of the painstaking attention to detail.

20.3 GAL. FUEL TANK 17 MPG (EPA) **$27,188.**

SEVILLE ELEGANTE.

Cadillac

Seville
BEST OF ALL...IT'S A CADILLAC

WITH CABRIOLET ROOF OPTION

WITH STANDARD ROOF

Full Cabriolet Roofs for Seville and Eldorado.
This dramatic treatment recaptures the dash and flair of the classic Cadillac convertibles. The simulated convertible roof design appears authentic in virtually every detail - from the canvas-look fabric to the welted seams. It is available in four colors: Black, Dark Blue, Dark Briar Brown (shown on Seville with Woodland Haze exterior) and White (shown on Eldorado with Balboa Blue exterior).

2 TONE PAINT, LEATHER SEATS and TRIM IN ELEGANTE

ELEGANTE $26183.

83

6KS69

$22304. *and up*

17 MPG EPA
21 MPG, DIESEL EPA

V.I.N. = 1G6A S698 X.D (-) 000001 UP

V.I.N. = 1G6A S698 XE (-) 000001 UP

Seville's Instrument Panel with elegant new Black Accent Interior Trim Moldings. (Available features also shown.)

NEW BLACK ACCENT TRIM ON DASH

Seville Aluminum Alloy Wheel.

GAS OR DIESEL V8s (135 OR 105 HP) 3.15 OR 3.36 GEAR RATIO (2.93 w. DIESEL)

84

WITH CABRIOLET ROOF OPTION

V.I.N. = 1G6A S698 XE (-) 000001 UP

SEDAN = $23,337.
ELEGANTE = $27,216.

Standard Seville Wheel Disc.

FUEL CAP'Y. 20.3 GAS 22.8 DIESEL

Standard Seville Elegante Wire Wheel Disc.

56

Cadillac
249 CID V8

S E V I L L E

DIESEL V8 AVAIL.

85

114" WB

V.I.N. =
1G6A S698
XF (-)
000001 UP

SEDAN $24,128.

6KS69

ELEGANTE
SEDAN $28,007.

"K" BODY   KS 698   KS 518   MPG:
                                17/25
TOTALLY   (249 CID V8)
RESTYLED **86-87**   1987
1986
110 MPH   **NEW**
new SHORTER 108" WB

CASHMERE CLOTH —
and-LEATHER COMBINATION
SEATING AREAS and new
REAR DOOR LOCK SWITCHES
IN 1987.

PRICED FROM
$27,256. ('86)
$27,405. ('87)

INTERIOR ('86)

(1986 EXAMPLES ILLUSTR.)

ELEGANTE
INTERIOR ←

SUSPENSION SOFTENED IN 1987.

Announcing the 1986 Seville.
The new essence of elegance

ELEGANTE
$30,851. ('86)

$101.
LESS
IN
'87!

108" WB
18.8 GAL. FUEL TK.

17/25 MPG ('89)

Cadillac SEVILLE

COMPACT DISC PLAYER OPTION → (STD. IN 1990)

16/25 MPG, 1990

OPTIONAL

SEDANS PRICED FROM
$29,057. ('88)
$30,300. ('89)
$32,380. ('90)

Cadillac Seville, America's ultimate luxury sedan.

Available Phaeton roof

■ Available Astroroof (now available with Phaeton roof), shown with standard painted metal roof. (Astroroof reduces headroom slightly.)

DASH

ROOF TREATMENTS

KS 515

88-90

NEW 155 HP V8   180 HP 4.5 L EFI V8 IN 1990

2.97:1 GEAR RATIO

■ Available gold ornamentation— available wheel cover wreath and crest (shown)*

"STS" INTRO. MID-1988 (TOUR. SEDAN IN 1990)

REAR (STS)

STS has DIFFERENT GRILLE OF ITS OWN. →

WHEEL TREATMENTS

■ Standard 15"x6" lace-look aluminum alloy wheels –Seville

■ Available 15" wire wheel discs–Seville (not avail. w/touring suspension)

■ Standard 15" x 7" exclusive fine-finish alloy wheels–Seville STS

■ Available 15"x6" aluminum alloy wheels–Seville (standard with touring suspension)

'89 "STS" $36,054.

1989 EXAMPLES ILLUSTR.

58

CHEVROLET (SINCE 1911)

Chevrolet / GM

1XX68

151 CID 4 (90 HP) OR 173 CID V6 (115, 135 HP)

1XX08 W. X11 PKG.

X-11 at a glance.
Vehicle type: front-engine, front-wheel-drive, 5-passenger, 3-door hatchback.
Engine type: V6, water-cooled, cast-iron block and heads, 1x2-bbl. carburetor.
Displacement . . . 173 cu. in. 2830 cc
Power (SAE net) . . . . . . 135 bhp
@ 5400 rpm
Transmission . . . 4-speed, manual
Wheelbase . . . . 104.9 in.
Length . . . . 176.7 in.
Curb weight . . . . 2650 lbs.

$9264.

CITATION X-11

P185/80x13/B TIRES
CITATION HAS FRONT-WHEEL DR.
(FIRST INTRO. SPRING, '79 AS 1980 MODEL)

1981 CHEVY CITATION
104.9" WB

MPG: 26/19 (V6)

$8377. UP

643-291

Monte Carlo

1AZ37

108.1" WB. V6, V8 ENGINES LIKE IMPALA, CAPR.

P195 75R14 TIRES

(NO MONTE CARLO DIESEL LISTED)

V.I.N. =
1GIA ( )0B-#

81

IMPALA

CAPRICE CLASSIC DASH

MOST IMPALA SPECS. SIMILAR TO
CAPRICE
116" WB
229, 231 CID V6
115, 110 HP
267, 305 CID V8

Caprice Diesel.

33 HWY EST   21 EPA EST MPG

WITH AVAIL. 350 CID DIESEL V8 (105 HP)

P205 (225) 7R15 TIRES

59

'82 CHEVY CAVALIER
THE COMPLETE CAR

Chevrolet New 82

V.I.N. ENDS WITH -C-#

CITATION
NEW ELECTRONIC FUEL INJECTION AVAIL. NEW 2-DR. COUPE JOINS EXISTING 3 DR. AND 5-DR. MODELS. CITATIONS PRICED FR. $7913.

CITATION, the country's best selling front-wheel drive, is available in '82 with electronic fuel injection.

15.9 GAL. FUEL TANK 26 MPG (EPA, CITATION)

(1982 CAVALIER INTRO. EARLY, ON THURS., MAY 21, 1981.)

WAGONS: CADET 1JD35/Z11 $8376.
CAVALIER 1JD35 8934.
CL 1JD35/Z12 9852.

WAGON 26 MPG (EPA)

CL DASH

101.2" WB 112 CID 4
CAVALIER
AVAILABLE IN CADET, CAVALIER, CL SER.
$7985. UP
14 GAL. FUEL TK.

CAVALIER FRONT

CELEBRITY DASH

CHEVROLET

BODY TYPES AVAILABLE IN THE ABOVE 30 MPG (EPA)

CAVALIER

SERIES

CAVALIER REAR END

MONTE CARLO

22 MPG (EPA)

CELEBRITY. NEW

104.9" WB $9387. UP
4 CYL. 151 CID EFI (90 HP)
173 CID V6 or 260 CID DIESEL V6

REAR OF CELEBRITY 15.9 GAL. FUEL TK.

1BL69 IMPALA $9172.
25 GAL. FUEL TANK 17 MPG (EPA)

MAYOR

SMART DIESELS.
Impala. 33 EST. HWY./22 EPA EST. MPG*

CAPRICE $9475. UP (2 DR.)

1BN69 4 DR. $9621.

60

$7852. UP (WAGON)

54.4"

66.3"

CAVALIER WAGON

24 MPG EPA, 27 DIESEL

CELEBRITY

1AW27 COUPE $9198.
(1AW19 SEDAN, $9348.)

CITATION

MPG: 42/27 (151 CID 4)

new CS LUXURY SERIES OF CAVALIER; CADET DISCONT'D.

$7589. UP

CAVALIER

26 MPG, EPA

83

120 MPH (MONTE CARLO SS)

V.I.N. ENDS WITH —D-#

new CAVALIER CONVERT. AVAIL., AT $12,380.

Citation 4-Door Hatchback $8664. V6 AVAIL.

CAPRICE CLASSIC DASH

SS version of the Monte Carlo available for the first time since 1971.

The 1983 Monte SS came in either white or blue with a blue bench seat interior and column shift. Only 4714 were built for '83.

CAPRICE CLASSIC

IMPALA GRILLE

(IMPALA WAGONS DISCONT'D.; IMPALA SEDAN ONLY, AVAIL. CRUISE CONTROL $9643.)
(1BL69)

SET COAST — CRUISE OFF ON RESUME

18 MPG EPA 23 MPG, DIESEL EPA

1BNG9 CAPRICE SEDAN (CLASSIC) $10,114. (NO 2-DR. CAPRICE IN '83)

Caprice Classic coupe dropped this year. Returns in 1984.

CAVALIER, TYPE 10, and CS MODELS

OFFICIAL U.S. CARS AND TRUCKS OF THE XIV OLYMPIC WINTER GAMES

CHEVROLET
taking charge

LET'S GET IT TOGETHER. BUCKLE UP.

$7933. to $12,694.
Cavalier

new GRILLE

V.I.N. ENDS WITH —E—#

84

1JD35

CS WAGON $8420.

CAVALIER INTERIOR

CITATION RE-NAMED AS
Citation II.

WITH 16 MECHANICAL IMPROVE- MENTS.

151 CID 4 (92 HP)   104.9" WB
173 CID V6 (112 HP)
173 CID H.O. V6 (135 HP)

CITATION II SEDAN CONTINUES FASTBACK STYLING

1XX68
$8786.
(CITATION II)

New

965 BCR

CELEBRITY
Our new Celebrity Wagon.
It can put 8 people in space.

CELEB. EUROSPORT

112 MPH

W. BLACK TRIM

STD. CELEBRITY GRILLE FOR 1984

MPG: 39/25
(2-DR. CAPRICE RETURNS)

1AW35 CELEBRITY WAGON $9358.

1BL69 IMPALA V6 SEDAN $10212.

SS (RESTYLED)
MONTE CARLO SS V8
$11,956. Z37G

(Z37A V6 COUPE RETAINS FORMER STYLE)

62

(CAPRICE) **CLASSIC ESTATE**
116" WB

305 CID V8 (150 HP)
(OPT. 3.50 CID DIESEL V8)   11,834.

The second generation SS Monte Carlo was an option package on the third-gen car, this time coded RPO 265.

Cavalier

TODAY'S CHEVROLET

CITATION II DETAILS

$8344
(C9 WAG., $8665)

101.2" WB

121 cid 4 (88 HP)
173 cid 6 (125 HP)

CAVALIER C8 SEDAN
(JD69P) $8499.

114 MPH (Z24)

V.I.N. ENDS WITH — F—#

CELEBRITY   104.9 WB

AW19W $10367.

XX68R
$8830. FINAL
CITATION II (last year)
151 cid 4 (V6 AVAIL.)
14.6 GAL. FUEL TANK
3.65 G.R.

104.9" WB
P215/60 R14 TIRES

85

NEW ENG. DAMPENER ON ALL GAS ENGINES (SILENCER)

173 cid V6 112,130 HP

2.84 GEAR RATIO

(AVAIL. 262 cid V6 DIESEL HAS 85 HP.) (88 HP w. 151 cid 4)

P195/75R14 TIRES
15.7 GAL. FUEL TANK

CELEBR. DASH $10558.

new "ESTATE" GRAINING AVAIL. ON CEL. WAG.

Monte Carlo

99 (GZ37G) $12524.

V8

SPORT CPE. $10684.

V6

117 MPH

(COUPE RETURNED TO CAPRICE CLASSIC LINE IN 1984.)

CELEBRITY

$11919.
BN35H WAGON

NEW

CAPRICE CLASSIC

262 cid V6 (130 HP)
305 cid V8 (165 HP)
OR 350 cid DIES. V8 (105 HP)

CAPR. CLAS. DASH

63

IMPALA (NOT SHOWN) (last year).

Chevrolet ('86)

$14010
JE67P
"RS"
CAVALIER
CVT.
115 MPH
(Z24)

"A" BODY
CELEBRITY

$11195
AW19W

MOST MODELS
CONTINUE
WITH FEW
CHANGES FR.
1985.

86
-87

IMPALA DISCONT'D.
CITATION II "

CELEBRITY MPG:
20/28 (173 CID V6)
(1987)

118 MPH

new CELEBRITY GRILLE ('86)
(COMPOSITE HEADLTS., 1987)

new BROUGHAM ADDED TO 1986 CAPRICE LINE
$12 654.

"J" BODY
CAVALIER
$10358
Z24
COUPE

CONVERTIBLE AVAIL.
SINCE 1983

CAVALIER MPG:
24/31
(121 CID 4, 1987)

"G" BODY
Monte Carlo.
SS
SPORT CPE.
$13630. ('86) GZ37H
14652. UP ('87)
GZ11H

1987
Monte
aero coupe-
over 6000 built.

now 1986

BN69Z

new FOR 1986
CAPRICE CLASSIC BROUGHAM

CAVALIER
RS
WAGON
('86)

108"
WB
305 CID
V8

MONTE CARLO LS LUXURY SPT. CPE (GZ37Z)
HAS DIFFERENT FRONT.
262 CID V6 (new FASTBACK AEROCOUPE ALSO, '87.)

only 200
built in
1986.

new
1986
GRILLE

('86)

CAPRICE CLASSIC
DASH
('87)

BU51Z
LS

('86)

1987 CAPRICE CLASSIC

WAGON
('86)

new 1987 "LS"
HAS LANDAU TOP
$15055.

$12642.

('87)

SPORT
COUPE

BN11Z "B" BODY

CAPRICE CLASSIC

CHEVROLET

1987
HAS
new 2-IN-ONE
"COMPOSITE" WIDE
HEADLIGHTS

V.I.N. ENDS WITH - G-# ('86)
"   "   " - H-# ('87)

1987 CAPRICE MPG: 18/27 (262 CID V6); 18/25 (307 CID V8)

For 1987, Monte Carlo production was actually extended through December 1987, as part of its phase out, so the last Montes were technically 1988 models. The car that replaced it became the 1190 Lumina coupe, with the SS tag replaced by Z34.

for 1986 over 41,000 Monte Carlo SS models were built — the highest yearly production number for these cars.

THE *Heartbeat* OF AMERICA ⬥ TODAY'S CHEVROLET

V6 OR V8

Chevrolet Cavalier Z24 Coupe   Chevrolet Celebrity Eurosport Coupe   Chevrolet Caprice Classic Brougham Sedan

CAVALIER Z24
$12,215.

4 OR V6

$14,900.

CAVALIER
(RESTYLED)

Cavaliers: the coupe, sedan and wagon; very stylish RS coupe and sedan; aggressive Z24 coupe and posh convertible.

You'll love the surprising new look that extends from Cavalier's new grille and hood, along its body-side molding, around its wheels, all the way to its new rear bumper.

$10,665.   CAVALIER RS CPE.   JE111

BERETTA DASH

2.0 L 4 OR
QUICK 2.8 LITER MULTI-PORT V6.

V.I.N. ENDS WITH -J-# (IN BAR. OR CORS.)

88

LV111

Grand Touring Beretta GT
$11,656.00*

New

BERETTA
(COUPES ONLY)

115-120 MPH   103.4" WB
1988
BERETTA AND CORSICA ("L" BODY)
INTRODUCED EARLY
(SPRING, 1987)

(CORSICA AVAIL. ONLY AS 4 DR.)

Touring Grand Corsica LT
$10,991.00**

(** REG. $11195.)
LT 511

110 MPH

New

103.4" WB

65

CHEVROLET

(THE FINAL CAVALIER CVT.)

THE *Heartbeat* OF AMERICA   TODAY'S CHEVROLET

CELEBRITY   AW51W
23/30 MPG (4)
20/29 (V6)

Celebrity
12,720.
(INCR. TO $13,350.)
WHEEL

25/36 MPG (4)

Plan 4:
Cavalier RS Wagon

Plan 3:
Celebrity Eurosport

Plan 2:
Cavalier RS Sedan

Celebrity. $11,495.*   STD. GRILLE

24/34 MPG (4)
18/29 MPG (V6)
CORSICA

Plan 1:
Corsica LT

JF11W $12,840.
18/29 MPG (V6)

Cavalier Z24.

JC111 $9/67.
VL

89

V.I.N. ENDS WITH – K – #

$11,650.

New Corsica hatchback.
$12,040.

PZG 524

BERETTA COUPE $12,240.

4 OR V6   LV111

24/34 MPG (4)
18/29 MPG (V6)

CHEVY BERETTA

V6   GT LW11W
$13,600.

LTG11

MONTE CARLO
DISCONTINUED

$17,340.
BU51E

CAPRICE CLASSIC

BROUGHAM
$16,120.
19/27 MPG (V6)
17/25 MPG (V8)

Caprice Classic Brougham. LS

THE *Heartbeat* OF AMERICA
TODAY'S CHEVROLET

66

Corsica LT Hatchback Sedan.

Corsica LT 2.5 L 4 **$11,640.** 5 SP. ISUZU TRANS. (OPT. 3-SP A/T)

CAVALIER RS DASH

Cavalier Wagon. $10382.

CHEVROLET

CAVALIER VL CPE. $9794

← CAVALIER

NEW

CORSICA DASH

Corsica LT Sedan.

BERETTA CVT. 4 OR V6 ('90½)

Beretta GTZ

→ HAS ITS OWN BLANKED -OUT GRILLE 180 HP QUAD 4 (138 CID)

$14715.

← BERETTA DASH

LUMINA **New**

90 107½" WB

V.I.N. ENDS WITH —L—#

(CELEBRITY WAGONS CONT'D. BUT NO SEDAN)

Lumina Euro

GRILLE and DASH

Caprice Classic Sedan.

Caprice Classic Brougham Sedan.

Caprice Classic Brougham LS Sedan.

Caprice Classic Wagon.

LUMINA DASH 151 CID 4 (110 HP) 191 CID V6 (135 HP) 27/21 MPG (4) 27/19 " (6)

Lumina **$14260.**

new Lumina APV. $15300. 120 HP V6

67

CHEVROLET CAMARO

Chevrolet

(SINCE 1967)

BERLINETTA DASH and CUSTOM CLOTH INTER.

| 28 Est. Hwy. | 20 EPA Est. MPG | (V6) |

1981 CHEVY CAMARO THE HUGGER

SPORT COUPE $8142.

IFP87 (J)

DELCO AM/FM STEREO

15 x 7" BODY-COLORED SPT. WHEEL

108" WHEELBASE

115 or 110 HP V6s, 120-190 HP V8s 229 CID V6, 267 CID, 305 CID OR 350 CID V8s. (231 CID V6 IN CALIFORNIA ONLY)

STD. SPT. CPE INTERIOR

WITH OPTIONAL CLOTH

V.I.N. = IGI (-) ( ) (-) B (-) I0000I UP

81

IFP87 (L)

Z-28

P205/75R x 14 or P225/70R x 15 TIRES

ALUMINUM WHEEL

Z-28 $9337.

Z28 SPOILER DETAILS →

BERLINETTA IFS87 $8938.

CAMARO

CAMAROS PRICED FR.

$ 9336.	'82
9862.	83
10,026.	84
10,237.	85
10,914.	86
11,674.	87
12,674.	88
13,199.	89
12,754.	90

(V6 PRICES;
V8s at EXTRA COST)

V6 SPT. CPE. →

Z-28

↑ 1982 Z28 $ 10,957. (V8)

New Z28 Camaro.

DASH ↘

16 GAL. FUEL TANK
24 MPG (EPA)
('82)

82 New FRONTAL STYLING
ON

V6 OR V8 ENGINES *
new SHORTER
101" WHEELBASE

* 4 CYL. ENG.
ALSO AVAIL.
1982-1986.

5 SPEED,
5 LITR.
V8 Z28
INTRO.
'83

Z28
134 MPH,
1983

BERLINETTA
HAS OWN
FRONTAL
STYLING

114 MPH, 1984   116 MPH, 1985

(1982 EXAMPLES ILLUSTR.
ABOVE)

1986 HAS 3RD BRAKE LT. (REAR WNDW.)

VEH. I.D. #s INCLUDE :
1982=1G1AP87 (2)(-)(C)(-)
1982 BERLIN.=AS987 (1)
1983=1G1AP87 (-)XD (-)
1983 BERLINETTA=1G1A987 (-) XD (-)
1984=1G1AP87 HXE (-)
1984 BERLINETTA=1G1A987 HXE (-)
1985 = HXF IN I.D. # OR
FP879, FS87S, OR FP87H IN I.D. #
(1986 SAME, BUT CHEV. I.D. #s
(F)(-)87(-)-G-)

1987=(FP()-H-#) 1988=(FP()-J-#) 1989=
(GENERAL CHEV. KEY NUMBERS) FP-K-
INCLUDE 1990=
FP
-L-

1987
MPG : 16/25 (V8)

RS SERIES REPLACES
BERLINETTA, 1987
(V6 OR V8)

RS CONVT. STARTS 1987,
PRICED FROM
$16,073.
FP31S

CPE. ALSO
AVAIL.

1987 =
3RD BRAKE
LIGHT MOVED
DOWN TO
BACK OF DECK,
ABOVE LIC. PLATE.

('89)   RS

NEW IROC Z28 1985

↓ FP87H
140 MPH
('85)

135-150
MPH
('87)

(IROC = INTERNATIONAL
RACE OF CHAMPIONS)

DRIVER AIRBAG IN 1990

"F"
BODY

26/16 MPG ('90)

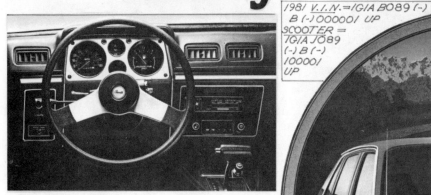

Chevrolet

Chevy Chevette

small car (1976 ~ 1987)

DELUXE DASH

1981 V.I.N.= IGIAB089(-)
B(-)000001 UP
SCOOTER =
7GIAJ089
(-)B(-)
100001
UP

COLUMN —
MOUNTED
"SMART
SWITCH"

97.3"
WHEEL-
BASE
ON
THE
4-
DR.

81-82

151 CID 4 OR 173 CID V8   98 CID 4
90 HP   115 HP   70 HP
                      12½ GAL. FUEL TK.

lower price!

$4595⁰⁰

REG. $5308.

"SCOOTER" ITJ08

FROM
$5730.
('82)

1981
MODELS
ILLUSTR.

39	**30**
HWY. EST.	EPA EST. MPG

2-DR. (94.3"
WHEELBASE)

P175/70 R13 TIRES
(ROOF RACK
OPTIONAL)

39-624

CHEVROLET

New
DIESEL
MODELS
ALSO
AVAIL. '82.
(116 CID
4 CYL.)

AM RADIO (BELOW)

**COMPUTER
COMMAND
CONTROL**

Every 1981 gasoline-
engined Chevrolet
passenger car includes a
sophisticated, thoroughly
tested on-board computer
as standard equipment.

(AM/FM ALSO AVAIL.)

FILLER DOOR

1982 V.I.N. =
IGIAB08C(-)C
(-)000001 UP
(SCOOTER=IGIAJ08C(-)
C(-)000001 UP)

70

60 EST. HWY.
43 EPA EST. MPG*

(WITH OPT. 4-CYL. DIESEL ENG. AVAIL. TO 1986.)

CHEVETTE

98 CID 4 (65 HP @ 5200 RPM) (1985)

3.36 GEAR RATIO (1985)

12½ GAL. FUEL TANK (1985)

CS SER. ONLY, 1985 ON

('83)

('83)

P155/80R13 TIRES (1985)

DASH ('83)

DIESEL

CHEVROLET

83-87

BLACK GRILLE

(FINAL CHEVETTE)
1987 MPG: 25/30 (w. 98 CID 4)

'83 DIESEL CHEVETTE FROM **$6535**.

FINAL "SCOOTER" **$5765**. ('83)

('86)

('84)

(2-DR. FROM **$5735**. IN 1987.)

"T" BODY

VEH I.D. #s INCLUDE:
'83 and
'84 — J or BO8C or 68C
'85 — TB08A or TB68A
(D SUFFIX = DIESEL)
'86 — TB08C or TB68C
'87 — TB21C or TB61C

71

CHEVROLET CORVETTE.

(SINCE 1953)

(V8-POWERED SINCE 1955)

(ALL CORVETTES WITH FIBERGLASS BODIES)

98" WHEELBASE

P225/70R x 15 B TIRES

NEW AUXILIARY ELECTRIC FAN CUTS IN WHEN EXTRA ENGINE COOLING NEEDED. IMPROVED BATTERY. 24-GAL. FUEL TANK

1981
V.I.N. =
1G1AY8760
B(-)100001
UP

1YZ87

81

NEW FIBERGLASS-REINFORCED "MONOLEAF" REAR SPRINGS. NEW STAINLESS STEEL, FREE-FLOW EXHAUST MANIFOLDS.

4-SPEED MANUAL TRANSMISSION, OR AUTOMATIC. 350 CID V8 (190 HP)＊
$16,141.

＊ CALIFORNIA 305 V8 ALSO (SINCE 1980)

New

STD. COUPE (1YZ87)
$19368.
(P225/70R x 15/B TIRES)

V.I.N. =
1G1AY878
(-) C (-)
00001/ UP

w. FRAMELESS GLASS HATCHBACK

COLLECT. ED. INTER AND EXTER. IN SILVER/BEIGE (METALLIC)

NEW "COLLECTOR EDITION" HATCHBACK COUPE (1YY07)

82-83

190 HP (OR 200)＊ WITH 350 CID V8

NO TRUE "1983" MODEL. CONTINUATION OF 1982 MODEL UNTIL 1984 READY (3~83)

$23,615.
P225/60R x 15/B TIRES

CHEVROLET CORVETTE

V.I.N.=1G1AY078 XE(-) 000001/UP

3.07 OR 3.31 TO 1 GEAR RATIO

142 MPH

2-CHOICE AIRCRAFT-TYPE BUCKET SEATS (INCL. LEATHER)

EMBLEM

INSIDE AND OUT, TOTALLY **NEW!**

1YY07

84

(AVAILABLE AT DEALERS SPRING, 1983.)

NEW SHORTER 96.2" WB

BIGGEST CHANGE IN CORVETTE SINCE THE 1960s

350 CID V8 (205 NET HP @ 4300 RPM)

The optional Delco-GM/Bose Music System ETR™ AM/FM Stereo with Seek and Scan, Cassette Tape and Clock.

$895. EXTRA

P215/65R15 TIRES

$24,405. (LATER $24,972.)

New Dash

SOPHISTICATED DASH HAS DUAL ANALOG AND DIGITAL READOUT OF SPEEDO. and TACHOMETER! SWITCH CONTROL OF OTHER GA. READOUTS.

ENGINE and FRONT AXLE

WE'RE TAKING CHARGE.

73

CHEVROLET CORVETTE

(YY078)

$26,501.*

96.2" WB

P255/50VR16 TIRES
20 GAL. FUEL TANK

(SHOWN WITH HEADLTS. OPEN)

DASHBOARD GRAPHICS IMPROVED, FOR CLARITY

* BASE PRICE = $24,891., EARLY IN YEAR

Z 51 SUSPENSION AVAILABLE

85

NUMEROUS MECHANICAL IMPROVEMENTS!

350 CID V8 IMPROVED
new 230 HP @ 4000 RPM
2.87, 2.73 OR 3.07 GR

TOP SPEED INCREASED TO 150 MPH
16 MPG. AVG. (EPA)

V.I.N. = 1G1AY078XF (-) 00000/ UP

YY78

144 MPH

COUPE
29,055

(COUPES ONLY, IN EARLIEST WEEKS OF MODEL YEAR)
OPT. GLASS ROOF PANEL, $615.
DUAL ROOF PANELS, $915.
MANUAL TRANS DELCO BOSE STEREO and LEATHER UPHOL. AVAIL.

V.I.N. ENDS WITH (YY67) OR (YY78) -G-#

HIGH-UP 3RD BRAKE LIGHT MANDATORY ON ALL 1986 and LATER CARS.

DASH

86

NEW

OFFICIAL PACE CAR
70TH INDIANAPOLIS 500·MAY 25, 1986

(YY67) ROADSTER (CONVERTIBLE)
$34,130.

new COMPUTERIZED BOSCH ABS II

Anti-lock braking power

CHEVROLET ✠ CORVETTE

"Y" BODY

"TURBO PORT INJECTION" INSCRIBED ON BELT TRIM STRIP

178 MPH WITH CALLAWAY TURBO ($50,865.)

STOCK TOP SPEED 152 MPH *

* 133-158 MPH IN VARIOUS OTHER TESTS, DEPENDING ON OPTIONS.

16 MPG (EPA)

87

240 HP @ 4000 RPM

NOW OFFERING 3 CHOICES OF SUSPENSION: BASE; Z51; and new Z52

REAR DETAILS (SHOWN WITH OPTIONAL BRIDGESTONE TIRES)

(YY 3/8) CONVERTIBLE $35,062.

V.I.N. ENDS WITH -H- #

DETAILS OF ENGINE COMPARTMENT

(YY 2/8) COUPE $29,889.

CHEVROLET CORVETTE

new 245 HP
TOP SPEED = 159 MPH

20.5 MPG (EPA)

V.I.N. ENDS WITH -J-#

88

new OPTIONAL REAR SPOILER and FRONT AIR DAM ("BODY KIT")

new WHEELS (6 OPENINGS)

COUPE (YY 2/8) $30,435.

HANDLING PKG. and 17" WHEELS AVAILABLE

(YY3/8) CONVERTIBLE 35,775.

TOP DETAILS

HIGH-PERFORMANCE, 190 MPH (380 HP)

16/25 MPG

NEW ZR1 OPT.

FOR 1990 HAS 17" WHEELS.

IN 1990, GLOVE BOX RETURNS ON new ANALOG/ DIGITAL INSTR. PANEL.

DRIVER AIRBAG IN 1990

COUPE (YY 2/8) $32,525.

CVT. (YY3/8) 37,765.

1989 V.I.N. ENDS WITH -K-# (1990-L-#)

15/24 MPG (EPA) w. 4 SP. AUTO. TR.

New WHEELS (MORE OPENINGS)

WITH

245-250 HP STD. in 1990

89-90

NEW 6-SPEED MANUAL AVAILABLE 16/25 MPG (EPA)

new OPTIONAL TIRE MONITOR WARNS OF AIR PRESSURE DEFICIENCY. (SIMILAR OPTION REPORTEDLY AVAIL. 1987)

1990 PRICES
3 DR. $32479.
CVT. $37764.
3 DR. ZR-1 = $58,995.

NEW

1990 DASH

CHEVROLET MALIBU
(1964 – 1983)
(ORIGINALLY *CHEVELLE*)

New Dash.

V.I.N.s START w. 1G1, END w. -B- #
WAGON V.I.N.= 1G1AW35K0B(-)100001 UP
1AT35 — MALIBU WAGON **$8178.**

INTERIOR

with optional vinyl roof.
SPT. SED.
1AT69 **$8001.**

SPT. CPE
$7885.

1AT27

108.1" WB
18.2 GAL. FUEL TANK

229 CID V6 (115 HP) OR 267 CID V8 (120 HP)

81 new GRILLE, TAIL-LIGHTS and DASH

Malibu Classic

LANDAU COUPE **$8479.**

← 1AW27
($82/5. CLASSIC SPT. CPE AVAIL.)

$8348.
CLASSIC SEDAN
↙ 1AW69

W. HEATED REAR WINDOW

"CLASSIC" WAGON LEFT REAR PANEL ↓

WOODGRAIN AVAIL. (CLASSIC ESTATE WAGON)
$8726. UP
1AW35

77

P185/75R x 14 TIRES (P195 ON WAGON)

MALIBU CLASSIC

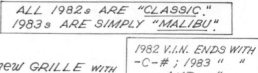

ALL 1982s ARE "CLASSIC."
1983s ARE SIMPLY "MALIBU"

NEW GRILLE WITH
CRISS-CROSS PCS.

1982 V.I.N. ENDS WITH
—C—#; 1983 " "
—AXD—#

82-83

NO MORE
2 DR. MODELS

'83 HAS "MALIBU"
NAME ON SIDE.

SPORT SEDAN
$9321. ('82) 9335. ('83)

GAS OR *DIESEL*
V6s and V8s
NOW AVAIL.

WAGON
$9450.
9468. ('83)

("ESTATE WAGON" STILL AVAIL. ALSO)

INTERIOR

Malibu Classic instrument panel.

1982 EXAMPLES ILLUSTRATED
21 GAL. FUEL TK.
(18.2 GAL. WAGON)
21 MPG (EPA)
23 MPG
DIESEL EPA

1983 HAS "MALIBU"
NAME ON SIDE,
JUST BEYOND FR.
WHEEL OPENING.

DISCONTINUED
1983

Malibu Classic standard notchback bench seat with folding center armrest.

CHEVROLET *JAPANESE - AMERICAN* NOVA - *SPECTRUM - SPRINT*

(AVAIL. 1985-1988)

Nova Hatchback Sedan.

New Chevy Nova. Imported from America.

Nova

93 MPH

NOVA NAME RETURNS 1985, FOR NEW GM/ TOYOTA CARS BLT. IN FREMONT, CAL.

"S" BODY

$9105. ('88)

1988 Chevy Nova

← NOVA →

95.7" WB
97 CID 4
$7485. ('85)

NOVA

24/46 MPG

1986 MODELS ILLUSTRATED, UNLESS OTHERWISE INDICATED.

NOVA SK194 4 DR. JOINED BY 9K684 HATCHBACK IN 1986. (AS SHOWN, UPPER LEFT) NEW TWIN CAM SEDAN ADDED 88, AT $11705. (110 MPH)

(BLT. BY ISUZU, JAPAN)
→ SPECTRUM ←
94½" WB

EARLY SPECTRUMS IMPORTED TO EASTERN USA ONLY. "R" BODY

90 CID 4
31/33 MPG

$6575. ('85)
8450. ('88)

1988 SPRINT TURBO GRILLE

89 MPH

$6295. ('85)
$6785. ('88) (EXPRESS)

1988 TURBO MR2I2

TURBO

(THESE CARS ALL REPLACED BY CHEVY'S NEW 1989 GEO LINE.)

$8470. 104 MPH

SPRINT.

$6026. ('86)

NEW SPRINT 5 DR. IN 1986

EARLY SPRINTS IMPORTED TO WESTERN USA ONLY.

SPRINT
31/58 MPG

'85 FROM $4949.

SPRINT 3 DR.
88.4" WB
3 CYL.
61 CID
48 HP
85 MPH

MFD. BY SUZUKI, JAPAN   "M" BODY

P145/80 SR12 TIRES

SPECTRUM

79

CHRYSLER

(SEE ALSO = CHRYSLER CORDOBA and IMPERIAL)

(SINCE 1924)

V.I.N. =
1C3BM ( )
EOB (-) 00000I UP

81

(NY = 318 CID V8 STD., INSTEAD OF 360 CID)

NEW YORKER (5 AVE. PKG.)
$13,526.

118½" WB

R57

1981 Chrysler LeBaron

M SERIES   **LE BARON**
$7840.

Chrysler LeBaron Town and Country. 26 est hwy, [17] EPA est mpg.
$9176.   M49

MINOR CHANGES ONLY, BETWEEN THESE FULL-SIZED, RWD CHRYSLERS, FOR 1980 and 1981. MAJOR 1981 CHANGES FOR CHRYSLER CORP. INVOLVED ITS ALL-NEW FWD DODGE ARIES and PLYMOUTH RELIANT "K CARS."

sedan

NEW YORKER
$11,704.

R47
NEWPORT
$9092.   118½" WB
(FINAL YEAR)

C SERIES
LeBaron
SEDANS FROM
$9664.
(MEDALLION SEDAN
$9929.)
C 56

new SHORTER 99.9" WB
13 GAL. FUEL TK.

THE FIRST 4-CYL. CHRYSLER SINCE THE 1928 "52" SERIES!
new 4 CYL. ENGINE (135 OR 158 CID)

82

TOTALLY RESTYLED AND DOWNSIZED

PART OF REAR QUARTER PANEL INCORPORATED INTO REAR DOORS.

[40 EST. HWY] [26 EPA EST. MPG]

80

CHRYSLER

V.I.N. = 1C3B
(C or F) ( )
(B or E) - C -
000001 UP

COUPE C42
$9570.
MEDALLION COUPE
$9835. C52

40 EST. HWY 26 EPA EST. MPG

A CONVERTIBLE
For 1982

LE BARON SERIES
(CONT'D.)

$10,852. ('82½)

WAGON V.I.N. = 1C3BC59D(-)C
(-) #

31 EST. HWY 23 EPA EST. MPG

C59

IMITATION
WOODGRAINED
WAGONS ONLY.
(1981 UN-
GRAINED
CHRYSLER WAGON
DISCONT'D.)

INTER.

New **TOWN & COUNTRY.**

WAGON (NOT AVAIL.
UNTIL MID-SEASON)
AM/FM w. 8-TRACK TAPE

17 MPG (EPA)

82

1982 LeBaron Convertible
is the first domestic-built ragtop since the
1976 Cadillac Eldorado.

LE BARON

NEW

31 EST. HWY 23 EPA EST. MPG **$14,900** (AVAIL.
SPRING, 1982)

W. MARK CROSS
LEATHER INTER.

NEW YORKER

$12,152.

AM/FM + CASSETTE

NEW YORKER
has 112.7" WB
225 CID 6
(90 HP @
3600 RPM)
OR'
318 CID V8 (130 HP @
4000 RPM, 2 BBL CARB.)
(IN CALIFORNIA,
4 BBL. CARB.
165 HP @
4000
RPM)

18-GAL. GAS TANK
2.9 G.R. (6)
2.2 G.R. (V8)
P205/75R
× 15
TIRES

F66

18 GAL. FUEL TK.
18 MPG (EPA)

F66

REAR
DETAIL

$13,799.
NEW YORKER
FIFTH AVENUE

5 AVE.

W. VINYL/
LEATHER
UPH.

LeBARON

It starts with great looks and it goes on to make great sense.

$ **12,097.** UP
CVT. (C55)

C51

CPE.
$ **10,055.**

$10,833.
WAGON

C59

$ **9892.**
SED.
C56

CHRYSLER TOWN & COUNTRY

ORIGINAL 1946 T+C CVT. SHOWN ABOVE. (NO T+C CONVERTIBLES BLT. SINCE 1949.)

26 MPG. EPA

C55

NEW

24 MPG, EPA

CVT.
$ **15,965.**

TOWN & COUNTRY CONVERTIBLE

WE'VE RE-ENGINEERED THE AMERICAN LUXURY CAR. THE NEW CHRYSLER CORPORATION. QUALITY ENGINEERED TO BE THE BEST

83 New

$10,487.
E CLASS

T46

E CLASS EXECUTIVE SEDAN (BELOW) NOT AVAILABLE DURING EARLY MONTHS OF 1983.

124" OR 131" WB

CHRYSLER EXECUTIVE SEDAN
Available for order this spring.

CHRYSLER E CLASS

WITH new ELECTRONIC VOICE ALERT SYSTEM (ALSO IN LE BARON)
$ **12,355.**
T56

24 MPG EPA

CHRYSLER NEW YORKER

new 4 CYL., 103" WB

NEW YORKER INT.

V.I.N. =
1C3B ( )
— XD (-)
000001 UP

5TH AVE.
$ **13,862.**
F66

18 MPG EPA

5TH AVE. RETAINS REAR WHEEL DRIVE.

112.7" WB (5TH AVE.)

NY 5 AVE.
225 CID 6 (90 HP) OR 318 CID V8 (130 HP)

NEW YORKER FIFTH AVENUE

82

CHRYSLER

"ELECTRONIC VOICE ALERT" MONITORS 11 VITAL FUNCTIONS

THE 1984 CHRYSLER NEW YORKER
Chrysler's most technologically advanced luxury car.

SIDE LOUVRES CONTINUE TO IDENT-IFY NY + 5 AVE.

BELOW: (5 AVE.) MFS41

DASH WITH NEW GRAPHICS

MPG 31 HWY 23 EPA

135 OR 158 HP 4 CYL.

$13,391.

ETP41 NEW YORKER DETAILS

84

FIFTH AVE.

318 CID V8 (130 HP) MPG: 25 HWY, 17 EPA

5TH AVE.

$15,269.

97" WB

"G" BODY

CHRYSLER LASER New

135 CID 4 (99 HP) OR 135 CID TURBO 4 (146 HP) STD. OR XE HATCHBACKS

LASER DASH GCH24

LASER TURBO AVAIL.

XE=GCP24

83

$10,456. UP

CHRYSLER

CHRYSLER

$16,893.

TOWN + COUNTRY CONVERTIBLE   KCP27

LeBARON

$10,202. SED.   KCP41

41 HWY.
27 EPA

COUPE
$10,357.   KCP22

CVT.
$12,730. KCP27

NEW
REAR QUARTER WINDOWS
and IMPROVED
TOPS ON
CVTS.

84

V.I.N.=1C3B ( ) -XE (-) 000001 UP

$15,893.
(MARK CROSS)
LEATHER UPH.

MPG
31 HWY
23 EPA
new LARGER
FUEL TANK

TOWN
and
COUNTRY
WAGON
KCP45
$10,991.

19,475.
EXECUTIVE
124"
WB
KCP48
CHRYSLER EXECUTIVE SEDAN

new

ETH41
$10,716.

CHRYSLER E CLASS
(FINAL YEAR FOR
E CLASS)

NEW

AJL LIMOUSINE $22,475.
131"
WB
4 CYL.

THRIFTY RENT-A-CAR

KCP48/AJL

In A Chrysler Limousine

84

Chrysler

(BELOW, LEFT): T + C CVT. $17,404.
CVT. KCP27 " WAGON KCP45 $11,510.

The turbocharged Chrysler Town & Country. the power of a V-8 with the efficiency of a 4.

TOWN and CTRY. V.I.N.= IC3BC59GXF (-) 000001 UP

AVAIL. TURBO P185/70R14 TIRES

LE BARON V.I.N.= IC3BC56 DXF (-) 000001 UP 100.3" WB

COUPE

135 OR 158 CID 4 (96 OR 101 HP) $10,607. KCP22

LeBaron

14 GAL. FUEL TANK 3.02 GEAR RAT.

$10,456. SEDAN KCP41

WAGON 23 HWY, 20 EPA

LEBARON GTS NEW

(STYLING DIFF. FR. OTHER CHRYSLERS)

REAR VIEW OF GTS

P185/70R14 TIRES

$13,036. CVT.

LE BARON KCP27

85

new GTS has 135 CID 4 99 HP (OR 146 HP WITH TURBO) (115 MPH)

GTS

Chrysler LeBaron GTS four-door sedan.

3.56 GEAR RATIO

14 GAL. FUEL TANK

HCH44 $10,701.

103.1" WB

(LS $11,597.) HCP44

GTS GRAPHIC INSTR. PANEL

GTS V.I.N.= IC3BH48 DXF (-) 000001 UP P185/70R14 TIRES

TURBO

MORE
GTS
DETAILS

LeBaron GTS.

SEATS

VIEW THRU
GTS
HATCHBACK

5
AVE.
AGAIN
FEATURES
TUFTED
CUSHION-
STYLE
CLOTH
UPHOL.
SEATS

(1985 LASER
SIM. TO 1984)
$10456.
(XE $12378.)
117 MPH

85

131.3" WB
EXECUTIVE
limousine. KCP49
$ **26,830.**
(FINAL YR.) 156 CID 4
MPG 23 HWY, 20 CITY
V.I.N.= IC3B C52 GXF (-) 00000I UP
P185/75R14 TIRES

1985 CHRYSLER FIFTH AVENUE
112.7" WB, 318 CID V8
(130 HP)
$ **15,496.**

MFS41
P205/75R15 TIRES
V.I.N.=
IC3BF64
PXF (-)
00000I UP

1985 Turbo New Yorker.
ADDITIONAL
LOUVRES
ATOP
HOOD

($610. LESS w. TURBO)

158 CID,
101 HP
(OR
135 CID
140 HP
TURBO
4)

4 CYL.
103.1" WB
P185/75R14
TIRES

$ **13,967.**
ETP41
NEW YORKER V.I.N.= IC3BT56GXF (-)00000I/
UP

86

CHRYSLER

V.I.N. = 1C3B ( ) ()
— G — #

(C59D) T+C WAGON **12,537.**

new... HIGH-MOUNTED 3RD BRAKE LIGHT ADDED

86

LE BARON (EXCEPT GTS) has **NEW** AMBER CORNER LIGHTS NEXT TO HEADLIGHTS.

C56D

CHRYSLER **LASER** $11051. UP

$11144. L.B. COUPE C51D

A64E

$11294.

H58D

LASER XT

XT IS TURBO 4

CHRYSLER LASER XE

A54K   LASER XE

LE BARON

TURBO

H48D GTS HIGHLINE **$11441.**

GTS PREMIUM (H58D) (ILLUSTR. ABOVE) **$12367.**

new WIDER 50/50 SEATS IN NEW YORKER

T56K

101 MPH

C55D **LE BARON** CONVERTIBLE **$13862.** (W. MARK CROSS LEATHER INTER., $17005.) (FINAL 1986 WOODGRAINED TRIM TOWN and COUNTRY CVT. $18005.)

103.3" WB

153 CID FUEL INJ. 4 CYL.

New Yorker. **$14,796.**

NY REAR CLOSE DETAIL

(EXECUTIVE LIMO. DISCONTINUED.)

CHRYSLER FIFTH AVENUE F66P **$16241.**

87   112.7" WB   318 CID V8

(LASER DISCONTINUED; RETURNS in PLYMOUTH 1990 LINE.)

CHRYSLER

"H" BODY

LE BARON GTS
HIGHLINE $11,889.
PREMIUM   12,722.

H48D HIGHLINE, H58D PREMIUM
(E SUFFIX W. TURBO 4 ENG.)

new WHEELS

$15,808.

"E" BODY   T56K

NEW YORKER
and ITS INTERIOR

(TOWN and COUNTRY CONVERT. DISCONTINUED)

LE BARON COUPE HIGHLINE C41K
$13,020.
PREMIUM C51K
$14,156.

LE BARON CPE. and CVT. TOTALLY RESTYLED ("CV" BODY)

87

MPG: 22, 27 (135 CID 4)
(19/24 " " " W. A/T)

LE BAR.

New DESIGN

135 CID 4
TURBO
148 HP
@ 5200 RPM

C55E

LE BARON PREMIUM CONVERTIBLE
3.02 GEAR RATIO

109-120 MPH

new WHEELS

(5TH AVE., LE BARON SEDAN, T+C WAGON STILL AVAIL.)

2.51 GEAR RATIO
14 GAL. FUEL TANK
P205/60 HR15 TIRES

new LTS. CONCEALED

FRONTAL
NEW LOOK

5TH AVE. ON NEXT PAGE

88

CHRYSLER

5TH AVE. MPG: 16/21 (318 CID V8)
TWN. + CTRY. WAGON " 19/24 (135 CID 4, A/T)

"M" BODY CONSERVATIVE STYLING RETAINED ON **5TH AVENUE** (4 DR. IS ONLY BODY TYPE.)

REAR DETAILS

F66P

DASH

87

TILT STEERING WHEEL

18-GAL. FUEL TANK

V.I.N. = - 1C3B (C46D) - H - #

OPT. AUTO. SPEED CONTROL

LIGHT-COLORED CAR GIVES ILLUSION OF APPEARING LARGER THAN DARK CARS.

318 CID V8 (140 HP @ 3600 RPM)

$17,831.

F66P

OPT. ILLUMINATED VISOR VANITY MIRROR

P205/ 75R15 TIRES

OPTIONAL AM/FM STEREO/TAPE and DIGITAL CLOCK

1230

5TH AVENUE BACK SEAT

INTERIOR TRIM

Standard Chrysler Fifth Avenue. Kimberly cloth 60/40 individually adjustable front seats with adjustable head restraints, folding center armrest, and passenger side seatback recliner. Available in Dark Blue, Red, Silver, Almond.

Optional Chrysler Fifth Avenue. Corinthian leather with vinyl trim 60/40 individually adjustable front seats with adjustable head restraints, folding center armrest, and passenger side seatback recliner. Available in Dark Blue, Red, Silver, Almond.

CHIMES REMINDER WHEN HEADLIGHTS LEFT ON, KEY IN IGN., OR SEAT BELTS UNFSTND. (A/R CONDITIONING STD.)

CHRYSLER LE BARON

J41D HIGHLINE or J51K PREMIUM

LE BARON COUPE, REG. $13,266. UP

CONVERTIBLE $15,752. UP

$9495. (SPECIAL PRICE.)

2.5-LITER EFI, OR A 2.2-LITER EFI TURBOCHARGED 4 CYL. ENG.

CHRYSLER INTRODUCES THE CRYSTAL KEY PROGRAM. BETTER OWNER CARE THAN EVEN ROLLS ROYCE OR MERCEDES.

MODELS:

| New Yorker Landau |
| New Yorker |
| New Yorker Turbo |
| Fifth Avenue |
| LeBaron Convertible |
| LeBaron Coupe |
| LeBaron Four-Door Sedan |
| Town & Country Wagon |
| LeBaron GTS |
| Conquest TSi |

LE B. TURBO WHEEL

88 A

new RESTYLED N.Y. / LANDAU

J45D HIGHLINE OR J55K PREM. (TURBO, _ E SUFFIX)

New safety

Air bags work quicker than you can blink your eye.

Air bags and seat belts.

H48D HIGHLINE OR H58K PREMIUM (TURBO, _ E)

LE BARON GTS
PERFORMANCE SEDAN

(LITTLE CHANGE FROM 1987) $12,591. UP

LE BARON 4 DR.

C 56 D

$12,522.

LE BARON

NEW
STARTING 5-15-88,
air bags standard equipment *

ON LE BARON CPE. and CVT.; 5TH AVE.; DODGE DAYTONA and DIPLO.; PLY. GRAN FURY

(* ON DRIVER'S SIDE)

STRIPE ALONG SIDE OF TURBO →

(T+C IS DISCONTINUED DURING 1988, RESUMES AS 1990 MINI VAN.)

C59K

$14,125.
TOWN and COUNTRY WAGON

90

CHRYSLER

When you think about it, the air bag is a truly remarkable device. It is made of nylon, with a neoprene coating to seal it. A coating of talcum powder covers the inside of the bag to help it expand fully when activated. It is neatly folded inside the steering wheel trim cover.

When sensors detect a front-end collision of sufficient force to trigger it, the air bag inflates to help protect the driver's head and chest. It all happens in about 50 milliseconds, just half the time it takes to blink your eye. Then, the bag partially deflates.

STEERING COLUMN ATTACHMENT
FOLDED AIR BAG
COVER
INFLATOR
STEERING WHEEL

4 CYL. NEW YORKER TURBO POWER.

THESE MODELS NOT RESTYLED.

U463

F66P

V8-ENGINED

FIFTH AVENUE

1988½ 5TH AVE. HAS DRIVER AIRBAG AS STD. EQUIP. **new**

$18,815.

$17,868.

$19,949.

NEW YORKER LANDAU

U663

New

New V6 ENGINE IN THESE 2 MODELS

INTERIOR DETAILS

new Chrysler New Yorker.

$17,856.

• Advanced front-wheel drive • Powerful new V-6 engine
• Electronic fuel injection • Four-wheel disc anti-lock braking system*
• Self-leveling suspension • Crystal Clear paint
• Adjustable front and rear seat headrests • Power rack-and-pinion steering
• Automatic temperature control air conditioning
• Power six-way driver's seat • Mark Cross leather seating
• Rear-seat stereo headphone controls
• Electronic instrument panel • Electronic speed control
• On-board travel computer • Crystal Key owner care

V.I.N.= -(1C OR JJ) 3B (C54N) -J-#

88

ALTERNATE WHEEL CHOICE

"Landau" NAME ON PADDED REAR QTR. PANEL

CLOSER DETAILS OF
NEW YORKER LANDAU

LE BARON CONVERTIBLE

18/31 MPG

LeBARON COUPE $12,698

CHRYSLER

L.B. CVTS.:

TURBO GTC

HIGHLINE = $15756. J45K
PREMIUM = 18645.
TURBO GT = 18956.
" GTC = 20116.

$17,921.

89
(5 AVE. 16/22 MPG)

(new LE BARON SEDANS AVAIL., 103.1" WB $13256. UP)

FINAL LE BARON GTS

19/34 MPG
$17370. H78A

N.Y. SEDAN C463

LANDAU $20,014. C663

18/26 MPG

SPEC. PRICE
BASE M.S.R.P. $17,416*
OPTION PACKAGE + $2,353
$19,769

V.I.N.
- (C, JJ or ZC)
3 - ( ) - K - #

1989 CHRYSLER NEW YORKER
CHRYSLER. DRIVING TO BE THE BEST.

INTRODUCING ULTRADRIVE, A CHRYSLER EXCLUSIVE. THE MOST ADVANCED FOUR-SPEED AUTOMATIC TRANSMISSION.

After years of development, Chrysler introduces Ultra-drive† The first and only fully adaptive electronic 4-speed automatic transmission. It constantly senses and adjusts for changes in your speed or driving situation. You could say, "It thinks for itself" as it delivers an amazingly smooth, quiet, responsive ride. **Other features include**†: Four-wheel disc anti-lock brake availability. Self-leveling rear suspension.** Vehicle Theft Security System. Power eight-way driver's seat with memory. An abundance of Mark Cross Corinthian leather. On-board travel computer. Crystal Key owner care. In a word, "Everything."

There Is No Luxury Without Engineering.

LE B. CVT. $16279. UP

19/28 MPG (EPA)

new

LeBaron Sedan

LE BARON DASH CPE. FROM $13779

note 2 DIFF. FRONT END STYLES

LeBaron Convertible

New Town & Country

119" WB

25515.

201 CID V6
150 HP
18/24 MPG

new WHEELS

luxurious new interior

LE BARON NOW AVAIL. W. Ultradrive.

↑ LARGE SIDE LIGHT IS new

DESIGN SIMILAR TO DODGE CARAVAN AND PLYMOUTH VOYAGER.

NY SALON $17734.
NY LANDAU 19315.
104.3" WB

5 AVE. INT.

new MITSUBISHI 181.4 CID V6 AVAIL. (141 HP @ 5000 RPM) AS WELL AS 4 and TURBO 4s.

V.I.N. ENDS WITH — L — #

90

U663

$23992.

201 CID V6
(147 HP @ 4800 RPM)

Fifth Ave.
109.3" WB

92

16 GAL. FUEL TK.

17/25 MPG

The New Chrysler Corporation

CHRYSLER CORDOBA

(1975 TO 1983)

DASH

INTER. →

SPECIAL PACKAGE:

Corinthian Edition

(1980 and 1981 ONLY)

$9047.

J52

Cordoba shown in Baron Red

CORDOBA

V.I.N.=1C3BJ (-) 2E0B (-) 00001 UP

J62

LS

$7765.

(REG. $8277.)

LS has DIFFERENT GRILLE, WITH "LS" IN CENTER DISC. (6 CYL. STD.)

W. CABRIOLET ROOF PACKAGE (ABOVE)

81

112.7" WHEELBASE

225 CID 6
318 CID V8
(140 or 155 HP)

P195/75R15 TIRES

AIR COND. CONTROLS

READING LIGHTS

2.7 GEAR RAT. (2.9 w. A/C)

LIGHTED VISOR MIRRORS

TURBINE WHEEL TRIM

17 EPA
26 HWY.
MPG (V8)

93

CHRYSLER CORDOBA

DASH

S52

$10,397.

2.9 GEAR RATIO

82
ALL NOW HAVE PADDED TOPS

CHRYSLER NAME NOW ON LEFT SIDE OF DECK LID

S62 LS $9458.

225 CID 6 (90 HP @ 3600)
318 CID V8 (130 @ 4000;
165 HP IN CALIFORNIA)

V.I.N. = IC3BS52
EOC (-) 00000/ UP

18 GAL. FUEL TANK   18 MPG (EPA)

LS
SHOWN WITH OPTIONAL
CABRIOLET ROOF TREATMENT

FINAL YEAR
FOR LS
MODEL

DASH

• Automatic Transmission • Power Front Disc Brakes • Dual Remote Mirrors • Glass Belted Radials • Halogen Headlamps • Electronic Digital Clock • Leather Wrapped Steering Wheel • Padded Landau Vinyl Roof • and 12 additional luxury features.

V.I.N. = IC3B S52 HXD (-) 00000/ UP

$11,006.
S52

24 EST HWY   18 EPA EST MPG
We've re-engineered the American luxury car.
THE NEW CHRYSLER CORPORATION QUALITY ENGINEERED TO BE THE BEST

83

225 CID 6 (90 HP)
OR
318 CID V8 (140 HP)

INTERIOR

(CORDOBA DISCONTINUED DURING 1983)

Chrysler

94

Chrysler Imperial.

(1926 – 1975;
1981 – 1983;
RETURNS 1990)

MARK CROSS INTERIOR ('81)

"Every luxury is standard. And there are more luxuries standard than any car in America."

KNOWN SIMPLY AS "IMPERIAL", 1954 – 1975 and 1981 – 1983.

112.7" WB
318 CID V8
140 HP @ 4000 RPM

('81) DASH

The New Chrysler Corporation.
CORPORATE SYMBOL

2-DR. ONLY

18 GALLON FUEL TANK
16 MPG (EPA) ('82)

it's time for Imperial.

$18,822. ('81)
21,513. ('82)
19,228. ('83)

NEW 81-83

MODEL Y-62

LITTLE CHANGE FROM 1981 TO 1983.
P205/75R x 15 TIRES
2.24 GEAR RATIO

NO IMPERIALS AVAILABLE 1984 TO 1989.

LEE IACOCCA, CHAIRMAN OF THE "NEW CHRYSLER CORP." FRANK SINATRA, MOVIE AND RECORDING STAR

('83) V.I.N. ENDS WITH —B-# (1981) —C-# (1982) —D-# (1983)

THEY APPEARED (AND WERE QUOTED) IN VARIOUS IMPERIAL ADS.

RETURNS 1990 AS "CHRYSLER IMPERIAL."

3.3L (201 CID) V6 (147 HP @ 4800 RPM) 17/25 MPG
16 GALLON FUEL TANK

90 New 109.3" WB
$25545.

4 DR. ONLY
V.I.N. ENDS WITH —L-#

195/75R x 14 TIRES

Mark Cross Ultrasoft leather.

95

(1989-1990)

CHRYSLER MASERATI "TC"

convertible
soft or removable hard top.

ASSEMBLED IN ITALY BY
MASERATI-INNOCENTI
IMPORTED BY CHRYSLER

1990 MPG. FIGS.
18/25 EPA w.
4 CYL. and 5 SP.
MANUAL TRANS.
17/24 w. V6 and A/T

('89) FP10

WITH
ITALIAN LEATHER UPH.

$30,000. UP

$33,000 IN
1990

4 CYL. DOHC
16-VALVE ENGINE
135 CID   7.3 COMPR.
200 HP @ 5500 RPM
3.47 G.R.   5 SP. TRANS.
(NEW 181 CID MITSUBISHI V6 (141 HP) ALSO
FOR 1990)

160 HP 4 ALSO
AVAIL. 1989

18/22
MPG ('89)

CLOSER
REAR
DETAILS

93" WHEELBASE

"Q"
BODY

89
-90

DRIVER'S
AIRBAG IN
NEW GRAINED
STEERING WHEEL FOR 1990

135 M.P.H.

14 GAL. FUEL TK.

MASERATI EMBLEM
AT CONSOLE

V.I.N.
ENDS
WITH
—K
—#
(1989)

—L
—#
(1990)

('89)

205/60 VR 15 TIRES

New

96

Imported for Dodge and Plymouth, built by Mitsubishi Motors Corp. in Japan.

COLT

(SINCE 1971)

4 CYL. (86 OR 98 CID, 64 OR 72 HP @ 5000 RPM)
90.6" WB

- Room for five
- MCA-JET engine
- 3-Door hatchback
- Front-wheel drive • Built by Mitsubishi Motors Corp., of Japan.

*Sticker prices higher: CA, LA, MA, MD, MS, NE, NJ, WI, AK, CO, TX, WA.

DE LUXE
$5300. ('81)
$5889. ('82)

note RUB RAIL ON SIDE OF DE LUXE (ABOVE)

(1982 EXAMPLES ILLUSTRATED)

1981
V.I.N. =
3B3BE (-) 4 (-) 0B10000I UP

COLT STANDARD
$5075. ('81)

INTERIORS

THE LOWEST-PRICED HIGH-MILEAGE JAPANESE IMPORTS... DODGE COLT & PLYMOUTH CHAMP...

$4995
*BASE STICKER PRICE. LOWEST PRICED OF ALL CARS OVER 37 EPA ESTIMATED MPG.

-400
FACTORY REBATE AT PARTICIPATING DEALERS

$4595
*SUGGESTED RETAIL PRICE WITH REBATE

*EXCLUDING TAX, TITLE, LICENSE, DESTINATION CHARGE AND OPTIONAL EQUIPMENT. NOT AVAILABLE IN AREAS WHERE HIGH ALTITUDE EMISSION PACKAGE IS REQUIRED.

MPG
39 EPA
51 HWY

DASH

COLT CUSTOM
$5606 $6211.
('81)   ('82)

51 EST HWY MPG 39 *EPA EST MPG
Use EPA estimate for comparison only. Your mileage may vary. Actual highway mileage will probably be less. CA mileage lower.

81-82

('82)

DODGE COLT ("IDL" BODY)

$5532.

('82½)
SIMILAR PLYMOUTH "CHAMP" AVAIL. '79-'82

$5632.

PLYMOUTH CHAMP
(FINAL CHAMP)

'82 V.I.N. JB3BE242(-)C(-)00000I UP

RS (ABOVE)
Dodge Colt RS
Our fun to drive, economical to run, top of the line Colt RS has a touch of class and a whole lot of sportiness and value almost everywhere you look.

RS WITH 2 TONE PAINT AND "RS" DECAL

These good-looking cast aluminum road wheels and P175/70R13 radial tires are part of the RS Package and Road Wheel Package, both available as options on Colt Custom. (Raised white letter—RS only.)

97

COLT

HIGH-TECH IMPORTS

Dodge · Plymouth

STARTING 1983, MITSUBISHI ALSO BEGINS IMPORTING OTHER MODELS UNDER ITS OWN NAME.

35 EPA* EST MPG 45 EST HWY

COLT GTS *new*

REGULARLY $5084. (2 DR.)

4 DR. FROM $5688.

51 HWY EST MPG 38 EPA** EST MPG

DELUXE 2-DR. HATCHBACK $5809.

CUSTOM 2-DR. HATCHBACK $6148.

CUSTOM 4-DR. HATCHBACK $6268

V.I.N. = JP3 BE242 (–) D(–) 000001 UP

83

Enter Colt GTS, imported only for Dodge and Plymouth. With black matte accents all around, rakish spoiler, side-glass louvres, wide tires, GTS badges and racing stripes, this Colt looks the part

V.I.N. = J(B) 3BE 24 AXE (–) 000001 UP

3.DPM45

IMPORTS WITH A PURPOSE

new

TURBO COLT:

VISTA WAGON 103.3" WB 4 CYL.

REG. $8205.

84

Vista is the wagon re-invented for today. Vista seats 7 passengers and those seats flip up or down, to handle just about any combination of people and things.

36 EST HWY 28 EPA* EST MPG

TURBO COLT (w. 1.6L TURBOCHARGED 4 102 HP @ 5500 RPM) WITH MICHELIN XVS 165/70 HR 13 TIRES

VISTA

53 EST HWY 41 EPA* EST MPG

WITH VARIOUS SEATING ARRANGEMENTS

TALLER and WITH MORE HEADROOM THAN OTHER COLT MODELS

$8,115 ADV. SPEC. PRICE

HATCHBACKS ARE NOW CALLED "3 DOOR" OR "5 DOOR" MODELS.

$4,995 SPECIAL AD. PRICE

98

DODGE Plymouth
IMPORTS

85-86

RESTYLED FOR 1985

98 cid TURBO 4 has 102 HP @ 5500 RPM   3.47 GEAR RATIO
11.9 GALLON FUEL TANK
185/60R 14 TIRES
('1985)

Colt

VISTA WAGON $8811. or $9899.
122 cid 4 (88 HP @ 5000)   103.3" WB   (WITH 4-WH DRIVE) new

3.19 GEAR RATIO
13.2 GAL. FUEL TK.

VISTA has P165/80R13 TIRES   ('85)

$5372

4WD COLT VISTA WAGON HAS TOP SPEED OF 84 MPH (1985)

('85)

$7624. ('86)

new

PREMIER SEDAN
I.D. PH41 (A4GF)

185/60 HR 14 TIRES

$7409.
7624. (1986)

1986 MODEL, WITH new WHEEL DESIGN

"TURBO" INSCRIPTION ON DOOR

1985 V.I.N. = J(B)3BE24AXF(-)000001 UP

1986 V.I.N.=(DODGE)
IB3B (A24K)-G-
(PLY.) (I or J) P3B (A24K)-G-

$5372. (SALE PRICE)

37 CITY EST MPG   41 HWY EST MPG

('85)

Colt. It's all the Japanese you need to know.

1987 MPG: 29/33 (90 CID 4); 24/26 (98 CID 4); 23/24 (VISTA WAGON w. 122 CID 4)

1987 V.I.N. = 1B3B (A24K)—H—#

Colt

(DODGE = "1DL" BODY)
(PLYMOUTH = "1PL" BODY)

Dodge Plymouth
IMPORTS

Four-wheel drive

4WD INTRO. ON VISTA DURING '85.

4WD $12108. H39D
('87)
$10864.
2WD
G39D

(OPT.)

Colts are built by Mitsubishi and sold exclusively at Chrysler-Ply. **Dodge**

VISTA: DODGE "3DM" BODY
PLYMOUTH "3PM" "

EXCEPT ON VISTA ABOVE, "COLT" NAME MOVED TO CENTER OF GRILLE.

Colt Premier
4-DR. $8926.
A46K (SHOWN ABOVE)
('87)

BELOW: E
3 DR. HATCHBACK
$6169.

TURBO DL HATCHBK.
A34F
(A34K W/O TURBO)

87–

new WHEEL DESIGNS

88

TURBOCHARGED ENGINE, $748. EXTRA
AUTO. TRANS. 455.
AIR COND.. $717.
POWER STEERING $236.

1988 V.I.N. =
JB3B
(A24K)
—J—#

"DL" wagon ('88)

INTRODUCED 1988

A24K E

25/46 MPG

$8859. SPECIAL PRICE

1988 COLTS PRICED FROM $6134. (DOWN $35.)

New

優秀 Colt
It's all the Japanese you need to know.

(REG. $8898.)

A39P

Buckle up for safety

1989 V.I.N. ENDS WITH -K-#

Colt **Standard** INTERIOR

Dodge Plymouth IMPORTS

$7760. E

28/38 MPG ('89) (1.5L 4)

Colt E is shown in Light Blue.

STD.

$6678*

13.2 GAL. FUEL TK.

**Base sticker price comparison of 1989 Colt vs. 1988 Nissan Sentra. Standard equipment levels vary. Buckle up for safety.

* REG. $6933.

VISTA

THESE MODELS RESTYLED (1989 EXAMPLES ILLUSTRATED) 93.9" WB

23/29 MPG

('89)   (ABOVE)   GT TURBO

wagons $9118. ('89)

← DL $9571. 2WD

$11,400. 4WD

STD., E, GT, DL, GT TURBO, VISTA MODELS (E NOT LISTED IN 1990.)

DL WAGON $9571. ('89) 12.4 GAL. FUEL TK.   10196. ('90)

89-90

23/36 MPG (EPA)

4WD

AVAIL. IN EITHER WAGON AT EXTRA COST

135 HP TURBO 4 NOT AVAIL. 1990.

FRONT DETAILS OF VISTA

13.2 GAL. FUEL TK. (14.5" w. 4WD)

2WD $11,773.   4WD $13,083.

12,913. ('90) VISTA HAS $13,880. ('90)

122 CID 4 (96 HP @ 5000 RPM)

22/28 MPG

NEW 1.5-LITER 4-CYL. EFI 90 CID ENGINE (STD. IN ALL BUT GT 1.6L TURBO, VISTA) (81, 87, OR 113 HP 1990)

STD.

優秀 Colt
It's all the Japanese you need to know.

1990 V.I.N. ENDS WITH - L -#

GT TURBO DASH

101

CONQUEST

(1984-1989)

MADE IN JAPAN BY MITSUBISHI and EXCLUSIVELY DISTRIBUTED BY

Dodge Plymouth

C4JE

new 84

95.9" WB
156 CID TURBO 4 (145 HP @ 5000 RPM) $13,464.
P195/70R14 TIRES (15" AVAIL.)

WHEEL DETAIL

DISC BRAKES (SINCE 1984)

"TECHNICA" PKG. AVAIL. (SINCE 1984)

$13,902.   123 MPH

C54H

85

5 SP. MANUAL or 2 SP. AUTO TRANS. (SINCE 1984)
V.I.N.=J(B)3BC44HXF(-)#

INTERIOR   ('84)

('84 V.I.N.=HXE INSTEAD OF HXF)

155.9 CID TURBO 4 176 HP @ 5000 RPM 3.54 G.R. 19.8 GAL. FUEL TANK

$14,756.

Dodge Plymouth

V.I.N. ENDS WITH —G—#

5 SP. TRANS.

3.54 GEAR RATIO

C54H

86

new INTERCOOLED ENGINE PKG.= $2200. EXTRA

TSi ILLUSTR.

18/24 MPG ('89)

DISTRIBUTED BY CHRYSLER, 1987 TO 1989.

C54H   C54N (1988 and 1989)

87-89

V.I.N. ENDS WITH
—H—# (1987)
—J—# (1988)
—K—# (1989)

('88)

1987 $16365. C54H

1988 TSi $19976. C54N

1989 TSi $20902. C54N

TSi INTERCOOLER PKG. OPT. '87

(DISCONT'D. DURING 1989)

102 (SIMILAR TO MITSUBISHI STARION)

DODGE and DODGE ARIES K.

6-passenger sedan. **$5,980** 41 / 25 EST HWY EPA EST MPG.

ARIES-K SEDAN

IN (STD., CUSTOM, SE SERIES)

6-passenger coupe. **$5,880** 41 / 25 EST HWY EPA EST MPG.

Dodge

ARIES-K COUPE

ARIES IS **NEW 81** K CAR (FWD)

INTER.

ARIES-K WAGON 6-passenger wagon. **$6,721** 40 / 24 EST HWY EPA EST MPG.

99.6" WB
135 OR 158 CID 4

P175/75 R13 TIRES

REGULAR ARIES PRICE FROM $ **7452.**

K59 GRAINED SE WAGON $8736.

ARIES V.I.N. 1B3K(--) BOB (-) #

$8838.

SALON DIPLOMAT WAGON M49

(M39 WAGON W/O GRAIN $8257.)

FARM FRESH

IN (SPEC., SALON, MEDALLION SERILS)

DIPLOMAT

112.7" WB
(COUPES, 108.7")
225 CID SLANT 6
(85 HP @ 3600)
318 CID V8 (130 HP @ 4000)
(90, 165 HP IN CALIFORNIA)

DIPLOMAT DASH

2.7 OR GEAR RATIO
P195/75 R15 TIRES

FINAL M22 SPT. CPE. $ **7663.**

DIPLOMAT V.I.N. = 1B3BM ( )OB(-) #

MIRADA V.I.N.= 1B3BJ62 EOB (-) 10000/ UP

R-47 # ST. REGIS

SEDAN

J62 **MIRADA** H/T
112.7" WB
6 OR V8

118½" WB, 6 OR V8
NEW RUB STRIP

$ **8778.**
($8083. SPEC.)

ST. REGIS

$ **8889.**
FINAL ST. REG. LITTLE CHANGE FROM 1980

Mirada CMX.
$ **9277.** UP
(SPECIAL PRICE)

24/18 MPG (6)

ARIES DASH

ARIES
FROM
$7690.

Dodge

ST. REGIS DISCONT'D.

America's Driving Machines

ARIES

D21

1982 ARIES HAS "D" MODEL DESIGNATION ("K" IN 1981)

13 GALLON FUEL TANK

26 MPG (EPA)

ARIES INTERIOR

D49 CUSTOM $8956.

Aries K 4-door—America's highest mileage 6-passenger sedan.

V.I.N.=1B3B( )-C-#

82

new "PENTASTAR" HOOD and DECK ORNAMENTS

NEW

Aries K wagon—America's highest mileage 6-passenger wagon.

D59-9E $9528.

New (First Dodge Convertible since 1971)
400 CONVERTIBLE
V45

13 GAL. FUEL TANK
26 MPG (EPA)

$13,727.

V46 (LS) V56

400 SEDAN (REAR DOORS EXTEND INTO QUARTER PANEL)

400 "LS" V51 COUPE $9735.

99.9" WB 135 OR 156 CID 4

Dodge 400's.
NEW

6 OR V8 (DIPLOMAT, DIPLOMAT MEDALLION SEDANS STILL AVAIL., FROM $8950.)

225 CID V6 OR 318 CID V8

(18 GAL. FUEL TANK 18 MPG EPA, MIRADA AND DIPLOMAT)

Mirada CMX

$9819. UP (CMX PKG. EXTRA COST)

X62

104

WITH A LOW PRICE: $6577.***

(REG. $8410. AND UP)

26 MPG EPA

$8551. UP

$9391. UP

Dodge
AMERICA'S DRIVING MACHINES

ARIES
(ABOVE, AND AT LEFT)

V51 COUPE $9592.

1983 DODGE
V.I.N. = (1 OR J)
B3B (E242) - D - #

V56 SEDAN $9555.

FINAL "400" MODELS IN 1983

DODGE 400

26 MPG EPA

LOTS OF MPGS:
41 EST. HWY.,
29 EPA EST. MPG:**

new 5-SP. MANUAL TRANSAXLE AVAIL.

CONVERTIBLE

V55 CVT. $13,602.

New

INTRODUCING DODGE 600.

E46 SED. $9987.

24 MPG EPA

102.9" WB   4 CYL.
13.5 OR 158 CID
94 OR 93 HP

TRANSVERSE-MOUNTED 2.2 LITER ENGINE 32 EST HWY, 24 EPA EST. MPG**

MANY DODGE DIPLOMAT SEDANS USED IN TAXI SERVICE.

Yellow

G26 18 MPG EPA

DIPLOMAT FROM $9674. CONTINUES GRILLE STYLE INTRODUCED 1980.

83

Dodge MIRADA $10,689* (AS EQUIPPED)

112.7" WB   225 CID 6 OR 318 CID V8
(100 HP)   (140 HP)

DASH

new "TALKING CAR" RECORDED VOICE WARNING SYSTEM

600 ES $9472*

(REG. $10,518.)
98 MPH

INCLUDES:
(600 ES)
FRONT-WHEEL DRIVE

38 EST. HWY. 23 EPA EST. MPG**

5/50 PROTECTION PLAN†

FIVE-PASSENGER SEATING

TRANSVERSE-MOUNTED 2.2 LITER ENGINE

ALUMINUM ROAD WHEELS

FIRM-FEEL POWER STEERING
(WITH QUICKER RATIO)

POWER BRA[KES]
(FRONT DISC, RE[AR]

SPORT SUSPENSION
(LARGER SWAY BARS, FRONT & REAR, HIGHER-CONTROL SHOCKS, FRONT & REAR)

5-SPEED MANUAL TRANSMISSION

STEEL-BELTED RADIALS

ELECTRONIC VOICE ALERT
(MONITORS 10 FUNCTIONS)

DUAL OUTSIDE POWER MIRRORS

AM RADIO

RECLINING BUCKET SEATS

DIGITAL CLOCK

PADDED DOOR TRIM PANELS

CARPETED TRUNK

SPORT STEERING WHEEL

POWER TRUNK RELEASE

ELECTRIC FUEL-FILLER DOOR RELEASE

BUMPER RUB STRIPS

105

X82 (FINAL MIRADA H/T AVAIL., $10437.)

600 ES

Dodge

84

400 SERIES IS DISCONTINUED

DODGE ARIES K.

INTERIOR

$8743. AND UP

Highest mileage: 41 est. hwy., [29] EPA

new 100.3" WB

ARIES SE INTERIOR

ARIES FRONT END, WITH CLOSE VIEW OF new WHEEL

1984 V.I.N.= IB3B (E24A) - E - #

600 ES $11115.

600 SERIES.

108 MPH

4 CYL. OR TURBO 4

new 600 CONV'TS.

$11949. UP

WITH new POWER QUARTER WINDOWS

600 DASH

CARAVAN WAGON 19

NEW "S" BODY 106

MPG 41 DIPLOMAT SE (RESTYLED FRONT) $11432.

DIPLOMAT

REAR WHEEL DR.

112.7" WB 318 CID V8 (130 HP)

Dodge

100.3" WB **ARIES.**
(RESTYLED)

FROM $**8842.**

73 IMPROVEMENTS
IN ARIES. 4 CYL.
135 OR 158 CID
(96 OR
101
HP)

INTERIOR

P175/80R
x 13 TIRES

3.05 GEAR RATIO
14 GAL. FUEL TANK

(DIPLOMAT
FROM $10748.)

28
MPG
(EPA)

HDS44

**LANCER
ES TURBO**
$11,317.

14 GAL. FUEL
TANK

New *Lancer*

P185/70R14
TIRES

600
ES CVT.
TURBO
4

HDH44
103.1" WB
135 CID 4 OR
TURBO 4 (99, 146 HP)

3.56 GEAR RATIO

85

$10,390.

KVP27/AGT
$15,142.

V.I.N. = (1 OR J)
B3B (A24K)
- F - #

Dodge
AN
AMERICAN
REVOLUTION

P185 (195) 70R14
TIRES

ARIES K

V.I.N. = 1B3B
(A24K)
G II

86

LANCER X48 SPT. SED.
$11113.
X68D "ES" SPT. SED.
$12009.
103.1"
WB

DODGE LANCER

4 OR
TURBO 4

SE, LE SERIES ALSO
(INCL. WAGON)

600
$9796.
UP

100.3"
WB
103.3"
4 DR.

9202.
UP

ARIES K (4 CYL.)   100.3" WB

600 MODELS :
V56D SEDAN
E31D COUPE
V55D CVT.
E46D "9E" SED.

NEW HIGH-MOUNTED 3RD BRAKE LT.

NOTE LOUVRES ON THE HOOD

Dodge 5/50
DIVISION OF CHRYSLER MOTORS

↑ THIS ES (CVT. ONLY) HAS 135 CID TURBO 4

(V8 DIPLOMAT SALON AND SE SEDAN AVAIL., FROM $11385.)

(SIMILAR TO 1984 ILLUSTRATED)

DODGE

AN AMERICAN REVOLUTION

(2 VIEWS)

86

DODGE 600 ES TURBO

V55E $15266.

"P" BODY 924D SHADOW COUPE $9104.

DODGE SHADOW 97" WB
4 CYL. OR TURBO 4 111 MPH New

928D SHADOW SED. AVAIL., AT $9304.

MPG: 23/27 25/33 (5 SP. 135 CID 4.)

87

SHADOW (REAR)

V.I.N. 1B3B (Z/8C) — H-#

SALON OR SE DIPLOMAT MPG: 16/21 (w. 318 CID V8) $11922 SALON G26P $13002 SE G56P (ILLUSTR. AT LOWER LEFT)

ARIES LE $9988.

D41D CPE.

"K" BODY

STD. AND LE ARIES ONLY; SE DISCONT'D.

ARIES MPG: 23/28 (135 CID 4, A/T) 22/27 (152 CID 4)

600 MPG 19/26 w. 135 CID 4 and A/T 22/27 (152 CID 4)

1987 DODGE LANCER.
LANCER MPG: 23/26 (135 CID 4, A/T) 22/27 (152 CID 4)

X48D SPT. SED. OR X68D ES SPT. SED. "H" BODY

"E" BODY

↑ 600 E30D SEDAN $11218. E46D SE SEDAN $11880.

1987 DODGE DIPLOMAT. SE "M" BODY 108

REG. $11589. UP ($9852. ADV. SPEYAL)

109

COUPE P24D

SHADOW

SED. P28D

19/34 MPG

SHADOW →

THE NEW SPIRIT OF DODGE

Dodge DIVISION OF CHRYSLER CORPORATION

SPIRIT DASH

SHADOW

$10050. (CPE.)
$10250. (SEDAN)

89

V.I.N. = (1 or J) B3 —
(P24D) — K — #

A46G or
"LE" A56G
SPIRIT

SPIRIT
FROM $11489.

18/34 MPG

SPIRIT REPLACES 600

New IN 1989
103.3" WB 2.5 L.
4 or TURBO 4

ES

Spirit. ES

3.0 L V6 AVAIL. ALSO

A76J SPIRIT ES
$14310.

SPIRIT ES
INTERIOR
and
REAR
DETAILS

SPIRIT SEDANS ONLY

ES HAS ADDIT'N'L.
LOWER GRILLE AND LTS.

ES
TURBO 4

LANCER SHELBY
$17670

H78A
19/24 MPG

Lancer Shelby is shown above in Bright White Pearl Coat.

DYNASTY FROM $13575.

ARIES AMERICA
FINAL 1989 MODEL
K41D

$9600.
23/34 MPG

16/22 MPG

DIPLOMAT

(ARIES, LANCER,
DIPLOMAT
DISCONTINUED 1990.)

110

DYNASTY

DODGE

SHADOW
P24D
LIFTBACK COUPE
$10525.
(SHADOW P48D
4 DR. AVAILABLE,
$10725.)
93 HP UP

SHADOW INTERIOR

SPIRIT INTER.

97" WB

2.2 OR 2.5L 4 OR
TURBO 4.
2.5 L 4 OR 150 HP
TURBO 4 OR 3.0L V6
AVAIL. IN
SPIRIT.

$14956.
SPIRIT ES

DODGE SPIRIT
ES TURBO

SPIRITS FROM
$12418.

103.3" WB

(ARIES, LANCER, DIPLOMAT
ARE DISCONTINUED.)

Spirit

A76J ES
2.5 L TURBO
4 OR 3.0L
OHC MPI V6
103.3" WB

3.3-liter OHV
MPI V-6

NEW 3.3 L OHV MPI
V6 ENGINE AVAIL. ON
DYNASTY
LE (3.0 V6,
4 CYL. 2.5L
ALSO)

V.I.N. ENDS
WITH — L—#

90

(ALL 4 DRS.
EXC. SHADOW)

(SPIRIT and SPIRIT LE
have 2.5 L 4 ENG.,
WITH ES ENGINES
OPTIONAL.)

MONACO ES INTERIOR
(LEATHER SEATS and POWER SEAT
CONTROLS OPT.)

100 OR 141 HP
OR 147 HP **DODGE DYNASTY.** 104.3" WB
$15034. UP

MONACO INTRO. FOR
1990½ SEASON

NEW MONACO
LE OR ES
106" WB

MONACO
SIMILAR TO
EAGLE
PREMIER

MONACO SERIES RETURNS
(FIRST SINCE 1978)

3.0 L OHC
MPI V6
4 SP. A/T   26 MPG EPA

(MADE IN JAPAN)

V.I.N.=
3B3B
D437
OB
10001
UP

New Dodge Challenger • Dodge

From Mitsubishi high technology
(1978–1983)

D 43 **81**

INTERIOR

99" WB
155.9 CID 4
105 HP
5-SP. TRANS.

$7516. UP *

195/70 HR × 14 TIRES
* (ILLUSTR. ALUMINUM WHEELS OPTIONAL.)

(PLYMOUTH SAPPORO IS SIMILAR)

HP CUT TO 100

D 43 **82**

V.I.N.=
JB3BD437
(-)C(-)
000001 UP

$8036.

AVAIL. UPH.

NEW

$8323.

"TECHNICA" INSTRUMENT PANEL

45 MPH

STANDARD DASH

The Anti-Shock Sticker

D 43 **83**

OPT. "TECHNICA" PKG. INCLUDES new GRAPHIC INSTR. PANEL, BLACK and SILVER BODY PAINT, ETC.

CHALLENGER & SAPPORO: MORE STANDARD EQUIPMENT

PRICES START AT ONLY $8323.

Cars shown, with aluminum road wheels, 4-wheel disc brakes with 9" vacuum booster, **$8698.** Sticker Price, excluding title, taxes, license and destination charge.

*Use EPA estimated MPG for comparison. Actual mileage may vary. Highway mileage probably lower. California mileage lower.

V.I.N.=
JP3BD437(-)D
(-)000001 UP

Dodge CHARGER

4 CYL.
104.7 or 133 cid
(63 or
94 HP)
96.6" WB

(RE-INTRO. 1981)
(ORIG. 1966 TO
1978)

REG. $7721. ('82)
80.54. ('83)

P175 75R x13 TIRES
FRONT WHEEL DRIVE

41 ⎹26⎸ mpg.
EST HWY | EPA EST MPG
THE 2.2 VERSION. $7438
MPG: 46/28
Z54
1982
1983

BASE MODEL
HATCHBACK
34/51 MPG

Z44 ('83)

$7213.
('83)

1981 MODEL
DOES NOT
HAVE EMBLEM
ON HOOD.

81 -83

SUNROOF
OPTIONAL

EACH OF THE 3 BASIC
CHARGER TYPES HAS ITS OWN
UNIQUE REAR QUARTER
PANEL and WINDOW STYLING
AS SHOWN. (SIMILAR TO PLY.
HORIZON TC-3 and TURISMO.)

1983 MODELS ILLUSTRATED

V.I.N.	1981	ENDS	WITH	B #
	1982	"	"	C #
	1983	"	"	D #

THE SHELBY VERSION. $8290*
(BELOW)

Dodge
AMERICA'S
DRIVING
MACHINES

CARROLL
SHELBY.

SPECIAL SHELBY COLORS:

RADIANT
SILVER WITH
SANTA FE
BLUE TAPE,
OR
SANTA FE BLUE WITH
RADIANT SILVER TAPE.

1983½
SHELBY HAS OWN
GRILLE DESIGN,
LESS WINDOW
SPACE, AND IS

NEW
IN MID
1983

MPG
40/25

CHARGER

SHELBY

117 MPH

P195/50 R x15 TIRES
GOODYEAR

113

Z64 SHELBY
REG. $8602.

107 HP
@ 5600 RPM

Dodge CHARGER

CHARGER 2+2

LZP24
$8101.
(SPECIAL PRICE $7288.)

LZH24

LZS924

BASE CHARGER SG49 REG. $7420.

SHELBY CHARGER S8541

↑ SHELBY CHARGER REG. $9534.

LZS24

EXCEPT FOR SHELBY LZS24 CHARGER, NOW WITH 4 HEADLIGHTS

FRONT-WHEEL-DRIVE SPORT COUPE.

96.6" WB
97.1 OR 133 CID 4 (94, 110 HP)
133 CID H.O. 4 AVAIL.

24/37 MPG

2+2 INTER. →

2+2 BASE CHARGER FRONT END

OPTIONAL CHARGER 2+2 INTERIOR

INTRO. new DODGE DAYTONA

84

97" WB (BELOW)
97.1 OR 135 CID 4 (99 HP)
135 CID TURBO 4 (142 HP)
(140 HP WITH A/T)

GVH24

DAYTONA

DAYTONA DASH

DAYTONA TURBO
$9898.

$11817. GVS24

01 GAL CONSUMED

↑ 1984½

122 MPH

SPECIAL MID YEAR PRICE: $9232.*

NOTE DIFFERING WHEELS AS WELL AS OTHER VARIATIONS ILLUSTR.

V.I.N. ENDS WITH —E— #

MPG: 24/43

DAYTONA INT.

P195/60VR x 15 GOODYEAR EAGLE GT TIRES STD. ON TURBO Z PKG.

2.2 LITER ENGINE
DAYTONA TURBO Z. PACKAGE

CHARGER, DAYTONA

32% NASTIER.

Dodge's incredible Shelby Charger now boasts an unfair advantage. Turbocharging.

V.I.N. ENDS WITH — F — #

85

LZS24 $9391.

P205/50VR 15 TIRES (SHELBY)

CHARGER 97.1 CID 4 (64 HP); 135 CID 4 (101 HP)

3.56 GEAR RATIO
13 GAL. FUEL TANK

AN AMERICAN REVOLUTION

124 MPH

DAYTONA INTER.

MPG (EPA)
34 HWY. /
23 CITY

DAYTONA

GVH24 ADV. SPEC. PRICE, (REG. $10107.) $8505.
5-SP. TRANS.; FUEL INJECT.

135 CID TURBO 4 (146 HP)

DAYTONA TURBO Z

ALUMINUM WHEELS, $322.

GV924 TURBO DAYTONA (W. "Z" PKG.)

$11,888., PLUS COST OF "Z" PKG.

NEW WHEELS

BASE MODEL CHARGER, 2.2, and SHELBY CHARGER TURBO CONTINUE ($7790. TO $9747.)

130 MPH (SHELBY GLHS)

A44D

DAYTONA Z TURBO HATCHBACK

$12,988.
(T-BAR ROOF OPTIONAL AT EXTRA COST)
146 HP

V.I.N. ENDS WITH — G — #

86

A64E

DAYTONA HATCHBACK
$10,700.

AN AMERICAN REVOLUTION

115

CHARGER, DAYTONA

DAYTONA MPG 22/27 (w. 152 cid 4)

$14,474. "L" BODY A64E

('87)

FINAL CHARGER AND SHELBY CHARGER ('87)

Z44C CHARGER, $7585. Z64E SHELBY CHR., $10,226. 134 MPH

DAYTONA SHELBY Z

AG4A, $15176. IN 1988

(SEE DODGE VEH. I.D. NUMBERS)

DAYTONA TURBO Z

CHARGER DASH

IT'S GOTTA BE A DODGE.

('87)

new

"G" BODY

DAYTONA PACIFICA

$15 637. ('87) A54E

DAYTONA PACIFICA

($15 488., 1988)

2 VIEWS ('88)

87-88

A44K

DODGE DAYTONA

$8995.* ('88)

SPECIAL PRICE

* REG. $11,807.

WHEELS SHOWN, $310. EXTRA

Daytona, shown in Daytona Blue Clear Coat

DASH ('89)

THE NEW SPIRIT OF DODGE
THE PERFORMANCE DIVISION OF CHRYSLER MOTORS

$14634. ('89) 16066. ('90)

G74A SHELBY ('90) (LEFT and BELOW) (G74C IN 1990)

('89) 174 HP 4 (TURBO)

89-90

19/32 MPG (EPA)

DRIVER AIRBAG STD. ↓

DAYTONA

SHELBY

G24K $11,045. ('89)
G44K (ES) 12,145. "
G64J (ES TURBO) 13,870. "
A44K $11,808. ('90)
ES   13,008. "
ES TURBO 15,218. "

Daytona Shelby and ES Turbo instrument panel ('90)

G74A
DODGE DAYTONA SHELBY

EAGLE

EAGLE MFD BY **CHRYSLER CORPORATION** (1988 ON)

**CHRYSLER · PLYMOUTH · DODGE
DODGE TRUCKS · JEEP · EAGLE**

MEDALLION — DL WAGON 12,317. (FF 48E)

DL SEDAN (FF45B) $11,589.
LX SEDAN (FF45C) 12,103.

V.I.N. = (VFI OR 2XM)(FF45B) — J — #

NEW 88

MEDALLION HAS 2.2 L 4-CYL. ENGINE

102.3" WB
(108.2" ON WAGON)

Designed by Giugiaro in Turin, Italy, Premier is distinguished by its beautiful styling. But it is more than a dramatic look that makes Premier unique. Under the hood of the Premier ES is a highly advanced, multi-port fuel-injected 3.0 litre overhead cam aluminum V6 engine. The only aluminum V6 you'll find on a North American-built car.

Premier's admirable European qualities, including a four-wheel independent suspension for wonderful agility and precise handling, are artfully combined with its more traditional American advantages.

Buckle up for safety

1988 Eagle Premier

Jeep Eagle
Expect the Best.

PREMIER

3.0 L V6 OR 2.5 L 4 106" WB

REAR DETAILS

LX SEDAN (JT559) 13,729.
LS SEDAN (JP557) 15,334.

V6 ENGINE (PREMIER)

PRE-1988 EAGLES IN AMC SECTION

EAGLE

SUMMIT MADE ('89) IN JAPAN BY MITSUBISHI

1989 SUMMIT DL $11,536. SUMMIT LX 11,872.

*113 HP @ 6500 RPM

SUMMIT

new SUMMIT has 96.7" WB, 1.5 or 1.6 L 4 CYL. ENG. (SIMILAR TO MITSUBISHI MIRAGE.)

THE NEXT STEP. THE ALL-NEW EAGLE SUMMIT.

PREMIER ES LEATHER SEATING!

A word about confidence. *Every Eagle carries Chrysler's exclusive 7-year/70,000-mile Protection Plan!*†

770

1989 V.I.N. ENDS WITH −K−# ; −L−# IN 1990

1990 STD. SEDAN $11,139 ; DL $11,625. LX $12,309. ES $13,347.

23/35 MPG SUMMIT '89

89-90

4-CYL. PREMIER ENG. NOT AVAIL. 1990.

PREMIER LX $14,556. ('89); $16,691. ('90)
" ES 16,539. ('89); 18,310. ('90)

106" WB 3.0 L V6 or 2.5 L 4

LX ('90)

22/31 MPG ('89) PREMIER 4 CYL.

PREMIER ES.

LX WAGON ADDED TO 1989 MEDALLION LINE. (NO 1990 MODEL)

PREMIER BUILT AT FORMER AMC FACTORY IN ONTARIO, CANADA. (150 HP RENAULT 180 cid V6) 18/27 MPG

('89)

Eagle Premier LX

Eagle Premier Limited

PRESENTING PREMIER ES LIMITED.

NEW

(SPECS. AS OTHER PREMIERS)

PREMIER ES LTD. (CB 66 U) $19,181. ('89)
20,737. ('90)

The ES Limited has independent suspension at all four wheels. And an advanced torsion-bar rear suspension. A major reason for its world-class ride and handling.
Inside: roomy, comfortable, and generously fitted with genuine leather. With functionally positioned instruments and controls.

Jeep Eagle

Expect the Best.

EAGLE TALON

JAPANESE-AMERICAN
TALON COUPE (4 CYL.) $13,449.
TALON TSi (4 CYL. TURBO) 15,207.
TALON TSi ALL-WHEEL DR. $16,891.

('90)

New Eagle Talon With All-Wheel Dr

Talon TSi's ergonomically designed cockpit features easy-to-read analog instrumentation, leather-wrapped steering wheel, and ideally positioned leather knob shifter grip.

(STARTS 1990)
TALON BUILT IN NORMAL, ILLINOIS BY CHRYSLER-AND-MITSUBISHI "DIAMOND STAR MOTORS."

122 cid 4 (135 OR 195 HP) 22/29 MPG (EPA) (20/25, 4WD)

118

(SINCE 1903) **FORD**

SELECTAIRE CONDITIONER

Wagon

LTD Wagon, Light Pine Glow (4E)

WOOD-GRAINED COUNTRY SQUIRE $9714.

GRILLE

DIGITAL CLOCK

11:53
DATE   E/T   TIME

UNGRAINED LTD WAGONS PRICED FROM $9016.

2 DR. $8681.

114.4" WB

81

V.I.N. = IFAB (P3/)
( )(-)600001 UP

3-Way Magic Doorgate

V8 OR 6

CROWN VICTORIA INTERIOR

4 DR. $9458.

Crown Victoria

CROWN VICT. HAS WRAP-OVER BRIGHTWORK BAND WHICH DIVIDES FRONT PORTION OF ROOF FROM REAR PORTION, "TOWN CAR" STYLE.

2 DR. $9325.

20-GAL. FUEL TANK

1981 LTD DOES NOT HAVE DUAL LOWER GRILLE OPENINGS IN THE BUMPER, AS 1980 HAD.

FORD

OPTIONAL "TRIP MINDER" COMPUTER ON DASH →

E M
S 07:51 R
58 ET
TIME TRIP ECON FUEL

(LTD "S" WAGONS AVAIL. FR. $9953.)

LTD   18 MPG
$9744.

85 MPH SPEEDOMETER

LTD WAGON →
$10,243.

GAS MILEAGE ESTIMATES
26 18

$10,750.
LTD COUNTRY SQUIRE

17 MPG (WAGON)

20 GAL. FUEL TANK (ON ALL)

CROWN VICTORIA 2-DR.

V.I.N. =
1FABP ( )
DOC (-) 000001
UP

82

255 OR 302 CID V8 s
114.3" WB

CROWN VICTORIA HAS REAR CHROME STRIP (new)

POWER SEAT CONTROLS

Ford

TRADITIONAL OVAL EMBLEM RETURNS (FRONT AND REAR)

FORD 82

120

LOOK OUT WORLD. HERE COMES FORD.

LTD V.I.N.=
 1FAB P31 BXD (-) 00000/ UP
LTD WAGON V.I.N. =
 1FABP37BXD (-) #

FORD

CROWN VICTORIA V.I.N. =
 1FABP34FXD (-) #
 CROWN VICTORIA WAGON V.I.N.
 1FABP38FXD (-) #
 P215/75R x 14 TIRES
 302 CID V8 IN
 CROWN VICTORIA

CROWN VICT.
"S" 4-DR.
P43/41K
$10334.
2-DR. SEDAN
P42
11298.
4-DR. SED.
P43
11298.
(S, STD.,
CNTRY SQ.
WAGONS ALSO)

114.3" WB

LTD Crown Victoria

has NEW GRILLE

83

STANDARD
LTD
SERIES
TOTALLY
RESTYLED
AND DOWNSIZED,
WITH new
105.6"
WB

FORD LTD

UN-
GRAINED

GRAINED

16 MPG
EPA

LTD Country Squire in Pastel Vanilla.

P44

Ford

OVAL
EMBLEM

19 MPG
EPA
P40

LTD Wagon

$ 9727. (GRAIN TRIM OPT.)

$ 11457.

LTD DASH

55 MPH

103 MPH

2.23
WED 24
TIME TRIP ECON FUEL

105½" WB

NEW
DOWNSIZED

LTD.

P39 SEDAN
$9605.

P39 60H BROUGHAM
SEDAN $9993.

NEW LOOK

140 CID 4
OR
LPG 4,
200 CID 6,
232 CID V6
(112 HP)

24 MPG EPA
(4 CYL.)
19 MPG EPA
(6)

P185/75R14
TIRES

Ford LTD
$10,271.

P185/75R
x14 TIRES

140 CID 4 (88 HP)
OR 232 CID V6 (120 HP) ON LTD

new LTD/LX SEDAN has BLACK WINDOW PILLARS, V8 ENG. 115 MPH

V.I.N. ENDS w. —E—#

Ford LTD
84

w. COUNTRY SQUIRE GRAIN OPTION

$12,084.

Ford LTD Crown Victoria Wagons

Ford LTD
FROM $10,183.

19 N346

LEATHER UPH. AVAIL. IN "INTERIOR LUXURY GROUP" PKG.

WITH TAILGATE DOWN

302 OR 351 CID V8s IN CRN. VICT. / SQUIRE (140 OR 180 HP)

Have you driven a Ford... lately? Ford

CTRY. SQUIRE $12,501. (WITH DUAL FACING RR. STS.)

$12,334. (6-PASS.)

VELOUR INTERIOR OF Crown Victoria

P215/75R x14 TIRES

FORD LTD CROWN VICTORIA

CR. VICT. 2 DR. OR CROWN VICTORIA 4-DR.

$12,177. VENT WINDOW OPT.

E   M
S   R
24
IN MPG
TIME TRIP ECON FUEL

122

FORD

FROM
$10461. ('85)
11220. ('86)

THIS 302 CID V8-POWERED LTD/LX NOT AVAIL. AFTER 1985. V6 LTD. NOT AVAIL. AFTER 1986.

('85)

$12,590

Ford LTD/LX high-performance

85-87

FORD EMBLEM MOVED TO CENTER OF GRILLE (ON LTD)

CRWN. VICT. and SQUIRE 302 CID V8

17/27 EPA MPG

('85)

LTD ↗

('85)

105½" WB
232 CID V6

LTD. AVAIL. W. 4, V6 OR V8

"S" CROWN VIC. FROM
$11832. ('85)
13430. ('86)
14340. ('87)

('87)

LTD Crown Victoria

302 OR 351 CID V8

"PANTHER" BODY

V.I.N. ENDS WITH	
— F — #	(1985)
— G — #	(1986)
— H — #	(1987)

WAGON INTERIOR

LTD

('87)

$13032. ('85)
13897. ('86)
15047. ('87)

Country Squire Wagon

"LX" SQUIRE WAGON ALSO, 1986 ON.

V8 ENGINES ONLY

88

RESTYLED FRONT END

V.I.N. ENDS WITH —J—#

CROWN VICT. SEDANS and WAGONS ONLY, SINCE 1987. NO MORE SEPARATE LTD SERIES.

P73F

'P72F "S": $15155.

Ford LTD Crown Victoria.

$15,721.

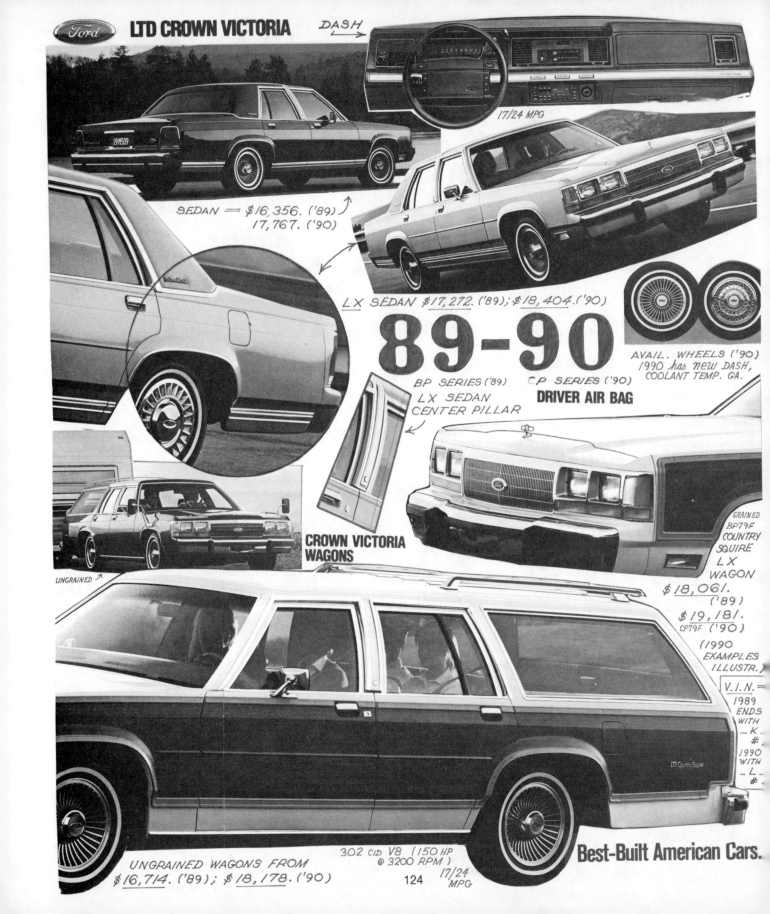

Ford **LTD CROWN VICTORIA**

DASH →

17/24 MPG

SEDAN = $16,356. ('89)
17,767. ('90)

LX SEDAN $17,272. ('89); $18,404. ('90)

89-90

BP SERIES ('89)   CP SERIES ('90)

DRIVER AIR BAG

AVAIL. WHEELS ('90)
1990 has new DASH,
COOLANT TEMP. GA.

LX SEDAN
CENTER PILLAR

CROWN VICTORIA
WAGONS

UNGRAINED →

GRAINED
BP79F
COUNTRY
SQUIRE
LX
WAGON

$18,061.
('89)

$19,181.
CP79F ('90)

(1990
EXAMPLES
ILLUSTR.)

V.I.N. =
1989
ENDS
WITH
_ K _
#
1990
WITH
_ L _
#

UNGRAINED WAGONS FROM
$16,714. ('89); $18,178. ('90)

302 CID V8 (150 HP
@ 3200 RPM)

124

17/24
MPG

Best-Built American Cars.

FORD ESCORT

(SINCE 1981)
REPLACES PINTO

FRONT WHEEL DRIVE AND ADVANCED TRANSAXLES

FOUR-WHEEL INDEPENDENT SUSPENSION SYSTEM

BUILT IN AMERICA

THE NEW WORLD CAR

Built to take on the world... and doing it!

V.I.N. =
IFA (-) PO5
(-) XBY
60000I UP

81 new

94.2" WHEELBASE

6723.

HATCHBACKS + WAGONS

STD. — FROM	$	5742.
L — "		6078.
GL — "		6422.
GLX — "		7060.
SS — "		6723.

ESCORT SS

OPT. INSTR. GROUP 19 STANDARD EQUIP. IN SS

UNLEADED FUEL ONLY

RPM   TRIP RESET   MPH

INTERIOR

SS WAGON
$7048.

4 CYL. 98 CID — **COMPOUND-VALVE HEMISPHERICAL HEAD ENGINE**

GLX
$7060

44	30
EPA EST HWY	EPA EST MPG

FORD ESCORT

DASH

SUNROOF AVAIL.

New

47 EST HWY	31 EST EPA MPG

IO GALLON FUEL TANK

4 DR.

2 DR.

HATCHBACK 4-DR. SEDAN ADDED

STD. — $6387.
"L" — 6919.
"GL" — 7181.
"GLX" — 7832.

GLX
WAGON
$8004.

WAGON INTERIOR

(GRAINED WAGON WAS ALSO AVAIL. IN '81.)

"GT" HATCHBACK 2DR. REPLACES "SS" SERIES

WAGON MPG:

44 EST HWY	28 EPA EST MPG

"L" WAGON $7116.
"GL" WAGON 7400.

At the heart of the World Car Wagon, the CVH engine.

82

OVAL "FORD" EMBLEM ADDED TO GRILLE

PRICED FROM $6180.

Ford

NEW Ford

V.I.N. = 1FAB P0520 C (-) 00000I UP

FORD ESCORT

Escort GT has the functional good looks of a serious road machine: rear spoiler, front air-dam, racing mirrors, TR-type steel wheels and a sporty blackout treatment.

P07

GT
$8010.

100 MPH

4-DRS. FROM
$6654.

"L" IS NOW LOWEST-PRICED ESCORT, AT $6447. and up.

fuel injected. Escort GT comes equipped with a 1.6 liter electronically fuel injected engine, hooked up to a 5-speed transaxle.

GRAINED "GLX" WAGON
$7897.

optional FS engine with improved mileage ratings

over 90 new improvements, ranging from a new luxury sound insulation package to a new fuel-conscious shift indicator light.

V. I. N. =
1FAB P052
XD (-)
000001 UP

P11

UNGRAINED GLX WAGON

43 EST HWY	29 EPA EST MPG

ESCORT WAGON

(GL 2 DR., $7131.)
(GLX, $7518.)

new 84 HP AVAIL. W. 5 SP. OR A/T

83

GL
$7348.
P14

NEW

GRILLE, WITH ADDED VERTICAL PIECES →

47 EST HWY	33 EPA EST MPG

HAVE YOU DRIVEN A FORD...LATELY?   127

ESCORT   **1983 FORD ESCORT**

FORD ESCORT

LX
$8412.

('84)

Escort Diesel:

('84)

NEW FOR 1984

| 46 | EPA EST. MPG. |
| 68 | EST. HWY. |

ALSO NEW DASH

(LX NOT AVAIL. IN LATER 1985)

STANDARD MODEL has PLAIN SIDES (above)
$5906. ('84)
5898. ('85)

Escort LX
$8322.

STEEL WHEEL

TR TYPE ALUMINUM WHEEL

84-85

NEW CHOICE OF GAS OR DIESEL ENGINES

Escort
← L
$6377.

| V.I.N. ENDS WITH |
| — E - # (1984) |
| — F - # (1985) |

Turbo GT
← $8799.

1985 MODELS ILLUSTRATED (UNLESS OTHERWISE NOTED)

Escort GL
4 DR. 7343.

Escort GT
$8066.

BLACK GT DASH →

128

(SIMILAR TO new 1986 MERCURY LYNX "XR-3")

FORD ESCORT

Escort GT

$8620.

HAS OWN "GT" ASYMMETRICAL GRILLE, new 4-CYL. HIGH-OUTPUT 1.9-LITER ENG.

UP TO 108 HP @ 5200 RPM

GT has AERO-DYNAMIC FRONT STYLING, FRONT and REAR STABILIZER BARS, 15" ALUMINUM WHEELS with P195/60HR15 TIRES

V.I.N. = 1FABP (319) — G-#

86

new "PONY" 2-DR. HATCHBACK IS LOWEST-PRICED 1986 ESCORT, AT $6229.

"L" and "LX" MODELS AVAIL. IN 3 BODY TYPES, and ALSO A new "SELECT L"

GT has REAR SPOILER

"GL" SERIES DISCONTINUED *

* FOR 1986 ONLY 129 **Ford Escort. The world's best-selling car.**

FORD ESCORT
WORLD'S BEST-SELLING CAR FOUR YEARS RUNNING.

(259) *V.I.N. ENDS WITH —H—#*

HATCHBK. 4 DR.
$7962.

(GL 2-DR.
HATCHBK.
$7748.)
(219)

GL →

(289) WAGON
$8243.

1.9 L 4 EFI ENG. w. "EEC IV"
ELECTRONIC ENG.
CONTROL SYSTEM
(DIESEL 4
AVAIL.)

ESCORT GL

"ERIKA"
BODY

87

"GL" SERIES
RETURNS,
REPLACES ALL
OTHER SERIES
EXCEPT FOR
"GT," 2-DR.
"PONY"
HATCHBACK,
ESCORT-
RELATED
"EXP."

CLOSE
DETAILS OF
HEADLIGHTS
AND
TAILLIGHTS

109 MPH (GT)

PONY = $6807.	(209)
GT = 9169.	(23J)
(EA. AVAIL. AS 2-DR. HTCHBK. ONLY)	

P259

(PRICED FR. $7297. =
P209 PONY 2-DR.
HATCHBK.)

88 GL

1988 V.I.N.
ENDS WITH
—J—#

$8078.

130

Ford Escort

LX 4 DR. HATCHBK.
$8256.
P959

(FINAL EXP :
P889 2 DR.
LUXURY COUPE
$8510.)

Ford Escort. The world's best-selling car six years running.

1988½ Ford Escort.

MIDSEASON MODEL CHANGE OFFICIALLY
LABELED 1988½ BY FORD MOTOR CO.

FRONT
END

OTHER MODELS :			
PONY 2-DR. HTCHBK.	$7472.	P909
LX " " "	7926.	P919
GT " " "	9402.	P93J
LX WAGON	8782.	P989

1988½ LX
NO LONGER INCLDS.
(AS STD. EQUIPMENT)
STYLED ROAD WHEELS
OR BUMPER GUARDS
(STD. ON 1988
GL)

('89)

1989 LX INCL. A/T, AM/FM and
CASSETTE PLAYER, DIGITAL CLOCK,
A/C, POWER STEER., and
OTHER EXTRAS AT N/C.

('89) $9030. ('89) LX Escort Wagon.

114 CID 4
90 HP
(110 HP, GT)

1989 LX SEDAN AND DASH (BELOW)

('89)

LX 2-DR.
HATCHBACK
$8174. ('89)

114 CID 4
(90 OR 110
HP)

1989 V.I.N. ENDS WITH —K—#

89-90

1990
V.I.N.
ENDS
WITH
—L
—#

	1989		1990	
PONY PP909	$7661.	P209	$8360.
LX PP919	8174.	P219	8837.
LX SED. PP959	8504.	P259	9167.
LX WAG. PP989	9030.	P289	9692.
GT P93J	9650.	P23J	10184.

(ALL MODELS ARE
HATCHBACKS ; 2-DR. UNLESS
OTHERWISE INDICATED.)

REAR SHOULD.
BELTS STD.
FOR 1990.

27/36 MPG (5 SP.)

131

FORD EXP

Brand-new

(1982 TO 1988)

ONE MODEL ONLY IN 1982

$8812. ('82)

w. FRONT-WH. DRIVE

1982 V.I.N. = 1FAB PO120 C (-) 000001 UP

94.2" WB

11.3 GALLON FUEL TK.

45 | 28
EPA EST. HWY. | EPA EST. MPG

('82)

INTERIOR

STORAGE SPACE BEHIND THE 2 FRONT SEATS

82-83

1983 V.I.N. = 1FAB PO12 XD (-) 000001 UP

4 CYL., 98 CID (70 HP.)
← CVH ENGINE

$7145. - 10004. ('83)

TWIN-SLOT GRILLE

4 ADDITIONAL MODELS IN 1983 ONLY (COUPES)

DASH

1984 V.I.N. = 1FABPO14 XE (-) 10000 UP
MPG: 42 HWY / 26 EPA

84-86

(FINAL TURBO CPE. 19 1985 0/8)

EXP Turbo.

1985 V.I.N. = 1FAB PO14XF (-) 10000 UP

PRICE RANGES

$6931. - 10863. ('84)
6975. - 10918. ('85)
7465. or 8514. ('86)

1986 V.I.N. = 1FABP (019) or (01J) - G - #

PRODUCTION SUSPENDED APRIL, 1985.

('84)

DASH

MID-1986, EXP BECOMES A PART OF **ESCORT** LINE

86 HP (108, GT)

86½-88

1987 V.I.N. = 1FA DD (179) or (18J) - H - #

109 MPH

1987 = 179 LUXURY CPE. $8100.
18J SPORT CPE.   9274.
ONLY REMAINING 1988½ ESCORT EXP IS P889 LUXURY CPE., AT $8510.

1988 (FINAL YR.) V.I.N. = (1FA) or (KNJ) B (P179) - J - #
(1988½ SUBSITUTE ⌐P179⌐ WITH ⌐P889⌐ IN V.I.N.)

25/33 MPG

132   **Escort EXP**

FORD FAIRMONT —MERCURY ZEPHYR

FAIRMONT V.I.N. = IFA(-)(P20)AXB(-)
60000I UP

ZEPHYR V.I.N. = IME(-)(P70)(A)XB(-)
60000I UP

(AVAIL. 1978-1983)

FAIRMONT DASH

FAIRMONT
FUTURA INTERIOR

Integral door pull
handles and armrests

THIS UNIQUE REAR
QUARTER WINDOW
TREATMENT EXCLUSIVE
TO FAIRMONT FUTURA and
MERCURY
ZEPHYR
Z-7.

81

105 1/2" WB
140 CID 4
OR 200 CID 6
(225 CID V8
AVAIL. ALSO)

FUTURA

34 EST. HWY.   23 EST. MPG   HAS ITS OWN
GRILLE DESIGN

$1667.

Fairmont 2-Door

P20

FUTURA   COUPE

$7982.

P23

↑
FAIRMONT
WAGONS
$8019.
and up

P21 SEDAN
OR P21/60.5
FUTURA
SEDAN

$7786.

14-GAL FUEL TANK
P175/75 R x 14 TIRES

ZEPHYR
PRICES
$7738.
and up

ZEPHYR has
ALL VERTICAL PCS.
IN GRILLE (AS
ILLUSTR. AT LOWER
RIGHT)

MERCURY ZEPHYR

SPECS.
SIMILAR
TO
FAIRMONT

Z-7

23 EPA EST. MPG, 34 ES

ZEPHYR

T. HWY.

4 DR.
ALSO AVAIL.

FORD FAIRMONT FUTURA and MERCURY ZEPHYR

14 GAL. FUEL TK.

SEATS IN MEDIUM FAWN CLOTH / VINYL (OPT.)

('83)

1982 FAIRMONT P22 COUPE

$8382.

A/C CONTROLS (OPT.)

DASH (FAIRMONT)

1982 V.I.N. IFABP22AOC (-) 000001 UP

AM/FM STEREO w. CASSETTE TAPE PLAYER (OPT.)

WAGONS NOT AVAILABLE. REMAINING FAIRMONTS NOW IN "FUTURA" SERIES.

FUTURA

1983 FAIRMONT V.I.N.: "S" FUTURA = IFABP 37 AXD (-) # FUTURA = IFABP37BXD (-) 000001 UP

STD. 2 DR. ROOFLINE

82-83

22 MPG (EPA)

STD. 140 CID OHC 4 ENGINE (88 HP)

(200 CID 87 HP 6 AVAIL.)

impressive fuel economy.

| 33 EST HWY | 22 EST EPA MPG |

MERCURY ZEPHYR

ZEPHYR MPG : 30 HWY/24 EPA ('82)

ZEPHYR HAS DECORATIVE FLAPS AS BEFORE. 16 GAL. FUEL TK. (NEW 20 GAL. FUEL TK. OPT.)

$8184. UP ('82)
8460. " ('83)
STD. and "GS" SEDANS, Z-7 CPES.

1982 ZEPHYR V.I.N. IMEBP71AOC (-) #
1983 ZEPHYR V.I.N. IMEBP71 BXD (-) #

FORD FAIRMONT

FRONT END

FORD

BODY CONSTRUCTION DETAILS

LOW-COST "S" MODELS ADDED TO '83 FAIRMONT LINE: 2 DR., $7825. (P35/41K) 4 DR., 7965. (P36/41K)

FAIRMONT SEDANS FROM $8284. ('82) $8608. ('83)

FRONT CLOSE-UP

$6419.* SPECIAL ADV. PRICE IN 1982.

FORD FAIRMONT 82-83

134

FORD FESTIVA

(1988 ON) (MFD. BY KIA MOTORS SEOUL, S. KOREA)

INTERIOR ('88)

90.2" WB
87 CID
OHC 4
(58 HP
@ 5000 RPM)
5-SP. TRANS. +
2.61 G.R. (LX)
10-GAL. GAS TANK

FESTIVA. THE FUN STARTS AT
$5765. (L)
(ADV. BASE PRICE)

1988 L =	$5882.
" L PLUS	6302.
" LX	7031.
1989 L	5954.
" L PLUS	6627.
" LX	7356.
1990 L	6824.
" L PLUS	7371.
" LX	8010.

35 / 41 MPG, 1990
(31/33 w. AUTO. TR.)

LX
91-95 MPH

165/70 SR12 TIRES

5 SP. TRANS. and FUEL INJECTION STD. FOR 1990, 63 HP @ 5000)

NEW
28/47 MPG
88-90

V.I.N. ENDS WITH —J—# (1988) —K—# (1989) —L—# (1990)

new 1990 GRILLE

1990 INTERIOR and "L" (BELOW)

REAR VIEW
('90)   L PLUS
19M352

OPT. AIR COND.

POP-OUT QUARTER WINDOWS

DASH

('90)

FORD **GRANADA** (1975 TO 1982)

A/C CONTROLS

DASH (GLX)

V.I.N. = 1FABPZ 6B (–)
B (–) 600001 UP

STD. "L" INTERIOR

L

L
2 DR.
$8167.

4, 6 OR V8

new SHORTER
105 ½" WB

RESTYLED
81

$8326. L
4 DR.

CLOSE-UP OF
new FRONT
END

FORD

↖ GLX has BLACK AROUND HEADLIGHTS.

GL

GLX 4 DR.
$8841.

GL
2 DR.
8568.

new MODEL SERIES

Built for a changing world.

136

FORD **GRANADA GLX** INTERIOR

L SERIES

new 232 CID 112 HP V6 REPLACES V8. (4, L6 STILL AVAIL.)

$9029.

22 MPG (EPA)

GL SERIES

GL WAGON $9678.

new "DEEP WELL" TRUNK INTERIOR

OPTIONAL GRAPHIC DISPLAY WARNS OF PROBLEMS. (LTS., WASHER FLUID, LOW FUEL SUPPLY)

LOW LAMP   WASHER FLUID
LOW FUEL
BRAKE LAMP   HEADLAMP

82
OVAL FORD BADGE RETURNS

A 4TH NEW WHEEL COVER "SUNBURST"-TYPE DESIGN IS AVAIL. IN MID-SEASON.

16 GAL. FUEL TK.

GLX 2 DR. $9569.

(140 CID 4, 200 CID 6 HAVE 88 HP)

UN-GRAINED L WAGON $9262.

| 33 EST HWY | 22 EPA EST MPG |

MPG

new "TOT-GUARD" RESTRAINT FOR SMALL CHILDREN AVAIL. IN MID-SEASON.

GRANADA WAGON

OPTIONAL 2-WAY LIFTGATE

1982

New BADGE **Ford**

19 MPG (EPA)

GRANADA WAGONS ARE

NEW

WARNING CHIMES OPTIONAL

V.I.N. ENDS WITH — C — #

1982 MODEL IS FINAL GRANADA. (BUT NAME COULD RETURN IN FUTURE)

137

Ford Mustang
(SINCE APRIL, 1964)

AVAIL. LEATHER WRAPPED STEERING WHEEL

CONSOLE

81

V.I.N. ENDS w. B (-) 600001 UP

POWER SIDE WINDOWS *new*

INTERIOR

100.4" WB 12½ GAL. FUEL TANK

P-10 2 DR. **$7581.**

P-12 GHIA

IMITATION CABRIOLET ROOF IS **NOT** CONVERTIBLE.

$7896. *and up*

(P-13 GHIA 3-DR. FASTBACK ALSO AVAIL. AT $8040.)

VARIOUS WHEELS AVAIL., AS SHOWN

P-15 COBRA TURBO **$9057.**

(W. 4 SP. TRANS. OPTIONAL)

AVAILABLE SUNROOF OR T-BAR TOP

3-DR.

COBRA

COBRA REAR

140 CID 4 or TURBO 4 200 CID 6 or 255 CID V8 (115 HP)

COBRA

OPT. BLACK LIFTGATE LOUVRES

HOOD DECAL

COBRA INTERIOR

37 EST HWY* · 22 EPA EST MPG* · 5-SPEED OVERDRIVE OPTION

138

Only 250 McLaren Mustangs were produced in 1981.

GLX SERIES — GLX INTER. — **Ford Mustang**

GLX
$8631. UP

ENGINES :
140 CID 4 (86 HP)
(ALSO 140 CID 4 "FS" ENG. AVAIL.)
200 CID 6 (87 HP) 255 CID V8 (111 HP)
302 CID HO V8 (157 HP)

CLOSER VIEW OF GLX DASH with GRAINED TRIM

new
302 CID V8 (5.0 L)
157 HP

NEW

$9678.
GT HAS OWN GRILLE and HOOD.

AUTOMATIC OR MANUAL TRANSMISSION →

P16

Mustang GT
(AVAIL. w. T-BAR ROOF)

33	22
EST HWY	EPA EST MPG

(WITH 140 CID 4)

P185/75R
× 14 TIRES (GT)

V.I.N. ENDS with
- C (-) 000001 UP

82

P175/75R 14
TIRES STD.

GT DASH and INTERIOR

MUSTANG GL

WITH T-BAR ROOF OPTION

MPG :
32 HWY
22 EPA
WITH
STD.
4-CYL.

GRAPHIC DISPLAY WARNING MODULE

RECARO SEATS AVAILABLE

TAIL LAMP   WASHER FLUID
LOW FUEL
BRAKE LAMP   HEADLAMP

GL
$8495.   139

Ford Mustang

24 MPG EPA (4 CYL. w. MANUAL TR.)

19 MPG EPA (V6)

15.4 GAL. FUEL TANK

L SERIES $8466. (2 DR.) P26

T-BAR

NEW 232 CID V6 AVAIL., WITH 112 HP (4 CYL. OR V8 ALSO AVAIL.)

3 DR. HATCHBACK FROM $9178. (GL)   P28/60C

P27/602 GLX CONVERTIBLE $13,767.

100½" WB

RESTYLED

New

CONVERTIBLE!

83

302 CID V8

V.I.N. ENDS WITH -XD (-) 000001 UP

New for '83—Sport Performance Bucket Seats. These special bucket seats are optional equipment in GL, GLX and GT.

OPENING QTR. WINDOWS

GT PRICES =
CONV'T. $14,602.
3-DR. HTCH.   10,426.
TURBO 2-DR.   10,712.
(MODEL NO. P27/932; P28/932)

GT PERFORMANCE-STYLE HOOD TREATMENT ↓

125 MPH (GT)

1983½ MPG (4 CYL.)

	49-States		California	
40 EST HWY	26 EPA EST MPG	36 EST HWY	24 EPA EST MPG

VARIOUS WHEELS AVAILABLE

Ford Mustang

USED BY POLICE FORCES IN 15 DIFF. STATES!

P185/75R×14 STD. TIRE SIZE

L 2-DR. $8856.
L 3-DR. (new) 9027.
LX (new)
2-DR. $9048.
3-DR. 9254.
CVT. 13,168.

GL, GLX DISCONTINUED

SVO

INTERIOR (SVO)

The 20th Anniversary Mustang

84

(SPRING, 1984)

Have you driven a Ford... lately?

Ford

ENGINES:
140 CID 4 (88 HP)
(145 OR 175 HP WITH TURBO)
232 CID V6 (120 HP)
302 CID V8 (HO) 175, 165 HP
AUTOMATIC OVERDRIVE AVAIL.

V.I.N. ENDS WITH -XE (-) 100001 UP

Mustang GT

GT 3-DR. $10,695.
GT CONV'T. $14,168.

175 HP V8

GT, TURBO GT WITH P205/70 HR×14 TIRES

REAR VIEWS OF SVO

SVO 3 DR. TURBO $16,713.

Get it together — Buckle up.

TURBO GT CVT. $14,362. (3 DR., $10,879.)
("SVO" MEANS "SPECIAL VEHICLE OPERATIONS")

SVO

SPECIAL VEHICLE OPERATIONS

SVO

NEW

WITH P225/50 VR 16 TIRES

128 MPH

Get it together — Buckle up.

141

Ford Mustang

('85) P26/602

ADVERTISED SPECIAL, LX $6885. ('85)

P27/602
LX CVT. $13,102. ('85)
232 CID V6
(V8 AVAIL.)

(L SERIES DISCONTINUED)

302 CID GT V8 has 210 HP 135 MPH

4 CYL. LX REG. ('85) $8441. UP

NEW HIGH BRAKE LT. IN 1986

GT CONVERTIBLE $16,281. ('86)

GT

OTHER 1986 MODELS:

LX 2 DR. (4 CYL.)	$8325.
LX HATCHBK. "	8880.
SVO " (TURBO 4)	15,646.
LX CVT. (V6)	13,957.
GT HATCHBK. (V8)	12,449.

85-86

Mustang GT. (V8) ('85)

1985 V.I.N. = 1FABP (28M) - F - #

3 DR. $11,553. (P28/932)
GT CVT. 15,253. (P27/932)

NEW GRILLE (SLOT TYPE)

1986 V.I.N. = 1FABP (26A) - G - #

1985 MUSTANG ENGINES = 140 CID 4 (88 HP); 140 CID TURBO 4 (175 HP); 232 CID V6 (120 HP); 302 CID V8 (165, 210 HP)

LX CVT. HAS PLAIN REAR DECK →

SVO ('85)

100½" WB ON ALL MODELS

3-DR. $14,895. P28/939

SVO

140 CID 4 CYL. W. TURBO (175 HP)

SVO INCREASED TO 205 HP @ 5000 RPM, NEW 3:73 TO 1 GEAR RATIO

(FINAL V6 ENGINE AND SVO IN 1986)

142

('87)

Have you driven a Ford...lately?

18/27 MPG, 1987
(302 cɪᴅ 5.0L V8)

GT

Ford Mustang

RESTYLED 1987

1987 MODELS
LX 2 DR. $ 9948.
LX 3 DR.   10367.
LX CVT.   14729.
GT "   17529.
GT 3 DR.   13783.

REAR SPOILER
(LX)

(GT HAS HORIZONTAL SLOTTED TAILLIGHTS.)

B.P45E $18914. (1989)

2-DR.

100.5" WHEELBASE

FRONT

LX VIEWS   LX

100.5"
179.6"
69.1"
52.1"
3 DR. REAR
56.6"   57.0"

V.I.N. ENDS WITH ═
—H—# (1987)
—J—# (1988)
—K—# (1989)
—L—# (1990)

87-90

3 DR.

"FOX" BODY USED

LX 5.0L

4 CYL. EFI has 90 HP @ 3800 RPM

('87)

DASH (GT)

136 MPH MODIFIED SALEEN MUSTANG AVAILABLE

5 0

ON COWL IDENTIFIES A V-8 POWERED CAR.

4 or V8 IN

MUSTANG LX

$11341. - 20297.

1990 PRICE RANGE (DRIVER'S AIR-BAG STD. IN 1990)

GT
5.0 L
V8

142 MPH

17/29 MPG ('90)

Ford   NO GRILLE ABOVE ON GT

GT

1989 MODELS ILLUSTRATED, UNLESS OTHERWISE NOTED.

143

(STARTS WITH 1989 MODEL)
JAPANESE-AMERICAN

NEW

Ford Probe

Have you driven a Ford...lately? *Ford*

GL
BT20C

ON LX and GT
STEERING WHEEL
AND INSTRUMENT
PANEL CAN BE TILTED
TOGETHER
AS ONE
UNIT.

$12655.
(ADVERTISED PRICE
SPECIAL OF
$10660. UP)

BLT. AT FLAT ROCK,
MICHIGAN, BY
MAZDA.

2.2 L
4 CYL. ENGINE

99" W.B.

1989
MODEL
STARTS
SPRING, 1988.

P185 70SR14 TIRES
ON GL and LX

BT21C

V.I.N. ENDS w.
—K—#

LX
$13362.

SMALL "PROBE" NAME
ON LOWER FRONT
CORNER OF SIDE
QUARTER WINDOW.

89

POWER DISC BRAKES ON FRONT WHEELS
OF GL and LX ; ON ALL 4 WHEELS OF
GT.

2.2 L TURBO 4
(145 HP @ 4300 RPM)
MPG : 27 HWY, 21 CITY (EPA)

$15,155. (GT)
(ADVERTISED SPECIAL,
$14,077.)

131 MPH

Probe GT
(GBT)
99"WB

P195 60VR15 TIRES

GT

FRONT
ENDS

WINDSHIELD CONFIGURATION

BT22L

GT has
HORIZONTAL
GROOVES
ALONG SIDES.

note "TURBO"

144

V.I.N. ENDS WITH — L — #

GT DASH w. ANALOG GAUGES

Probe GT instrument panel in Titanium with Preferred Equipment Package 261A. Some equipment shown is optional.

FORD PROBE LX

(RIGHT, and BELOW)

LX

GT AND DASH (ABOVE)

$16,570. (new GRILLE)

90

133 CID 2.2 L TURBO 4 (145 HP @ 4300 RPM)
(STD. 2.2 L 4 has 110 HP @ 4700 RPM)
182 CID 3.0 L V6 has 140 HP @ 4800 RPM (new)

FORD PROBE GL w. 2.2 L 4 (110 HP @ 4700)

$13,434.

15.1 GAL. FUEL TANK
19/31 MPG

LX   *LX*

↑ GT WHEEL (ABOVE)

REAR DETAILS (new TAILLIGHTS)

ELECTRONIC CONTROLS

145   WITH 3.0 L V6 (140 HP @ 4800)   LX **$14,852.**

FORD TAURUS

(SINCE 1986)

MFD. BY **Ford Motor Company**

NEW $10,833. UP
(L SEDAN) 29D

| MPH km/h |
| ODO SEL |
| TRIP RESET |
| SPEED ALARM |
| FUEL ECON |
| DTE |
| ECON RESET |

"TAURUS" BODY

1986 SEDANS FROM $11,464. (MT5 29D)

1987 MODELS, PRICES

MTS SED. 51D $12543.	GL SEDAN 52D $12836.
" WAG. 56D-13104.	" WAGON 57U-14016.
L SEDAN 50D-11864.	LX SED. 53U-15059.
" WAGON 55U-13084.	LX WAG. 58U-15669.

86-87

106" WB   182 CID V6 (140 HP)   *INTERIOR*
OR 153 CID 4 (90 HP)   24-27 MPG (EPA, CITY)

114 MPH

MECHANICALLY SIMILAR TO *new* MERCURY **SABLE**

SEDAN (29U) $13,777. (LX)

WAGONS FROM $11,929.

MT5, L, GL and LX SERIES

113 MPH

1986 EXAMPLES ILLUSTR.

CLOSER VIEW OF ELECTRONIC INSTR. PANEL

1986 V.I.N. ENDS WITH -G-# 1987 w.-H-#

146

FORD TAURUS

Quality is Job 1.

3.0 OR 3.8 LITER V6
(2.5 L. 4 AVAIL.)

88

115 MPH WITH
3.8 L V6

Dealer Service:

1988 FORD V.I.N. =
(IFA OR KNJ) B (P51D)
—J—#

ELECTRONIC
DIAGNOSIS
(TAURUS ENGINE
COMPARTMENT ILLSTR.)

LX SED. (P53U)
$15,392.

MT5 SED. (4 CYL.) (P51D)
          $12,926.
L SED. (P50U) $13,266.
  WAG. (P55U)   13,898.
GL SED. (P52U)   13,773.
  WAG. (P57U)   14,381.
  (MODEL NUMBERS
      END IN "D," IF 2.5 L
  4-CYL. ENGINE USED)

(4-CYL. WAGON NO LONGER LISTED IN 1988.)

LX WAGON (P58U)
$16,124.

wagon

WITH
REAR
DETAIL

LX

GL WAGON and SEDAN (BELOW)
1989 V.I.N. ENDS WITH —K-#; 1990 WITH —L-#

FORD TAURUS

19/29 MPG ('89)

ELECTRONIC DASH

L →

ANALOG DASH

TAURUS L, GL, LX

(1990 EXAMPLES ILLUSTRATED)
L = $13688. UP ('89)
    13912. UP ('90)
GL= 14112. UP ('89)
    14385. UP ('90)
LX= 15732. UP ('89)
    16635. UP ('90)

↑ LX

BP--U SERIES
SHO $20189. ('89)
22088. ('90)

89-90

FORD TAURUS SHO

(new) IN 1989

P--U SER.
(1990 POLICE SPEC. HAS 4 HORIZ. COOLING SLOTS ON EA. SIDE OF EMBLEM.)

(1990 DASH SLIGHTLY CHANGED)

TAURUS

19 M359

SHO

TAURUS SHO

(REPLACES _FAIRMONT_)

Ford TEMPO

STARTS WITH 1984 MODEL (INTRO. 5-26-83)

Front-wheel drive.

GL 2-DR. (P19) $8962.
(GL 4-DR., P22 $8962.)

Tempo GL 2-Door Coupe

L 4-DR. (P21) $7557.

Tempo L 4-Door Sedan

L 2-DR. (P18) $7557.

SUNROOF AVAIL.

GLX 2-DR. (P20) $9424.

NEW

(OPT.)

"HIGH SWIRL COMBUSTION" ENGINE

84

99.9" WB
P175/80 R x 13 TIRES

L, GL, GLX MODELS
(2 DR. OR 4 DR.)

140 CID 4
(HSC FS = 84 HP,
HSC = 90 HP)

MECHANICALLY SIMILAR TO new MERCURY TOPAZ.

Tempo's new tach. (OPT.)

V.I.N.
1FAB
P18RXE (-)
100001 UP

100 MPH

Tempo GLX 4-Door Sedan

GLX 4 DR. (P23) $9424.

THE ALL-NEW 1984 FORD TEMPO
STYLE AND TECHNOLOGY IN TOTAL HARMONY

HAVE YOU DRIVEN A FORD...LATELY?

New diesel option.
121 CID, 4-CYL., 52-HP DIESEL ENG. AVAIL. LATER IN 1984.

| 41 EPA EST MPG* | 56 EST HWY. |

INTERIOR

Get it together—Buckle up.

149

Ford Tempo

V.I.N.=IFA (-) P (-)(-)(-) XF (-) 000001 UP

The forward thinking car.

DASH

L
7415.
(2 OR 4 DR.)

GL

85

GLX 4 DR. $9771. (2 DR. 9723.)

NEW WHEELS
P175/80 R13 TIRES

140 CID 4 IN
86 HP EFI OR
100 HP EFI
VERSIONS. (121 CID, 52 HP DIESEL 4
CONT'D.)

$8629.

GL NOW AVAIL.
IN STANDARD,
SELECT,
LUXURY
OR SPORT
PACKAGES.

GLX IN
STANDARD
OR
LUXURY
PACKAGES.

14 GALLON
FUEL
TANK

3.73/2.73 GEAR
RATIO

New

Sport GL.

150   Electronically fuel-injected
2300 HSC engine

Ford Tempo

"TOPAZ" BODY

L SERIES DISCONTINUED.
GL and LX ONLY.

OPTIONAL DIESEL ENG.
(H) STILL AVAIL.
1986, NOT
LISTED 1987.

('86)

new 2-SLOT GRILLE w.
FORD EMBLEM ABOVE IT.

GL

86- Sport

1986 MODELS
GL : 19X 2.DR. $9128.
     22 X 4 DR.   9278.
LX : 20 X 2 DR. 10,119.
     23 X 4 DR. 10,318.
1987 = 31X GL 2-DR. $9813.
       36X GL 4 DR. 9963.
       339 SPT. GL 2DR.
                  $ 10,589
       38S SPT. GL 4 DR. 10,739.
       32X LX 2DR. 10,974.
       37X LX 4.DR.
                  11,173.

87

new
4-W-D
LX MODELS
(1987)
34S 2-DR.
$11,215.

39S 4-DR.
11,365.

1987 MPG:
22/27
140 cid 4
w. A/T

('86)

TEMPO
ALL WHEEL DRIVE

NEW FOR 1987

ALL WHEEL DRIVE   OFF ON

There's something new about this
Ford Tempo. Four wheel power at
your finger tips. It comes into play
through a simple switch and it's
a move you can make while on
the move.

V.I.N. ENDS WITH
-G- # (1986)
-H- # (1987)

SINCE MID-'86,
AIR-BAG
RESTRAINT SYST.
AVAIL. (1987 MODEL)

1987
DASH

TEMPO GL

29 M172

GL

4 DR. (ILLUSTR.)
(22X) $9278. ('86)
(36X) 9963. ('87)   104 MPH
                     (1987, 4WD)

151

1988 MODELS =
GL : P31X 2 DR. $10,311.
P36X 4 DR. 10,461.
GLS : P33S 2 DR. 10,902.
P38S 4 DR. 11,053.
LX : P37X 4 DR. 11,390.
4WD : P39S 4 DR. 11,584.

Ford Tempo

(SAME MODELS
and NUMBERS
IN 1989
$10,785. TO 12,073.)

GL

('88)

1989 GLS
INTERIOR

GLS

$11053. ('88)
$11576. ('89)

PP38S
$12258.
(1990)
GLS   ('89)

1989
GLS
ILLUSTR.

88-90
RESTYLED

V.I.N. ENDS WITH
—J—# (1988)
—K—# (1989)
—L—# (1990)

141 CID 2.3 L 4
(98 OR 100 HP @ 4400 RPM)
21/32 MPG (VARIABLE AS TO
TRANSMISSION 5 SP. O/D,
3 SP. AUTO., 4WD)
15.9 GAL. FUEL TANK
(14.2 "   "   " w. 4WD)

(LX 2 DR.
DISCONT'D.
1988)

Buckle-up–together we can save lives.

LX

('88)

$11390. ('88)
11884. ('89)
12415. ('90)   152

THUNDERBIRD

BY FORD MOTOR CO. (SINCE 1955) (2-DR. MODELS ONLY)

(A) DASH   TOWN LANDAU (LOWER LEFT) $9702.
HERITAGE (CENTER) $11,733.

CLOSE-UP OF WARNING LTS. ATOP DASH (B) 108.4" WB
"KEYLESS ENTRY" COMBINATION DOOR LOCK

OPT.
new 81
200 CID 6, OR
255 OR 302
CID V8s

← "CARRIAGE ROOF" OPT.

ELECTRONIC FUEL GAUGE
AND DIGITAL SPEEDOMETER
OPTION (ABOVE) (C)

V.I.N. =
1FAB P42 (-) 0B (-)
600001 UP
P195/75R14
TIRES

TRUNK

WHEELS AVAIL.

STD. TOP →

THUNDERBIRD

FROM $8564.

THE THUNDER'S STILL THERE.

153

THUNDERBIRD
Ford

W. "CARRIAGE TOP"

MPG : 24 HWY, 18 EPA EST.
30 HWY, 18 EPA (V6, O/D)
CALIF.: 30 HWY, 19 EPA

THUNDERBIRD SERIES

$9823.

ENGINES
200 CID 6
(88 HP)
255 CID V8
(111 HP)
OR
NEW
232 CID V6
(112 HP)
SHOWN
BELOW, LEFT

21 GAL.
FUEL TANK

"TRIPMINDER" COMPUTER

new (OPT.)

82 TOWN LANDAU

$11,034.

V.I.N.= IFAB (P42) BOC
(-) 000001 UP

V6 IS **New**

VENT WINDOWS OPT.

$13,156.

HERITAGE SERIES

154   1982

THUNDERBIRD

V.I.N.= IFABP463XD UP ; TURBO = IFABP46WXD UP

HAVE YOU DRIVEN A FORD...LATELY?

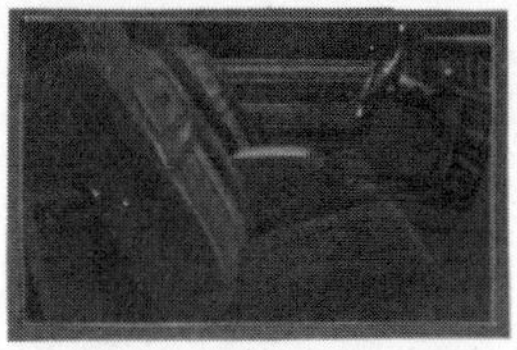

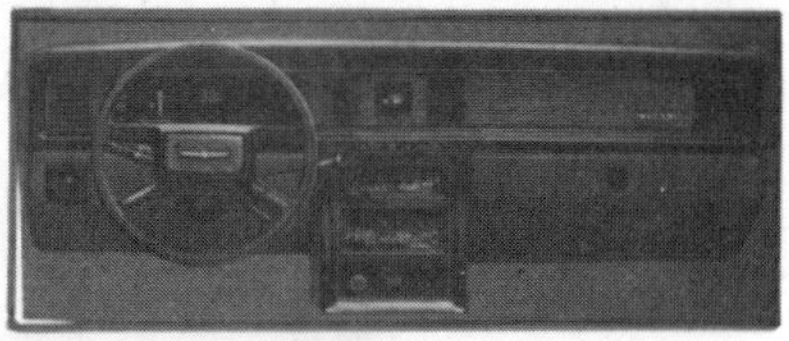

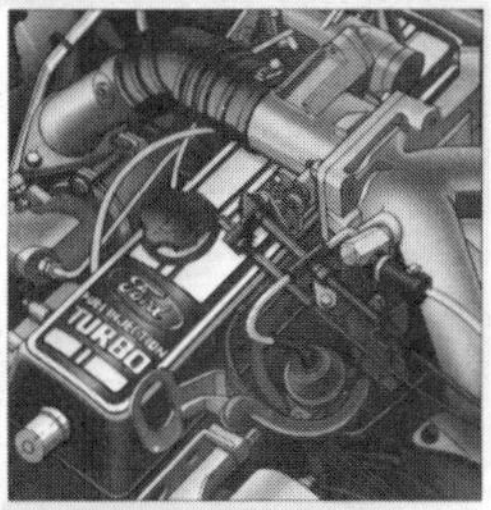

TURBO 4, 232 CID V6 OR 302 CID V8

New
The turbocharger.

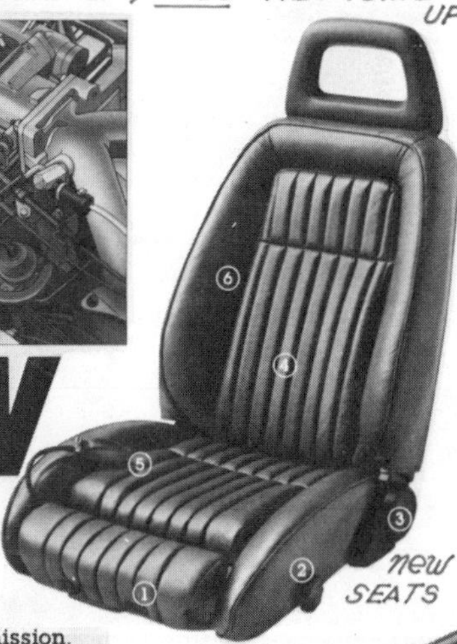

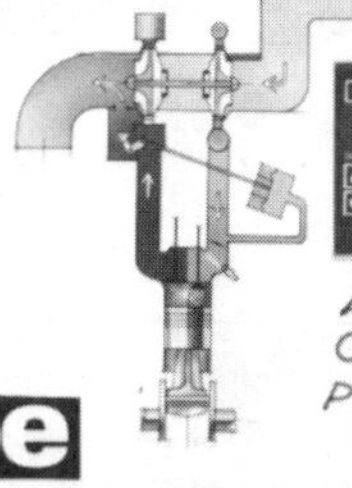

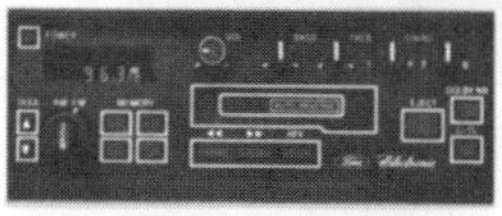

AM/FM STEREO w. CASSETTE PLAYER

PRICED FROM $10,401.
20 MPG EPA (V6)

NEW

4-CYL. TURBO ENG. (145 HP)

new SEATS

83
new shape
new 104" WB

5-speed transmission.

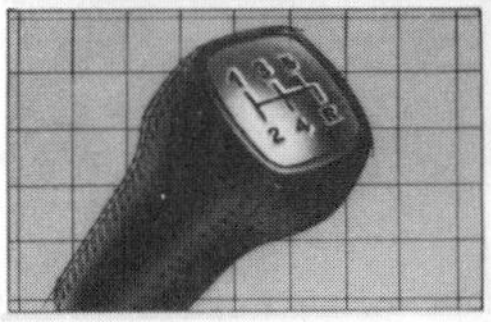

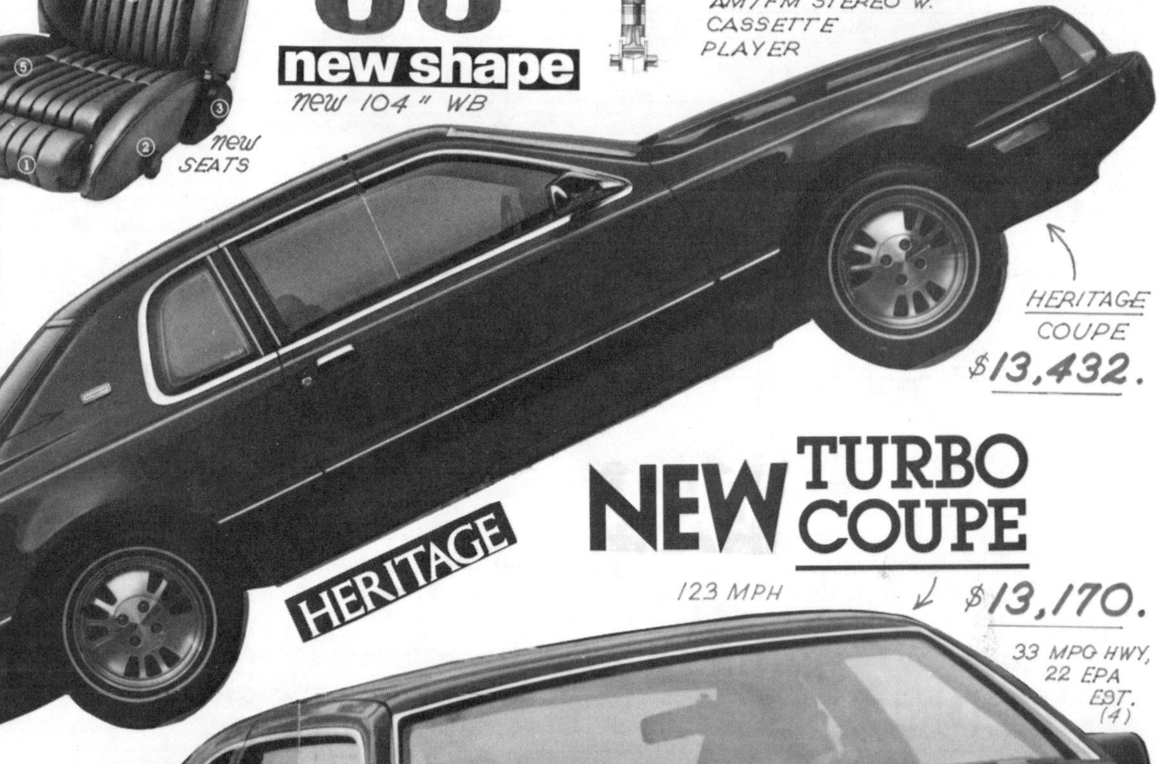

HERITAGE MODEL HAS THIS EMBLEM

HERITAGE

HERITAGE COUPE $13,432.

NEW TURBO COUPE

123 MPH

$13,170.

33 MPG HWY, 22 EPA EST. (4)

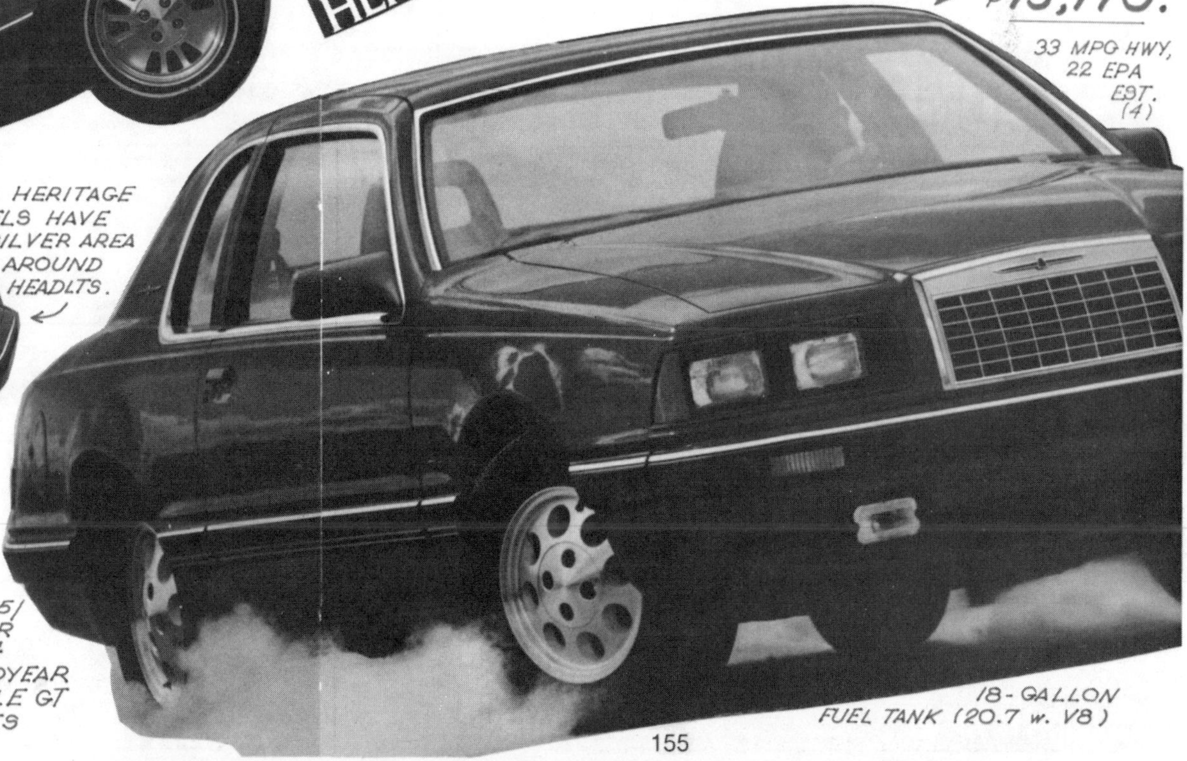

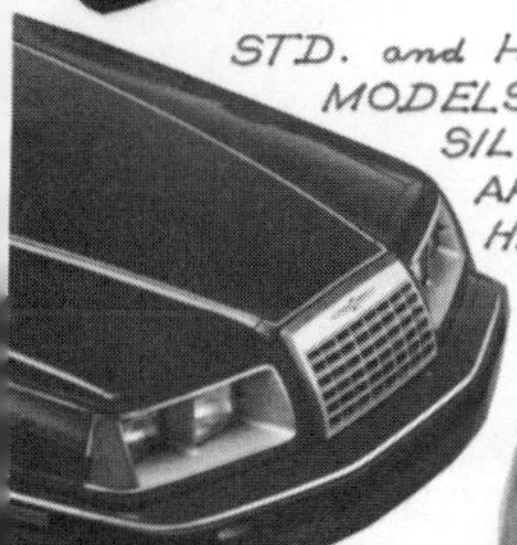

STD. and HERITAGE MODELS HAVE SILVER AREA AROUND HEADLTS.

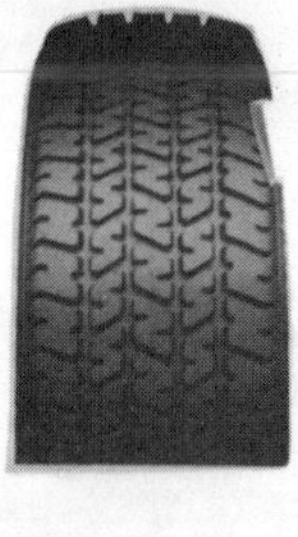

HAS P205/70HR x 14 GOODYEAR EAGLE GT TIRES

18-GALLON FUEL TANK (20.7 w. V8)

Thunderbird

Ford

V.I.N. = IFABP46TXE (-) 10000I UP (SAME FOR TURBO)

STD. COUPE **$10,808.**

↑ TRX ALUM. WHEEL

New ELAN

(REPLACES HERITAGE)

$13,836.

4 CYL. TURBO (145 HP)
232 CID V6 (120 HP)
302 CID V8 (140 HP)

P195/75R × 14 TIRES STD. *

84

FRONT END

The FILA Thunderbird.

New

FILA = **$15,646.**

* note: FILA HAS P205/70 HR × 14 TIRES, COLOR-COORDINATED WHEELS

FILA

FILA INTERIOR

CAST ALUMINUM WHEEL

Turbo Coupe

$13,820.

P R N D 2 1

156 AVAIL. w. AUTOMATIC **shift**

Thunderbird

30th Anniversary Thunderbird

STD. $11,424.

ELAN $13,091.

85

157

Thunderbird

FILA (FINAL FILA) $16,149.

FILA V6

EVERY 1985 FILA INCLUDES A FILA CANVAS SPORT BAG w. LEATHER PORTFOLIO, BEACH TOWEL, OTHER MISC. ITEMS.

85

6 WAY POW. SEAT IN GRAY SUEDE CLOTH or WHITE LEATH. 1985 FILA has NEWLY-DESIGNED DIGITAL INST. PANEL.

FILA IN EITHER BLACK, RED MEDIUM CHARCOAL, or THE UNIQUE "PASTEL CHARCOAL" WITH DARK CHARCOAL LOWER ACCENT TREATMENT. PINSTRIPING AND FILA EMBLEM ALSO.

note BLACK GRILLE, "BLACKED-OUT" FRONT END TREATMENT.

V.I.N.= IFAB (P46)TXF (-)10000I UP

$14,540.

Turbo Coupe
140 CID TURBO 4

TURBO COUPE DASH

12:38

Ford Thunderbird 86

STD. CPE. (463) $12,214.
ELAN CPE. (463) 13,748.
TURBO CPE. (46W) 15,652.

V.I.N. = 1FABP (46W) -G-#

137 MPH

140 C.I.D. TURBO 4 has 155 HP @ 4600 RPM and P225VR60/15 GOODYEAR "GATORBACK" TIRES

18/23 MPG (302 CID V8) (1987)

(FILA DISCONTINUED)

Have you driven a Ford... lately? Ford

V.I.N. ENDS WITH -H-# (1987); -J-# (1988)

LX ('87) (REPLACES ELAN)

LX

LX 623 ('87) P624 ('88)

"S" BODY

1987/1988 MODELS =
COUPE (V6) $13460./13927.
LX (V6) $15789./16214.
SPORT COUPE (5.0L V8) (61F) $15497./ (P61F) 16359.
TURBO COUPE (2.3 L TURBO 4 $17547./17578. (FINAL 1988, P64T)
64W (1987)

87-88

new FRONT

('87) TURBO HAS ABS BRAKING, COMPUTERIZED SUSPENSION and INTERCOOLED TURBOCHARGER

Turbo Coupe.

TURBO INCREASED TO 185~190 HP IN 1987 (190 HP IN 1988)

131 MPH

('87) REAR INT. (TURB.)

159

SC.*

(* "SUPER COUPE")
SUPER-
CHARG.
INTER-
COOLED
210
HP
V6

$20278. ('89)
P64R

$21413. ('90)

Ford

Thunderbird

TURBO 4 and
V8 SPT. CPE.
DISCONTD.

"SC"
ON FRONT
BUMPER

Have you driven a Ford...lately?

V. I. N. ENDS
WITH -K-# ('89)
"-L-# ('90)

17
TO
23
MPG

('89)

NEW

19 GALLON
GAS TANK

COUPE (P604)
$15067. (15440. '90)

3.8 L, 232 c/d
V6
(140 HP @
3800 RPM ON
STD., LX)
(19/27 MPG)

REAR-
WHEEL
DRIVE
RETAINED

89-90

LX INTERIOR ('89)

new
WHEELS

new SHEET METAL   new 113"
WHEELBASE,
BUT BODY LENGTH 4"
SHORTER

new POWER EQUIP.
OR LUXURY GROUP
OPTIONS FOR
1990

LX

('90)
LX CPE. (P624)
$17272. ('89) 17723. ('90)

160

(INCL. SPECTRUM, REPLACES SPRINT)

GEO

(STARTS 1989)
(DISTRIBUTED BY CHEVROLET DEALERS)

Japanese

3 CYL. METRO LSi 5 SP. MPG 46 CITY / 50 HWY. (38/40 w. AUTO TRANS.)

NEW 89

METRO
(FORMERLY SPRINT)
MFD. BY SUZUKI, JAPAN

MPG 58 HWY 53 CITY

FRONT VIEW

DASH

GEO METRO LSi

MS212 BASE METRO **$5995.** (REG. $6250.) (ABOVE)

note DIFFERENCES IN WHEELS OF EACH OF THESE TWO MODELS.

"BRAIN-POWERED"

THINKING MAN SYMBOLIC FIGURE SEEN IN 1989 GEO ADVERTISE-MENTS.

PERFORMANCE · QUALITY · VALUE · PROTECTION

THE LOGIC OF GEO-LOGIC

'89 Geo Spectrum

METRO LSi 2-DR. **$6895.** (4 DR., $7195.) (REG. $7150. and $7450.)

BLT. BY ISUZU, JAPAN

EARLY 1989 4-CYLINDER **SPECTRUM** 4 DR. NOTCHBACK $8110. (2-DR. HTCHBK., $7610.)

GEO KNOWN AS "PASSPORT" IN CANADA.

V.I.N. ENDS WITH — K-#

TRACKER BLT. BY SUZUKI, JAPAN, OR BY GM/SUZUKI, CANADA

GEO TRACKER

(JAPANESE-AMERICAN NOVA REPLACED BY 1990 GEO PRIZM, INTRO. IN EARLY 1989.)

12,495. LSi MODEL 10,495. HARDTOP 10,195. CONV'T.

TRACKER DASH

WITH 4-WHEEL DRIVE MPG = 28 CITY, 29 HWY (5 SP.); 25 CITY/HWY (AUTO TR.)

METRO DASH

GEO

METRO LSi

$8351.
93.1" WB (SEDANS)
89.2" WB (COUPES)

Geo Metro XFi. $6551.

3 CYLINDERS
58/53 MPG (40/38 w. A/T)
61 CID 55 HP @ 5700 RPM

1990 GEO V.I.N. ENDS WITH — L — #

Geo Tracker.
97 CID 4
86.6" WB (80 HP @ 5500)
GRILLE
SIMILAR TO SUZUKI SIDEKICK

Geo Storm
96½" WB
4 CYL. (95, 130 HP)
BLT. BY ISUZU, JAPAN
$11,297. UP

New

90

$10,705.
UP
24 TO 36 MPG, DEPENDING ON ENG. + TR.

Geo Tracker Convertible's 2-position soft top is available in black or white, depending on exterior color selected.

DASH

STORM DASH

STORM (REAR)

TRACKER

GEO PRIZM HATCHBACK SEDAN

Geo Prizm. = BLT. IN USA BY GM/TOYOTA
4 CYL. (102, 130 HP) 98 CID
95.7" WB
$11,369. UP new
34/28 MPG

PRIZM DASH

GEO PRIZM LSi
4-DOOR SEDAN

162

Get to know
Geo

SILHOUETTES

STD.

MISER

HORIZON *and* **OMNI**

Plymouth

Dodge

The New Chrysler Corporation

Trans-4 engine
front-wheel-drive

4 CYL., 104.7 CID
OR 133 CID

(1978 - 1990)

HORIZON V.I.N.= IP3BL18
AOB (-) 0000/ UP

TC3 V.I.N.=
IP3B L24
AOB — #

PLYMOUTH HORIZON MISER
L18 $5,299†
50 EST HWY   30 EPA EST MPG

(MISER HAS
NO CHROME
TRIM ON
ROCKER
PANEL.)

REG.
$6002.

('81)

96.6" WB

PLYMOUTH TC 3 HATCHBACK
L24 $6,149†
41 EST HWY   27 EPA EST MPG

"MISER"
MODELS
AVAILABLE IN
1981 and 1982 ONLY.

TRANVERSE
ENGINE
PLACEMENT

Dodge Omni Miser
as shown $5499.**
L18

EURO
SIDE -
TRIM

99.1"
WB

OMNI V.I.N.=
IB3BL24
AOB (-)10000/ UP

DASH DETAILS

L SERIES

81

PREMIUM
TRIM

Omni Euro-Sedan: as low as $6722.**
41 est. hwy.   25 EPA est. mpg*
Fuel efficiency enhanced by
advanced computer technology.

with Premium Exterior Package.

L28

with Custom Exterior Package.

CUSTOM
TRIM

Horizon

HORIZON
GRILLE has
ALL
VERTICAL
PIECES.

L28

163

HORIZON and OMNI

M SERIES — *Z SERIES*

Horizon Custom 47 EST. HWY. 30 EPA EST. MPG.

M48

HORIZON MISER: 35 EPA EST MPG, 52 ESTIMATED HIGHWAY.*

Horizon Miser 52 EST. HWY 35 EPA EST. MPG

82

"PENTASTAR" new EMBLEM ON GRILLE

TURISMO 2 + 2 (BELOW)

MODEL		Prices Start at*	Prices as shown**
Horizon Miser	M18	$5499	$5639
Turismo 2.2	M54	$7345	$7345

TRI-COUNTY RALLY

$7,345*

Turismo 2.2 41 EST HWY 26 EPA EST MPG

0 to 50 in 6.4 seconds* 41 EST. HWY 26 EPA EST mpg**

DASH

Plymouth

13 GAL. FUEL TK.

OMNI

HORIZON new GRILLE EMBLEMS

OMNI 50 EST. HWY. 30 EPA EST. MPG mpg.*

Z18 Omni Miser

V.I.N. ENDS WITH AOC (-) #

HORIZON E-TYPE:

1982 OMNIS and HORIZONS REGULARLY PRICED FROM $6103.

NOTICE THAT 024 MISER (RT.) HAS MORE WINDOW AREA THAN 024 CUSTOM (BELOW)

024 MISER

024

Z14 $6486.

HORIZON DASH (E)

34* EPA EST MPG, 51 EST. HIGHWAY.

DODGE 024...

024 CUSTOM ← $7027. Z44

FINAL YR. FOR **Euro-Sedan**

164

RALLYE CLUSTER (OPT.)

("MISER" MODELS DISCONTINUED)

HORIZON and OMNI
M SERIES   Z SERIES

AND WE'VE ADDED 13 NEW FEATURES FOR $626 LESS.

DASH

HORIZON CUSTOM INTERIOR
$7039.

HORIZON CUSTOM

NEW TAILLIGHTS

83

HORIZON – $6809. UP
OMNI —— 6675. UP

CONTROL STALK
(W. "SPEED CONTROL"
DESIGNATION
SINCE '82)

NEW
5-
SPEED
TRANS-
AXLE
OPT.

ENGINE IMPROVED FOR 8% BETTER HWY. MPG

REAR DETAILS

HORIZON V.I.N.
=1P3BM18
BXD (-)
000001
UP

DODGE OMNI

(1982 "024" REPLACED BY 1983 CHARGER)

OMNI
V.I.N.=
1B3BZ48
BXD (-)
000001/ UP

EXTRAORDINARY MILEAGE: 51 EST. HWY., 34 EPA EST.

important new standard features such as power brakes, reclining bucket seats, and halogen head-lamps.

PRICE: $5841.

HORIZON and OMNI

OMNI GRILLE — LM SERIES

LZ SERIES

MPG:
43 EST. HWY,
27 EPA
EST.

OMNI
(SAME PRICES AS HORIZON)

LZE44 / AGB

new GLH (OMNI ONLY) $7658.
106 MPH
110 HP 2.2 L ENG.

Plymouth Turismo 2.2 for 1984.

0 ~ 50 IN 5.85 SECONDS

new GRAPHICS, 2-TONE PAINT, SPOILER, 14" RALLYE ROAD WHEELS, GOODYEAR EAGLE GT TIRES, ETC.

TURISMO 2.2 - $8101.
STD. TURISMO - 7420.

HORIZON DASH and INT.

84

new GRILLES

1984 V.I.N. ENDS WITH AXE (-) #

HORIZON SE $6895.

HORIZON $6690.

REAR DETAILS

109 MPH

PLYMOUTH TURISMO'S DODGE COUNTERPART IS CHARGER. (SEE DODGE CHARGER / DAYTONA PAGES)

DASH

HORIZON and OMNI
M SERIES   Z SERIES
"L" BODY

(STD., SE, or GLH OMNIS,
1985-1986 ;
"AMERICA" ONLY,
STARTING 1987.)

STD. WHEEL

HI-PERFORMANCE
OMNI
GLH
('85)

(STD.)
M18A
HORIZON
$6871. ('85)
7146. ('86)

('86)

$7940.
LZE44/AGB

Horizon SE

$7101.
('85)
7382.
('86)

$872. EXTRA FOR
TURBO 4
ENG.

HORIZON

M48A

OPT. AUTOMATIC
SPEED
CONTROL

COOL   TEMPERATURE   WARM   HI
OFF MAX A/C A/C VENT HEAT   LO

AIR COND. CONTROLS

85-87

TURISMO
DASH

2+2:
M54F
('85)
M54A
('86)

OPT. SUNROOF AND REAR
WINDOW SUNSHD.

2+2
$8622. ('86)

TURISMO

(CONT'D.
NEXT
PAGE)

FINAL TURISMO and DUSTER ARE 1987 MODELS.

('87)

TURISMO... "L" BODY

HORIZON and OMNI

55.7"

DUSTER CONSIDERED AN OPT. "PACKAGE" IN 1985 -1986

Turismo Duster $8894. ('86)

1987 MPG: (TURISMO) 23/27 (135 CID 4 w. A/T)

V.I.N. = ENDS WITH
— F → # 1985
— G → " 1986
→ H → " 1987

(1987 MODEL YEAR BEGINS JUNE, 1986) ("AMERICA" SERIES, 1987 ON)

85-87

AM/FM SET 9:4.0
VOL BASS TREBLE TUNE SPKR
A BALANCE 1 2 3 4 5

CLOCK / RADIO

('86)

4 CYLINDER ENGINES : (STD.)   (OPT.)   TURISMO/ DUSTER DASH

20/43 MPG

1987 OMNI "AMERICA" NOW HAS 2.2-LITER ENG. + 5 SP. TR. AS STD EQUIP.

OMNI "AMERICA."
REG. $6895.
('87)

106 MPH (HORIZON AMERICA, 1987)

1.6-liter (97.1 CID) four-cylinder engine: 64 hp @ 4,800 rpm; 87 lb-ft torque @ 2,800 rpm.

2.2-liter (135 CID) Trans-4 engine: 96 hp @ 5,200 rpm; 119 lb-ft torque @ 3,200 rpm.

Dodge DIVISION OF CHRYSLER CORPORATION

AN AMERICAN REVOLUTION

GET MORE IN AMERICA, WITH DODGE OMNI "AMERICA."

DODGE OMNI "AMERICA"

THE LOWEST PRICED AMERICAN CAR YOU CAN BUY.

SPECIAL PRICE: $5499.

LEASE Zero down. $99 month!

168

HORIZON and OMNI

(SOLD IN CANADA UNDER THE NAME OF "EXPO", THEN AS "CANADA.")

With over fifty standard features, a 2.2-liter four-cylinder engine now with electronic fuel injection, front-wheel drive, and hatchback versatility,

(AS OF 1988)

Horizon America

NEW 1990 DASH (AT UPPER RT.)

DRIVER'S AIRBAG STD. FOR 1990.

STD. INT. NOW INCL. FR. RECLINING CLOTH BUCKET SEATS WITH VINYL TRIM. ('88)

INTERIOR

Horizon America is packed with such conveniences as a standard rear window wiper/washer, a standard deluxe intermittent wiper, and even a standard passenger vanity visor mirror.

7/70 LIMITED WARRANTY

V.I.N. ENDS WITH
−J−# 1988
−K− " 1989
−L− " 1990

Horizon America, shown in Garnet Red Clear Coat.

(UNLESS OTHERWISE INDICATED, 1988 EXAMPLES ARE ILLUSTRATED)

THE AMERICA SERIES

(JUST 1 BASIC 5-DR. HATCHBACK IN HORIZON/OMNI LINE, SINCE 1987.)

OMNI/HORIZON REG. PRICE ═ $ 7116 / 7719 / 9443
(1988, 1989 and 1990 CONSECUTIVELY)

88-90

135 CID 4
93 HP @ 4800 RPM

26/35 MPG (24/30 WITH AUTO. TRANS.)

note TAILLIGHT DIFFERENCES FROM PLY. HORIZON (AT UPPER LEFT.)

OMNI DASH (1988)

625 BGL

('89)

(1990s ARE FINAL MODELS)

13-GAL. FUEL TANK

WE JUST WANT TO BE THE BEST.

169

LINCOLN (SINCE 1921)

OPTIONAL "KEYLESS ENTRY SYSTEM" 4 SP. AUTO. OVERDRIVE TRANS.

$14,560. 2 DR.

(NEW MODEL NAME) TOWN CAR

$14,958. 4 DR.

V.I.N.=
ILN (–)
P93FXB (–)
600001 UP
(MK. VI, P95)

$23,144.

HOOD ORNAMENT

CONTINENTAL MARK VI 2-DR. "SIGNATURE" (OVAL OPERA WINDOWS)(4 DR. ALSO)

"INSTANT FUEL ECONOMY" READOUT ON DASH IS NEW

81

302 CID (5.0 LITRE) EFI V8 ENGINE

117.3" WB (114.3" ON 2-DR. MODEL OF MK VI)

18-GAL. FUEL TANK

MARK VI DESIGNER SERIES (FROM $20,554.

"BILL BLASS" EDITION (GIVENCHY, PUCCI, and CARTIER EDITIONS ALSO AVAIL.)

MARK VI HAS HEADLIGHT COVERS

16 EPA EST. MPG 24 HWY EST

CONTINENTAL MARK VI

170

LINCOLN

18 GAL. FUEL TANK
17 MPG
(EPA)

Lincoln Town Car

P94
TOWN CAR
$16,880.

V.I.N. ENDS WITH
— OC (-)
000001/ UP

82

MARK VI FRONT
FENDER DETAIL,
SHOWING CONTINENTAL
EMBLEM ON CORNER
LIGHT

TOWN CAR FRONT DETAILS

new DOWNSIZED CONT'L.
WITH 108½" WB

"CONTINENTAL"
NAME ON IMITATION
TIRE COVER

CONTINENTAL
REAR DECK DETAILS
20 GAL. FUEL TK.
18 MPG
(EPA)

1982 CONTINENTAL

New

REAR
EMBLEM

(ALL 3 SERIES AVAIL. IN
SIGNATURE OR
DESIGNERS MODELS
ALSO.)

CONTINENTAL $21,808.
UP
P98

18
GAL.
FUEL
TK.

17
MPG
(EPA)

1982 MARK VI

MARK VI COUPE
$19,958. UP
P95

LINCOLN

16 MPG EPA

TOWN CAR $17,916. (P96)
(SIGNATURE $19,258; DESIGNER $20594.)
60 U   CARTIER
                          605

83

302 CID V8 has 134 HP

TOWN CAR REAR

V.I.N. ENDS WITH — FXD (-) #

CLOSE-UP FRONT DETAIL OF MK. VI

New ANTI-THEFT ALARM (OPT.)

1983 MARK VI

("SIGNATURE" and "PUCCI" MK. VIs ALSO)

60 N BLASS

BILL BLASS ED. w. CABRIOLET ROOF
$25,242.

$23,285.
60 R

TYPICAL MK. VI OPERA WINDOW
MK. VI PRICES =
$20,939. and up

CONTINENTAL

New

"VALENTINO" ADDED TO THE DESIGNER" ED. LINE (WALNUT MOON-DUST OVER GOLDEN MIST COLOR SCHEME)

OPT. AUTOMATIC DIMMING DAY/NIGHT MIRROR
New
P97 $21,694.

AP10240

(60 M "GIVENCHY" MODEL ALSO)

117.3" WB
P96

302 CID V8 OR 8 CYL. new DIESEL (BMW) TURBO AVAIL.

LINCOLN
TOWN CAR
19,069.

CLOSE VIEW OF HOOD ORNAMENT

SIGNATURE, $21039.
DESIGNER, $22516.

DESIGNER CONTINENTAL HAS 2-TONE COLORS

VALENTINO $24926.

'84
P97

(new MK. VII STARTS)

new CONT'L. INTERIOR w. REAL WOOD TRIM, new OVERHEAD CONSOLE w. WARNING LTS. and READING LAMPS.

CONTINENTAL
$22478.

GIVENCHY INTERIOR IN ADMIRAL BLUE (EXTERIOR IN SLATE BLUE METALLIC over MIDNIGHT BLUE METALLIC

$24,951.

New
FRONT STYLING

V.I.N. ENDS WITH FXE (-) 000001 UP

CONTINENTAL and new MK. VII w. 108½" WB, 302 CID V8 (130 HP @ 3200 RPM)

111 MPH

BILL BLASS, VERSACE MK. VIIs ALSO, AS WELL AS STD., LSC.

REAR DETAILS OF

Mark VII P98

MARK VII INT. (ABOVE) HAS NO WOODGRAIN TRIM, LSC MODEL, $24415.

$22416.

NEW

173

CONTINENTAL MARK VII.

MPG: 26 HWY, 17 EPA

LINCOLN

NEW GRILLE ON **Town Car,** $19,756.
P96/700A
(CVT.-STYLE "CARRIAGE" ROOF ALSO AVAIL.)

TOWN CAR SIGNATURE SERIES
P96/705A $22,991.
TOWN CAR DESIGNER EDIT.
$24,229.
P96/710A

V.I.N. = ILNBP96FXF UP (TOWN CAR)

302 CID V8 (140 HP) (180 @ 4200 IN MK. 7)

GIVENCHY DESIGNER SERIES CONTINENTAL $26,430. (VALENTINO, $26725.)
P97/865A
P97/860A

CONT'L. V.I.N. IMRB P97FXF UP

P215/70R15

P97/850A **CONTINENTAL** $23,683.

146 CID 6 CYL. TURBO DIESEL ENG. AVAILABLE (115 HP)

GOODYEAR EAGLE GT
IS STD. EQUIPMT. TIRE ON MK.VII. (P215/65R x15 ON LSC)

85

P98/800A **MARK VII** $23,571.

(MK. VII LSC, BILL BLASS, and VERSACE ALSO AVAIL.)

MK. VII OVERHEAD CONSOLE AND DASH

AVAIL. ANTI-LOCK BRAKE SYSTEM

V.I.N. = IMRB P98FXF UP (MK.VII)

(note: MOST LSCs HAVE AUX. LTS. BELOW FRONT BUMPER, AS SEEN ON 1984 EXAMPLE.)

174

LINCOLN

COMPACT DISC PLAYER OPT. IN 1987 TOWN CAR.

('87)

STD. SIGNATURE, or DESIGNER

V.I.N. (1986) ILNBP(96F) -F-#
(1987) ILNBM(81F) -H-#

('86) "PANTHER" BODY

TOWN CAR 1987 MPG: 17/27

(V8)

('87)

TOWN CAR.

TOWN CAR

1986 PRICES FR. $21,473.
1987 " " 23,361.

86 - 87

CONTINENTAL WHEEL DETAIL

302 CID V8 (17/27 MPG) 1987

"LS" BODY CONTINENTAL FRONT DETAIL ↓

110 MPH

Lincoln Continental.

"LS" BODY

('86)

Lincoln-Mercury Div.

1987 FINAL YR. FOR CONT'L. w. V8

120 MPH

STD. MK. VII, LSC or BILL BLASS

"FOX" BODY

MARK VII (LSC)

CONT'L. SED. or "GIVENCHY" SEDAN, FROM $24556. ('86) 26008. ('87)

new Ford JBL Audio System.

140 WATTS, 12 SPEAKERS (OPT.)

MK. VII FROM $22399. ('86) 23770. ('87)

LINCOLN. What a luxury car should be.

175

LINCOLN

1988 V.I.N. = 1LNBM
(81F)-J-#
81F SEDAN, 82F SIGNATURE ", OR 83F DESIGNER / CARTIER SED.

('88)

$25,591. UP ('88)
26,806. UP ('89)

1988 TOWN CAR HAS "LINCOLN" NAME ABOVE LT.

88-89 NEW

1989 V.I.N. =
1LN - M
(81F)
- K - #

TOWN CAR 5.0 L V8
117.3" WB

17/24 MPG ('89)

1989 GRILLE HAS RELOCATED "LINCOLN" NAME

New

STYLING FOR 1988

Continental →

new
109" WB
3.8 L
V6 (new)

V6 ENG. IN CONTINENTAL ONLY

974 SEDAN
28,852. ('89) $26,602. ('88)

CONTINENTAL
SIGNATURE SEDAN $28,468.
984
30,460. ('89)

new GRILLE ON MARK VII

108 1/2" WB 5.0 L V8
17/24 MPG ('89)

MARK VII
93E BILL BLASS OR LSC 92E
EACH $26,904.
$28,119 ('89)

LINCOLN. What a luxury car should be.

176

LINCOLN

MK.VII

TOWN CAR SEDAN 8IF $29156.
" " SIGNATURE 82F 31276.
" " CARTIER 83F 33364.

TOTALLY RESTYLED **TOWN CAR**

TOWN CAR IS MOTOR TREND'S 1990 "CAR OF THE YEAR."

117.4" WB
302 CID V8 (150 HP @ 3200 RPM)
18 GAL. FUEL TANK
17/24 MPG

CELLULAR TELEPHONE OPTIONAL

V.I.N. = ILN-M (8IF)-L-#

90

(MK. VII HAS 22.1 GAL. FUEL TANK.)

V8 MARK VII BILL BLASS (93E, $29801.)
and LSC (92E, $30023.) 2-DR. SEDANS
CONTINUE (WITH LITTLE CHANGE.) new DASH.

CONTINENTAL new DASH
GRILLE

DRIVER AND RT. FRONT PASSENGER AIR BAGS ON ALL 1990 LINCOLN CARS.

V6 **CONTINENTAL**
SEDAN $30796. 974
SIGNATURE SED.   31901. 984
232 CID V6 (140 HP @ 3800 RPM) 19/28 MPG 18.6 GAL. FUEL TANK

LINCOLN. What a luxury car should be.

REAR DETAILS

MERCURY

(BY LINCOLN-MERCURY DIVISION **Ford**)

A/C CONTROLS

INTERIOR (C.P.)

DASH DETAIL

P87

MERCURY MARQUIS WAGON in Dark Cordovan Metallic

$10,182.

8891.

VOLUME — 98.8 — TONE SET/TAPE

RADIO (AM/FM)

MARQUIS →

P81

18* EPA EST MPG   26 HWY EST

81

114.3" WB
255, 302, OR
351 CID V8s
AUTO. OVERDRIVE AVAIL.

P82

P205/75R x 14 TIRES

MARQUIS BROUGHAM

$10,418.

V.I.N.= 1MEB
P820B (-)
60000/ UP

• POWER ANTENNA
• POWER DOOR LOCKS
• POWER SEATS
• POWER WINDOWS*

OPT.

GRAND MARQUIS

$11,315.

P85

MARQUIS COLONY PARK WAGON

P88

$11,177.

SEAT (WAGON)

ORNAMENT

VEHICLE IDENTIFICATION NOS. =
IMEBP81 DOC (-) (MARQUIS)
IMEBP98 DOC (-) (MARQ. BROUGHAM)
IMEBP84 DOC (-) (GRAND MARQUIS)
IMEBP88 DOC (-) (WAGONS)
NUMBERS FOLLOWED BY
00000I UP

MARQUIS, 53 CUBIC FEET | 17 EPA EST MPG | 26 EST. HWY
(WAGON)

MERCURY

COLONY PARK WAGON
← P88

82

255 OR 302 CID V8s

$12,071.
($12,238.,
W. DUAL-FACING
THIRD
REAR SEATS)

P85 4 DR.
GRAND MARQUIS
$12,520.

20 GAL.
FUEL TANK

18 MPG (SED.)
EPA

An advanced Automatic Overdrive Transmission
cuts engine speed on the highway by 30%. And options
run the gamut from luxury cloth or leather seats to a
formal roof (shown), digital electronic sound

SIDE-LT.
DETAIL

NEW ENGINES
140 CID 4
200 CID 6
OR
232 CID V6
(112 HP)
WITH 4-SP.
O.D. TRANS.

(RESTYLED
1983 MARQUIS
← P89

NEW SHORTER
105 1/2" WB

$9939.

MARQUIS V.I.N. =
IMEBP81, ETC.
"TRIPMINDER" COMPUTER OPTIONAL.

MARQUIS
WAGON V.I.N.=
IMEBP87BXD
(-) 000001 UP

83

24 MPG EPA
(MARQUIS 4)
19 MPG EPA
(MARQ. 6, V6)
16 MPG EPA
(GRAND M. V8)

GRAND
MARQUIS   P93

GRAND MARQUIS
NEW WHEELS →
SEATBELT WARNING CHIMES
V.I.N. IMEBP84 FXD (-) 000001 UP
GRAND MARQUIS
LS

MORE HORIZONTAL
BANDS ADDED TO
TAIL-LIGHTS.

$13,172.

MERCURY

OPTIONAL ELECTRONIC INSTRUMENT CLUSTER is IMPROVED.

P90

MARQUIS WAGON
$10,393.
2-WAY LIFTGATE is OPTIONAL.

MARQ. WAGON V.I.N. =
IMEBP903XE (-)
000001 UP

INTERIOR

P89

MARQUIS 4 DR.
$10,305.
MARQ. BROUGHAM
4 DR.
10,608.

MARQUIS V.I.N. =
IMEBP893XE (-)
000001 UP

MARQUIS
BROUGHAM
WAGON (P90/60H)
$10,667.
GR. MQ. LS 4-DR.
$14,159.

GRAND MARQUIS 2 DR. $13492.
  "   "   4 DR. 13604.
  "   "   LS 2 DR. 14047.

P95/60H

GRAND MARQUIS LS INTERIOR

GRAND MARQUIS COLONY PARK
LS WAGON $13790. UP

84

V.I.N. = IMEBP93FXE (-)
000001 UP (GR. MARQ.)
P94FXE (-)(COL. PK.)

P94

180

903 MARQUIS WAGON $10,675.

MERCURY

MARQ. BROUGH. WAGON $10,974.

(GRAND MARQUIS and COLONY PK. SER. CONT'D. WITH FEW CHANGES)

V8

903

85

V.I.N. = 1MEBP893 XF(-)000001 UP

105½" WB

$10,583. UP

new TAIL LTS.

AVAILABLE WHEEL STYLES

893

MARQUIS

CLOSE DETAILS OF new GRILLE (MARQUIS)

"MERCURY" NAME MOVED

MERCURY MARQUIS
LINCOLN-MERCURY DIVISION Ford

181

MERCURY

FROM $**11,342.** ('86)

114.3" WB

GRAND MARQUIS LS 2-DR. $**15,917.** ('86)

FROM $**16,588.** ('87)
17/27 MPG (302 CID V8)
"PANTHER" BODY
1986 EXAMPLES ILLUSTRATED

MERCURY. The shape you want to be in.

1986 MARQUIS RESEMBLES 1985 MODELS
1986 IS FINAL YR.
FOR MARQUIS V6 OR 4
(NOT SHOWN)

COLONY PARK LS

GRAND MARQUIS

CHILD RESTRAINT

1986 V.I.N.= IMEBP (93F TO 903) —G— #

86-
HIGH-MOUNTED 3RD BRAKE LT. ON ALL 1986 and LATER MODELS

87
1987 V.I.N.= IMEBM (M72F TO 79F) —H— #

Mercury NAME AT TOP CORNER OF GRILLE

WHEEL TYPES

COLONY PARK
LS

MERCURY
(2-DR. MODELS DISCONTINUED)

GRAND MARQUIS ROOFLINE →

GS OR LS MODELS AVAIL.

1990 DASH IS **NEW**

CLIMATE CONTROL AIR CONDITIONING SYSTEM OPTIONAL

REAR

1988 V.I.N. = (IME OR 3MA)
BM (74F) - J - #

88-90

79F
COLONY PARK
WAGON, LS
$18939. ('88)
19309. ('89)
20782. ('90)

74 F
COLONY PARK
WAGON, GS
$18355. ('88) 18727 ('89)
20210 ('90)

GS SEDAN/WAGON | LS SEDAN/WAGON

1989 V.I.N. =
IME-M (74F)-K-#
-L-# IN 1990 V.I.N.

1990 AUDIO SPEAKERS NOW IN DOOR PANELS INSTEAD OF ON DASH.

GRAND MARQUIS
SEDAN
$19475.
UP ('90)

RESTYLED,
1988
114.3" WB
5.0 L V8
302 CID
150 HP @
3200
RPM

18 GAL.
FUEL TANK

OTHER WHEELS AVAILABLE →

1990 EXAMPLES ILLUSTRATED

17/24
MPG,
EPA

183

(1969-1986)
(NAME TO RETURN IN 1991)

(MFD. BY FORD OF GERMANY UNTIL 1978 ; MFD. IN U.S.A. 1979 TO 1986.)

MERCURY CAPRI

CAPRI
LINCOLN-MERCURY DIVISION

100.4" WB
140 CID 4
OR TURBO 4,
200 CID 6,
OR 255 CID
V8 IN 1981.

P175/80R x 13 TIRES

STD. $8095.

"GS" $8277.

"RS" 8329.

"RS"

WITH T-BAR ROOF OPT.

1981 EXAMPLES ILLUSTR., UNLESS OTHERWISE INDICATED.

"BLACK MAGIC" 3-DR. HATCHBACK IS new, PRICED AT $ 8739.

"RS" TURBO* 8937.

81-82

V.I.N. = 1ME (-) P67 (A) XB 60000/ UP

V.I.N. = 1MEB P67 B0C (-) 00000/ UP ("RS" has -P67F0C- V.I.N.)

"BLACK MAGIC" CPE. and INTERIOR (T-BAR ROOF OPT.)

"TR" PERFORM. PKG. OPT.

new 1982 H.O. (HIGH OUTPUT) CAPRI w. new 157 HP 302 CID V8 (RS)

For power, you've got choices ranging from a 2.3-liter overhead cam four to a 5.0-liter V-8 that still remembers it's a V-8.

A five-speed overdrive transmission is standard. There are four different sound systems available, a flashy T-roof, special wheels, special paint, even a choice of steering wheels.

FROM $ 8362 ('82)

MPG : 21 EPA CITY, 34 36 HWY. (WEST COAST) 2.3 L., 5-SPEED

('82)

('82)

184

4 CYL. CAPRI V.I.N.= IMEBP79AXD (-)000001 UP
R9 (V8) V.I.N.= IMEBP67FXD (-)000001 UP

CAPRI

83

NEW
"BUBBLE BACK"
DESIGN, WITH
UNIQUE
WRAPAROUND
BODYSIDE
MOLDING
100.4" WB
CONTINUES

$8895. TO $10368.

STD.
L, G9,
BLACK MAGIC
CRIMSON CAT
OR R9 MODELS,
ALL 3-DOOR
HATCHBACKS

GS INTERIOR
P79/602
$9653.

5.0 LITER
(302 CID) 4 BBL. V8 has 178 HP
(232 CID V6 has 112 HP) 19 MPG EPA

(140 CID 4
AND TURBO 4
ALSO AVAIL.)
TO 24 MPG EPA

AVAILABLE WHEELS

84

GS (4 CYL.)
V.I.N. =
IMEBP793
XE (-)000001
UP

RS (V8) V.I.N. =
IMEBP79MXE (-)000001 UP

DASH

TURBO R9
INTERIOR

TURBO RS
$11,443.

140 CID 4 CYL.
TURBO ENG.
145 HP @ 4600
RPM

TURBO V.I.N. =
IMEBP79WXE
(-)000001 UP

New

(FRONT VIEW OF TURBO RS
ON NEXT PAGE)

1984 IS FINAL YR.
FOR R9 MODELS.

1984 Capri Turbo RS,
FRONT VIEW

RS REPLACED BY 5.0L (V8) IN 1985.
(1985 V.I.N. ENDS w. — F — # ; 1986 " " — G — #)

Mercury **CAPRI**

Options

AM/FM RADIO w. CASSETTE

T-ROOF

↙ SUN ROOF   1986 DASH

1984 EXAMPLES ILLUSTR.

84-86

GS OR 5.0 L 3 DR. HATCHBKS. ONLY, IN 1985 and 1986.

A/C OPT.

1985 $9500. OR 11891.
    GS (79A)   5.0 L (79M)
1986 9977. OR 12708.

ENDS 1986

186 '84 V8 **RS** $11,306. ↑

(IN SAN FRANCISCO, CALIF.)

MERCURY COUGAR

(SINCE 1967)

new

Introducing the Cougar 4-door.

INTERIOR

Premium Sound Systems. And many other options. With the standard engine and automatic transmission required on Cougar with LS option (shown below), the new Cougar is rated at 22* EPA EST. MPG, 31 EST. HWY. The 1981 Cougar 4-door. A 4-door car is one thing. But a Cougar is another.

4 DR. RETURNS, AFTER BEING OMITTED FROM 1980 SERIES.

105½" WB

139 CID 4, 200 CID 6, OR 255 CID V8

81

PARTIALLY RESTYLED

V.I.N. =
IME (-)
P76 (A)
XB (-)
60000I UP
XR-7 =
IME (-)
P90 (-) XB
60000I
UP

$**8387.** P77 4 DR.

($8228. P76 2 DR.)

Notice the new two-tone paint treatment, the electronic instrument cluster, and the unique convertible-like carriage roof options.

COUGAR XR-7
LINCOLN-MERCURY DIVISION

COUGAR XR-7

108.4" WB (XR-7)

255 OR 302 CID V8s OR 200 CID 6

$**8762.** (P90 CPE.)

GS OPTION $320.

LS OPTION $715.

RECARO SEATS, "KEYLESS ENTRY" LOCKS AVAILABLE ALSO.

CABRIOLET OPTION, XR-7

The standard engine/drive train is rated at 18 EPA EST. MPG, 24 EST. HWY. Compare to estimated MPG of other cars. Your mileage may differ depending on speed, weather, and trip length. Actual highway mileage probably lower.

FRONT DETAIL

STD. XR-7 CAB DETAIL

options like the TR-type tires, cast aluminum wheels, and a special suspension. AM/FM cassette stereo with Dolby® NR. And your choice of three engines: the 3.3 liter 6,° or the optional 4.2 and 5.0 liter V-8's...both available with Automatic Overdrive Transmission.

GS 4 DR. WAGON $9495. (P78)

New

COUGAR WAGON

82

(WAGON AVAIL. 1982 ONLY)

6, new V6, or V8 (4 CYL. DISCONT'D.)

OTHER MODELS (GS, LS, XR-7) CONT'D., $9262. UP (2 DR. and 4 DR. AVAIL.)

"MERCURY" INSCRIPTION ON new 1982 GRILLE

V.I.N. = IMEBP76BOC UP
XR-7 = " P90DOC UP

187

MERCURY COUGAR

LINCOLN-MERCURY DIVISION *Ford*

(4 DR. SEDAN and WAGON DISCONTINUED)

ALL-NEW SHAPE

2.0 MPG EPA (V6)

83

TOTALLY RESTYLED

new 104" WB.
2.47 GEAR RATIO

(ILLUSTRATED)
LS COUPE (P92/603)
$12,054.

MERCURY. THE SUBSTANCE SHOWS.

V.I.N.= 1MEBP923XD(-) 00001/UP

232 CID V6
5 LITER EFI (V8 AVAILABLE)

STD. COUPE (P92)
$10,725.

note UNIQUE new ROOFLINE

UPRIGHT COUGAR-HEAD DISC HOOD ORNAMENT ON 1983 COUGAR

2.73 GEAR RATIO IS **New**

XR-7 RETURNS AS TURBO 4. (next pg.)

84

New FLAT RADIATOR BADGE (ROUND) (INSTEAD OF UPRIGHT ORNAMENT)

188

MERCURY COUGAR

LINCOLN-MERCURY DIVISION Ford

V.I.N.=IMEBP923XE
(-) 000001 UP
XR-7=IMEBP92WXE (-)
000001 UP

INTERIOR (XR-7)

ELECTRONIC FUEL INJ.
NOW ON ALL COUGAR
ENGINES.

XR-7

XR-7 TURBO 104" WB

XR-7
TURBO-
CHARGER

$14,240.

WHEELS

NEW "CHECK
OIL" LIGHT
ON DASH

21 GAL.
FUEL
TANK
(18 ON
XR-7)

POWER TRAIN COMBINATIONS		REAR AXLE RATIO		
ENGINE	TRANSMISSION	49-STATES	HIGH ALTITUDE	CALIF.
3.8L EFI V-6 (STD.)	3-speed SelectShift Automatic with lock up torque converter (STD.)	2.73(a)	NA	2.73(a)
2.3L EFI Turbo I-4 (XR-7 Only)	3-speed SelectShift Automatic (STD.)	3.45(b)	3.45(b)	3.45(b)
2.3L EFI Turbo I-4 (XR-7 Only)	Manual 5-speed Overdrive (OPT.)	3.45(b)	3.45(b)	3.45(b)
5.0L OPT. EFI V-8	Automatic Overdrive (OPT.)	3.08(a)	3.08(a)	3.08(a)

STD. P92
COUGAR →
$11,153.

189

MERCURY COUGAR

OPT. "KEYLESS ENTRY" DOOR LOCK

GRAINED LS DASH

new CRISSCROSS PCS. IN GRILLE

new TAILLIGHTS

ELECTRONIC (DIGITAL) INSTRUMENT CLUSTER OPTIONAL, BUT NOT AVAIL. ON XR-7.

(XR-7 HAS BLACK DASH, CIRCULAR ANALOG GAUGES)

$15,089.
XR-7
(P92/934)

STD. CPE (P92)
$11,825. (P92/603)
LS CPE.
$13,025.

P205/70R x14 TIRES ON STD. OR LS. (P215 OPT.)

P225/60 VR15 TIRES ON XR-7 ONLY.

V.I.N. ENDS WITH —XF(–) #

85

new GRILLE
new TAILLIGHTS
new 20.6 GAL. FUEL TANK

XR-7 HAS DIFF. SIDE TRIM

140 CID TURBO 4
145 HP

232 CID V6 (120 HP)
302 CID V8 (140 HP)

2.73 GR w. V6 OR V8.
3.45 WITH TURBO 4 (XR-7)

STANDARD ON XR-7.

STANDARD ON LS

WHEEL CHOICES

STANDARD ON XR-7.
PEFORM. ALUMINUM

TR ALUMINUM WHEEL

WIRE LOCKING W.W. CVR.

POLYCAST ROAD WHEEL

LUXURY WHEEL CVR.

190

MERCURY COUGAR

XR-7 92W **$15886.**

232 CID V6 (V8 AVAIL.) IN GS OR LS (20.6 GAL. FUEL TANK)

XR-7 HAS 140 CID TURBO 4, 18.2 GAL. FUEL TANK

86 New

MERCURY TRADEMARK →

(GS CPE. [923] $12615.)

V.I.N. = IMEBP (92W) - G - #

1986 CARS HAVE HIGH-UP 3RD 3RD BRAKE LT.

$13951.
LS ↓

MERCURY. The shape you want to be in.
LINCOLN-MERCURY DIVISION *Ford*

104.0" WB

WT.= 3033 LBS. ('87)

LS HAS 3.8 L. V6 OR 5.0 L. V8.
XR7 HAS 5.0 L. V8 (150 HP)
and 4-SP. AUTOMATIC OVERDRIVE TRANS.
120 HP   150 HP

(603)

1987 LS CPE. $**14,062.**
↓ " XR7 CPE. **16,092.**
(62 F)

1987 V.I.N.
IMEBM (62 F)
- H - #

('87)

"S" BODY

new 104.2" WB

RESTYLED

87-88

1987 MPG: 18/27 (302 CID V8)

new 22.1 GAL. FUEL TK.

1988 V.I.N.
ENDS WITH - J - #

← 1988 GRILLE and DASH →

1988 LS INTERIOR

1988 LS CPE. (604)
$**14,458.**
XR7 CPE.
16,589.
(62 F)

1988 WEIGHTS:
3137 LBS. (LS)
3385 " (XR-7)

POWER MIRRORS STD. EQUIPMENT

Cougar XR-7 instrument panel. Some features shown may be optional.

191

PULSE-QUICKENING COMFORT.

MERCURY COUGAR

LS and DASH

V.I.N. =
IME—M
(62R)
— K—#

"KEYLESS ENTRY" DOOR LOCK OPTION ↓

89

new 113" WB

BODY RESTYLED

new 19-GAL. GAS TANK

LS
$15,903.
(60)

XR-7 and DASH (BELOW) $20,105. (62)
(PAINTED GRILLE on XR-7)

MERCURY

SUPERCHARGED COUGAR XR7.

MERCURY COUGAR

new CONTOURED HEAD RESTRAINTS

V.I.N. ENDS WITH — L — #

19 / 27 MPG
19-GAL. GAS TANK

(604) LS
$16,276.

90

XR-7 has 3.8 L. V6 (210 HP, 232 CID SUPERCHARGED)

LS has 140 HP VERSION OF 3.8 L V6.

XR-7 (62-F) $21,236.

AVAIL. WITH 15" OR 16" WHEELS.
P205/70R15 TIRES STANDARD ON LS.
P225/60R16 STD. ON XR-7.

XR-7 CONTINUES PAINTED GRILLE. — XR-7 WHEEL

note new WARNING LTS. BELOW GAUGES ON XR-7 DASH

Cougar XR7 instrument panel. Some features shown may be optional.

XR-7 DASH
17/23 MPG WITH SUPERCH.

ELECTRONIC DASH (OPT.)

193

MERCURY LN7

(1982-1983)

(SPECIAL SPORT VARIA-TION OF *LYNX*.)

11.3 GAL. FUEL TK.

1982
MPG: 29 EPA
STD. 46 HWY.
3-DR. HATCHBACK IS ONLY MODEL FOR 1982.

NEW

94.2" WB

1982 V.I.N.= 1MEBP6120 C (-) 000001 UP

DASH

LN7 WHEEL STYLE ON CAR ABOVE

(1982 EXAMPLES ILLUSTR.)

DETAIL OF SIDE

$9258.
('82)

4 MODELS IN 1983:
3 DR. — $8875.
SPT. HTCHBK. COUPE —
$9559.
GR. SPT. HTCHBK.
CPE.- $9940.
"RS" —
$10,240.

82-83

98 CID 4 70 HP
"HO"('83) 80 HP

FRONT
MULTI-PORT E.F.I. AVAIL. '83

(WIDTH EXAGGERATED)

1983 V.I.N.= 1MEBP612XD (-) 000001 UP

MERCURY LYNX

(1981-1987)

(MECHANICALLY SIMILAR TO FORD ESCORT)

made in America. 26 *EPA EST. MPG 36 HWY. EST.

(REPLACES BOBCAT)

27 EPA EST. MPG 42 EST. HWY.

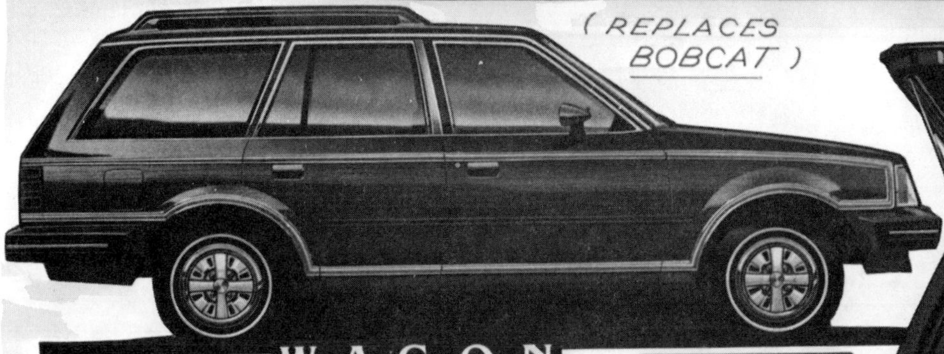

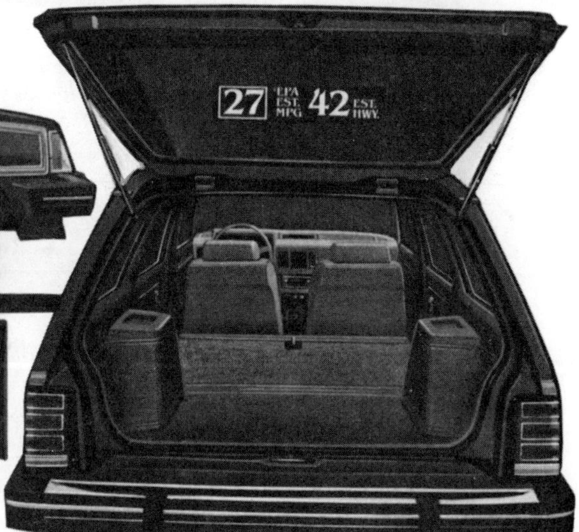

WAGON

WAGONS FR. $6515.

Full-door trim panels. And such tailored optional touches as woodtone bodyside treatment, liftgate wiper and washer, roof rack, even speed control.

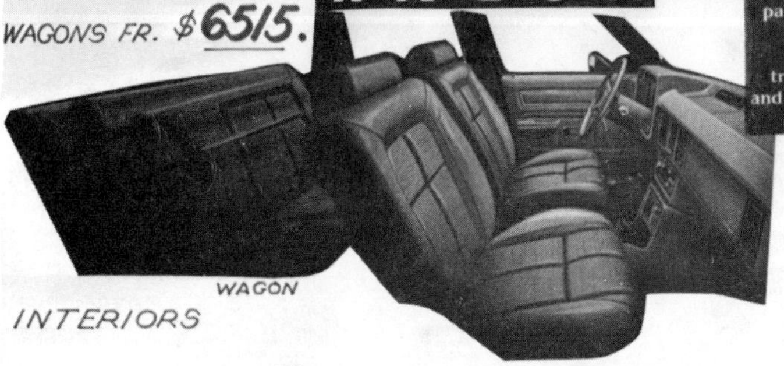

WAGON

INTERIORS

81 NEW

94.2" WHEELBASE

2 DR.

TRANSVERSE ENGINE
HALOGEN HDLTS.
FRONT WHEEL DRIVE
FRONT DISC BRAKES

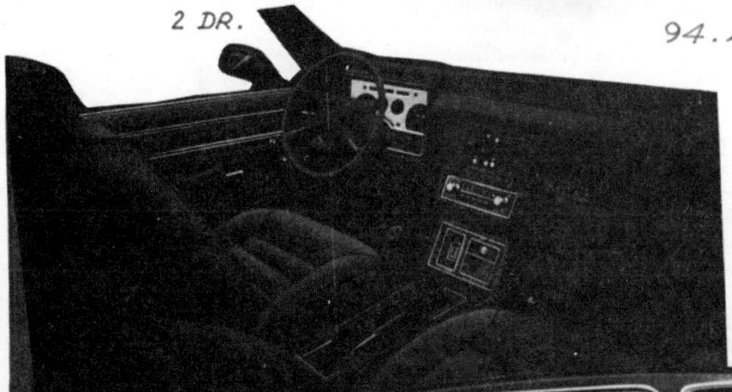

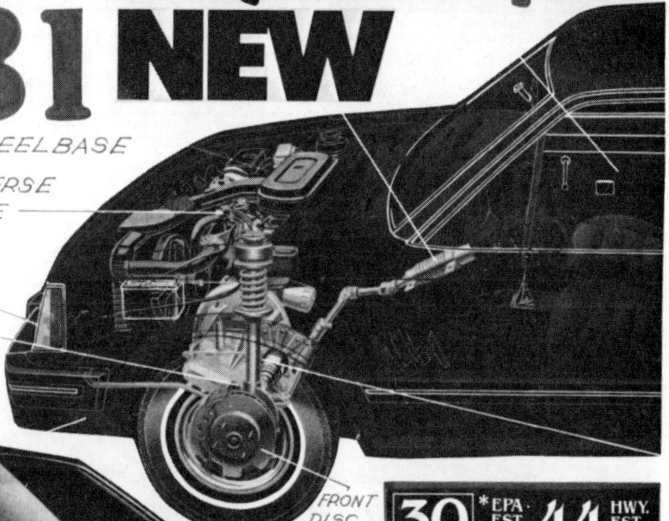

30 *EPA EST. MPG 44 HWY. EST.

STD., L, GL, RS, GS or LS SERIES

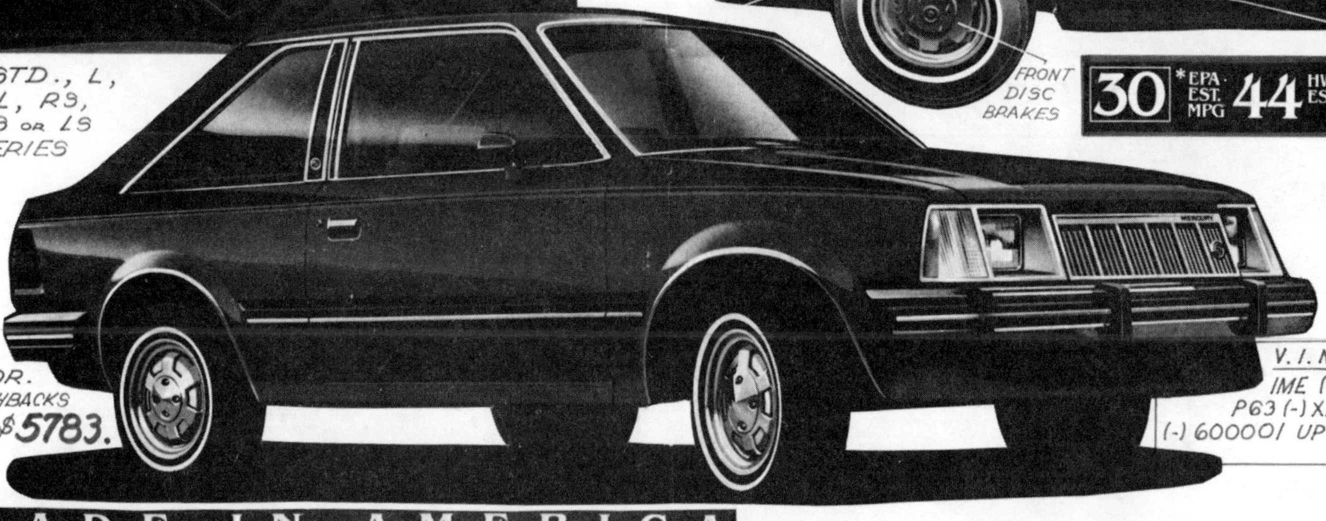

2-DR. HATCHBACKS FR. $5783.

V.I.N.
IME (-)
P63 (-) XB
(-) 600001 UP

MADE IN AMERICA

2-DR. HTCHBK. PRICES:
STD.=
$ 6212.
L=
6860.
GL=
6871.
GS=
7658.
LS=
8163.
RS=
7220.

WAGONS:
L = $ 7282.
GL = 7298.
GS = $ 7995.
LS = 8500.

V.I.N.= IMEBP 6320 C
(-) 00000I/ UP

LYNX

2-DR.

LYNX

the Lynx wagon has the best gas-mileage rating of any American-built wagon— either manual transaxle or optional automatic transaxle.

| MANUAL | 28 EPA EST. MPG 44 EST. HWY. |
| AUTOMATIC | 29 EPA EST. MPG 41 EST. HWY. |

P 165/80R13 TIRES

GS INTERIOR

10 GAL. FUEL TANK

31 MPG (EPA)
2-DR.

STD.
$ 6419.
L 7077.
GL 7088.
GS 7875.
LS 8379.
(ABOVE PRICES FOR NEW 5 DR. MODELS)

82

4-DR.
31 EPA EST. MPG 47 EST. HWY.

NEW LYNX 5-DOOR

MERCURY **LYNX RS**

LINCOLN-MERCURY DIVISION · Ford

P165/70R 365 TIRES ON RS.

98 CID 4 CYL. ENGINES

CVH 70 HP
HO 80 HP
EFI 88 HP
FEC ENG. ALSO AVAIL.

RS 3 DR.

83 NEW GRILLE

$7996.
P57

V.I.N. = 1MEBP632XD (-) 000001 UP

GROUND CONTROL: The standard TR performance package of Michelin TRX tires, TR sport steel wheels, and a TR sport suspension lets you hug corners and straighten out sharp curves.

POWER EQUIPMENT: The standard 1.6 liter multi-port electronic fuel-injected engine gives you a clean, crisp, fast start. One touch of the accelerator and you're off!

MAXIMUM EFFICIENCY: The standard five-speed manual transmission gives you all the excitement of close-ratio shifting, while maximizing the power of the engine.

"EFI 5-SPEED"

MPG: 44 HWY. 25 EPA w. 1.6-LITRE HO ENG. and 5-SP. MANUAL O.D. TRANS.

P54	L 3 DR.	$6516.	
P65	L 5 DR.	6818.	
P60	L WAGON	6931.	
P55	GS 3 DR.	7178.	
P66	GS 5 DR.	7489.	
	GS WAGON	7574.	P61
	LTS 5 DR.	8055.	P65/934
	RS 3 DR.	7996.	P57
	LS 3 DR.	8231.	P58
	LS 5 DR.	8543.	P68
	LS WAGON	8611.	P63

LTS 5 DR.
$8055.
P65/934

LYNX LTS

P165/80R13 TIRES

MERCURY. THE SUBSTANCE SHOWS.

197

MERCURY LYNX

OPTIONAL 7-BAND GRAPHIC AUDIO EQUALIZER →

196 IMPROVEMENTS IN LYNX SINCE THE FIRST MODEL OF 1981!

DASH

LTS 5 DR. $8725.

"EFI" MEANS ELECTRONIC FUEL INJECTION ↓

EFI

V.I.N. IMEB P542 XE (-) 000001 UP

new 4 CYL. DIESEL ENG. OPT.

70, 80 or 88 HP WITH 98 CID 4

GS VILLAGER $7551. UP

LYNX GS 3-DOOR
LYNX GS 5-DOOR
LYNX GS STATION WAGON

84

L WAGON $7110.

(STD. 3-DOOR FROM $5790.)

L $6772.

TAILLIGHT DETAIL

LYNX

MPG: 56 HWY 37 EPA

TR SPORT CAST ALUMINUM WHEEL →

LYNX L 3-DOOR
LYNX L 5-DOOR
LYNX L STATION WAGON

198

MERCURY LYNX

(1984 EXAMPLES ILLUSTRATED)

TAILGATE (WAGON)

LIFETIME SERVICE GUARANTEE

L, GS, LTS INTERIOR COLORS
Charcoal
Canyon Red
Academy Blue
Desert Tan

Perhaps the most intelligently designed 102 cu. ft. you've ever seen. With 85 cu. ft. of passenger space and approximately 26 cu. ft. of cargo space with the rear seat down," it will never make you wish you bought something bigger.

OPT. CHILD RESTRAINT

SPEED CONTROL STEER. WHEEL AVAIL.

DIESEL MPG. = 68 HWY, 46 EPA

GS INTERIOR

New
(AVAIL. THROUGH '87)

OPT. 4-CYL. DIESEL ENGINE

POWER VOL BASS TREB SPKRS
SEEK AM FM MEMORY AUTO·REVERSE EJECT DOLBY NR CrO₂

ELECTRONIC AM/FM STEREO w. CASSETTE

84 **NEW** INTERIORS

13 GAL. FUEL TANK (10-GAL. ON 5-DR. w. "FUEL SAVER" OPTION)

GS CONSOLE

RS DASH

RS INTERIOR IN "DESERT TAN"

RS = (FINAL '84)
$8652.
(RS TURBO ALSO AVAIL.)

MERCURY

RS AND RS TURBO INTERIOR COLORS
Charcoal
Desert Tan

VENT WINDOWS OPT.

RS HAS 165/70R365 TRX MICHELIN TIRES

MERCURY. A MORE ENLIGHTENED APPROACH.

LINCOLN-MERCURY DIVISION Ford

199

Mercury Lynx

$5986 ⁺

† ADVERTISED 1985½
STARTING PRICE
REG. $6057. UP

NEW 113 cid 4 CYL. ENGINE

STD. 3 DR. HTCHBK.	$5930.
L " "	6796.
L 5 DR. "	7010.
L WAGON	7133.
GS 3 DR. HTCHBK.	7243.
GS 5 DR. "	7457.
GS WAGON	7507.

1985 V.I.N. IMEPP (-)(-)(-) XF (-)000001 UP
1986 " IMEBP ——— G-#
1987 " IMEBM ——— H-#

MERCURY

SPRING, 1985 ("1985½") MODELS with "EURO STYLE" HDLTS. and STYLIZED EMBLEM

85 **NEW** XR3 HAS OWN GRILLE (STARTS 1986)

MPG: 33 CITY, 43 HWY.

GASOLINE 33 49

-87

XR3 113 cid 4 (108 HP @ 5200 RPM)

$8243. (9251. 1987)

GS GRILLE

RPM x 1000 — FUEL — TEMP — UNLEADED FUEL ONLY — TRIP RESET — MPH — 00087 — TRIP

LYNX L 5 SPEED MERCURY LYNX

1986 DASH

FINAL 1987 MODELS $6870. UP

L 3 DR. $7034. ('86)

FRONT WHEEL DRIVE

Mercury Sable. (SINCE 1986)

LS SEDAN (87U)
$13,762.
115 MPH

GAS FILLER ON RIGHT

INTERIOR

MECHANICALLY SIMILAR TO new FORD TAURUS

86 New

106" WHEELBASE new type 182 CID V6 ENGINE

V.I.N. = IMEBP (87.D) — G - #

UNIQUE "LASER" LIGHTBAR EXTENDING BETWEEN HEADLTS.

Mercury Sable LS Sedan

X-RAY VIEW, WITH DETAILS OF FRONT WHEEL DRIVE, TRANSVERSE V6 ENG., ETC.

(GS HAS PLAINER LOWER SIDE TRIM.
87-D SED.= $11,888.
88U WAGON = 12,964.)

Sophisticated new shape. The 1986 Mercury Sable.

ROOF RACK DETAIL

LS wagon. (88U) $14,256.

MERCURY. The shape you want to be in.

Mercury Sable.

GS WAGON

"TAURUS" BODY

$13,554. ('87)

$14,198. ('88)

$14,118. ('87)
$14,839. ('88)

GS

New SERIES MODEL NUMBERS (50 U)

SABLE WAGON

87-88

1987 V.I.N. ENDS WITH —H-# (—J-# 1988)

('88)

(55 U)

Sable's optional digital instrumentation. Some features shown may be optional.

$15,515. ('87)
15,858. ('88)
LS WAGON (58 U)

Sable LS instrument panel. Some features shown may be optional.

UPHOLSTERY (SEDAN)

1987 EXAMPLES ILLUSTR. (UNLESS OTHERWISE NOTED.)

LS

SEDAN (53 U)

$14,970. ('87)
15,191. ('88)

MERCURY. The shape you want to be in.

202

Mercury Sable.

1989 V.I.N.=
IME — M (50U)
—K—#

('89)

('89)

GS SEDAN (50U)
$14,551. ('89) 15,520. ('90)

GS SEDAN INTERIOR

GS
SABLE WAGON. (55U)
$15,254. ('89)
16,465. ('90)

16-GALLON FUEL TANK
19 TO 21 MPG, EPA (CITY)

Ford **MERCURY** **LINCOLN**
Quality is Job 1.

('90)

89-90

1990 has new DASH, DRIVER'S AIR BAG, and new OPTIONAL ANTI-LOCK BRAKING.

LS SEDAN (53U)
$15,544. ('89)
16,522. ('90)

1990 V.I.N.=
(1M or 3A)
—(P or C)
M (50U)
—L—#

3.0L, 182 CID V6	OPT. 3.8L, 232 CID V6
(140 HP @ 4800 RPM)	(140 HP @ 3800 RPM)
21/29 MPG	19/28 MPG

LS WAGON (58U)
$16322. ('89)
17493. ('90)

Sable LS interior in leather.
Some features shown may be optional.

203

MERCURY TOPAZ

LINCOLN-MERCURY DIVISION — Ford

(P73) LS 2 DR. $10638. →

(SAME PRICE FOR LS 4 DR.) (P76)

('84)

(REPLACES MERCURY ZEPHYR.) FRONT WHEEL DRIVE

STARTS WITH 1984 MODEL.

GS 9144. P72 2 DR. OR 4 DR. P75

43 EST. HWY. 28 EPA

90 HP, 140 CID 4 "2300 HSC" ENGINE is new with HIGH SWIRL COMBUSTION CHAMBER DESIGN. →

121 CID 4 CYL. DIESEL (52 HP) ALSO AVAIL.

(INTRO. MAY 26, 1983 AS EARLY 1984 MODEL.)

CROSS SECTION VIEW OF A CYLINDER

note THAT GS has THINNER RUB STRIP ON SIDE THAN LS. (GS ADVERTISED SPECIAL PRICE OF $7991.)

15.2 GAL. FUEL TANK (14 GAL. ON EARLY MODELS)

1984 V.I.N.= 1MEB (P72) RXE (-) 000001 UP

1985 V.I.N.= 1MEPP7 (-) (-) XF (-) 000001 UP

99 MPH

Ford's EEC-IV* is the most advanced on-board automotive computer in the world.

NEW 84-85

(MECHANICALLY SIMILAR TO FORD TEMPO.)

1985 PRICES : GS 2DR. OR 4-DR. $9013. LS 2 DR. (P73) $10619. LS 4 DR. (P76) 10668.

LS INTERIOR ('84)

EMBLEM

ACCORD. TO VAR. SOURCES 1984-1985 TOPAZ MODEL NUMBERS HAVE "P" PREFIX OR "R" SUFFIX. (H SUFFIX IF EQUIPPED WITH DIESEL ENGINE.)

P76 (R) ('85)

TOPAZ GS

$9465. UP ('86) = GS 2 DR. ('86) (72X)
10,206 UP ('87) = " " " ('87) (31X)
" 4 DR. ('86) (75X)
$9615.
" " " ('87) (36X)
$10,356.
1987 GS SPORT
2 DR. (33S) $10850.
4 DR.
(38S)
$11000.

"TOPAZ" BODY

SPORT DASH

Mercury Topaz

33.S

GS SPORT
(new in 1987)

1986 V.I.N.=
IMEBP (72X)
—G—#

1987 V.I.N.=
IMEBM (M31X)
—H—#

22-27 MPG (w. A/T)

(GS SPORT PACKAGE AVAIL. 1986)

(1987 EXAMPLES ILLUSTRATED)

140 CID
(2.3 L) 4 CYL.
ENGINES
HSC =
86 HP @ 4000
HSO =
100 HP @ 4600
(4 CYL. DIESEL ALSO
AVAIL. 1986)

new
GRILLE

37 X
LS
4 DR.
$11830.
('87)

AVAIL. IN 1987:
DRIVER AIRBAG

86-87

(LS 2 DR. NOT
AVAILABLE 1987)

LS DASH

1986 LS
2 DR. (73X)
$10621.
4 DR. (76X) $10891.

4WD CONTROL

ALL WHEEL DRIVE OFF ON

205   NEW TOPAZ ALL-WHEEL-DRIVE OPTION, 1987

Mercury Topaz

ALL-WHEEL DRIVE
OPTIONAL

new LTS SEDAN (38S)
$12,421.
('88)

('88)

LTS INTERIOR

new DASH in 1988 WITH ALL ANALOG GAUGES IN FIELD OF DRIVER'S VISION

XR5 SPT. SED. (2-DR.)
ALSO new IN 1988
(33S) $11,711.

DRIVER'S AIRBAG OPTIONAL

88-90
RESTYLED

XR-5 INTERIOR ('88)

1988 V.I.N.= (IME OR 3MA) BM (31X)- J- # 1989 V.I.N. ENDS WITH K #; 1990 WITH L #

GRILLE
('88)

BLACK—PAINTED SIDE PILLARS CREATE THE APPEARANCE OF A 4-DR H/T.

MODELS = GS (2+4 DOOR) LS (4 DR.) XR5 (2 DR.) LTS (4 DR.)

XR5 ('88)

Topaz LTS instrument panel.
Some features shown may be optional.

NEW SHAPE
OF REAR UPPER BODY

('89)

15.9- GALLON FUEL TANK

MERCURY SYMBOL ON WHEEL (1989)

$11462.
('89) GS

REAR DETAILS

The Shape You Want To Be In.
MERCURY

1990 FROM $11817. (GS 2-DR.)

141 CID (2.3 L) 4 (98 OR 100 HP @ 4400 RPM) 23/31 MPG (22-26 w. A/T)

TOPAZ GS

206

ASSEMBLED BY FORD OF MEXICO; SOME MAZDA COMPONENTS (JAPAN)

MERCURY TRACER (1988 ON)
(REPLACES LYNX)

28/35 MPG (MANUAL 5 SP.)
26/29 (A/T)
('89)
$9592. ('88)

#135 WAGON

SPORT HATCHBACK #115

104-105 MPH

small car
88-90

UPHOLSTERY →

(EXCEPT FOR WAGON, 1990 EXAMPLES ILLUSTRATED)

PRICED FROM $8409. ('88)
8891. ('89)

1.6 L OHC
4 CYL.
82 HP @
5000
RPM

94.7" WB
11.9 GAL.
GAS TANK

P175/70R13
TIRES

V.I.N. ENDS WITH
-J-# (1988)
-K-# (1989)
-L-# (1990)

TRACER

#125 4-DR. HATCHBACK

NEW

| | | | | | | | | | | | | | | | |
|1 2 3|4 5| | 6 7 8| | 9|10|11 12 13| |14 15 16|

| | |
|17|18 19 20 21 22 23 24 25|

1	Fog lamp switch	13	Low washer fluid level indicator
2	Rear window defroster switch	14	Low oil level indicator
3	Rear window wiper washer switch	15	Low fuel level indicator
4	Flash to pass high beam control	16	Seat belt indicator
5	Instrument panel illumination control	17	Right/left remote electric mirror control
6	Low oil pressure indicator	18	Easy access fuse panel
7	Discharge indicator	19	Parking headlamp control
8	Low brake fluid level indicator	20	Windshield wiper/washer control
9	Ice alert warning indicator	21	Interval wiper control
10	Door ajar/exterior bulb failure graphit warning display	22	Heated front seat switch (optional)
11	Disc brake pad wear indicator	23	Grundig AM/FM/stereo cassette
12	Low coolant level indicator	24	Power window control
		25	Cassette storage trays

EMBLEM
MERKUR

New *MERKUR* (INCL. SCORPIO)

(STARTS 1985)

15 GAL. FUEL TK.

Merkur XR4Ti from Germany.

(3 DOOR HATCHBACKS ONLY, UNTIL 1987.)

note DUAL REAR SPOILERS ON XR4Ti (ALSO, *DUAL PAIRS OF REAR QUARTER WINDOWS* ARE AN IDENTIFYING FEATURE.)

1985 V.I.N. = WF11P (80W) -F-#
1986 " = " " -G-#
1987 " = "1PT " -H-#

85- 87

129 MPH ("SIERRA" BODY)

$16965. ('85)
16788. ('86)
18401. ('87)
XR4Ti

102.7" WB 2.3L TURBO 4 (170 HP) MFD. BY FORD MOTOR CO. OF GERMANY, IMPORTED BY LINCOLN-MERCURY

New

81V "GRANADA" BODY **SCORPIO** 5 DOOR SED.

INTERIOR

('88)

$19,711. ('88)

MERKUR INT.

(INTRO. SUMMER, 1987) 108.7" WB 2.9L V6

117-130 MPH (SCORPIO)

X4Ti ('88)

$24,782. ('88) 25,772. ('89)

$20,408. ('89)

SCORPIO

('89)

V.I.N. = 1988: WF1PT(80T) -J-# 1989: WF1-T(80W) -K-# 1990: _L-#

88-90

144 HP   new 145 HP
ONLY SCORPIO IMPORTED IN 1990. 17/23 MPG

80W 208

MERKUR XR4Ti

Oldsmobile Cutlass

INTERMEDIATE-SIZED
108.1" WB (ESTABL. 1897)

V.I.N. = IG3A
( ) OB 10000/ UP

2 VIEWS OF CUTLASS SEDAN

AVAIL. T-BAR TOP

STANDARD V6
21 / 30
EPA Est. / Hwy. Est.
mpg

3K47 CALAIS
$9042.
(CALAIS COUPE ONLY)

81

231 CID V6
(110 HP)
260 OR
305 CID V8s
(105, 155 HP)
350 CID DIESEL
V8 (105 HP)

diesel

"DIESEL" HOOD ORNAMENT IDENTIFIES DIESEL CARS.

THIS OPTIONAL GAUGE PACKAGE IS STANDARD EQUIPMENT ON "CALAIS" MODEL.

$8342.

P195 (185)/75R x 14 TIRES

UN-GRAINED "CUTLASS CRUISER" WAGON HAS GRILLE LIKE CUTLASS SEDAN (ABOVE, RT.)

AVAIL. WHEEL STYLES

Cutlass Cruiser Brougham. wagon with luxury touches.

WITH GRAINED SIDES

$8763.

(STD. CUTL. CRUISER, #3G35 $8454.)

DASH (W/O OPT. GAUGE PKG.)

SUPREME HAS OWN OUTSWEPT GRILLE WITH ALL VERTICAL PCS. $8522.
3R47 COUPE

CUTLASS SUPREME BROUGHAM

(BROUGHAMS HAVE GRILLE LIKE ILLUSTRATED WAGON.)

CPE. 3M47 $9007.

$ 8674.

Delta 88

3L69

116" WB
P20575R×15
TIRES

GM

Oldsmobile

We've had one built for you.

FULL-SIZE MODELS

DELTA 88 DASH

STANDARD V6	REMEMBER: *Compare* the "estimated mpg" to the "estimated mpg" of other cars. You may get different mileage, depending on how fast you drive, weather conditions and trip length. Actual highway mileage will probably be less than the estimated highway fuel economy. Diesel estimates lower in California. Oldsmobiles are equipped with GM-built engines produced by various divisions. See your dealer for details.	DIESEL V8
19 EPA Est. mpg **28** Hwy. Est.		**23** EPA Est. mpg **34** Hwy. Est.

IMPORTANT: Computer Command Control is on all standard 1981 gasoline engines. It helps reduce exhaust emissions while allowing good fuel efficiency.

V6, V8 OR DIESEL V8

(3L37 STD. DELTA CPE. AVAIL. AT $8578.)

$11,208.

98 REGENCY COUPE

3X37

119" WB

81

DELTA 88 "ROYALE" CPE.
$ 8842. 116" WB

3N37

Buying a luxury car need not mean giving up economy.

Oldsmobile Ninety-Eight Regency's standard V6 engine offers an EPA estimated **18** mpg, estimated highway 29. With available diesel engine, an EPA estimated **21** mpg, estimated highway 33.

98 DASH

98 INTERIOR WITH TUFTED SEATS

NINETY-EIGHT REG.

98 GRILLE

3P35

CUSTOM CRUISER
Functional utility? It takes on luxurious forms.

FROM $ 9602. P225/75R15 TIRES ON WAGON

3X69
$11,365.
(3X37 CPE: 11,208.)

210

NEW *CIERA SERIES*

Oldsmobile
We've had one built for you.

A new diesel V6 for 1982.

CUTLASS CIERA BROUGHAM SEDAN

$10,673.

DASH

AVAILABLE RALLYE WHEEL

$10,471.

CUTLASS CIERA BROUGHAM COUPE

➤ note GRILLE IS DIFFERENT FROM STD. CIERA GRILLE ON SEDAN ILLUSTR. BELOW.

CLOSER DETAIL OF DASH

CUTLASS CIERA

82

CIERA IS *new* FRONT-WHEEL DRIVE SERIES

$9921.

151 CID 4 CYL. ENGINE
(173 CID V6 AVAIL.)

$10,071.

104.9" WB

DIESEL 260 CID V6 ENG. AVAIL. (V8 ALSO, IN LARGER OLDSMOBILES.)

$10,231.

CUTLASS CIERA LS SEDAN

Oldsmobile

108.1" WB

CUTLASS SUPREME

Cutlass Supreme.

3R47 COUPE $9761.

DIESEL V6 — 36 Hwy.Est. / 25 EPA Est.mpg

STANDARD V6 — 30 Hwy.Est. / 21 EPA Est.mpg

V.I.N. ENDS WITH — OC — #

CUTLASS CRUISER WAGON INTERIOR

$10,078.

CUTLASS CRUISER 3H35

82

Split-tailgate. Top swings up. Bottom drops down for a loading platform on Cruiser.

CUTLASS CALAIS (COUPE ONLY) 3K47

231 CID V6 (110 HP)
260 CID V8 (105 HP)
307 CID V8 (155 HP)
263 CID DIESEL V6 OR 350 CID DIESEL V8 (105 HP)

$10,552. (T-BAR TOP OPT. AT EXTRA COST)

$10,333.

BROUGH. SEDAN INTER.

$10,428.

CUTLASS SUPREME BROUGHAM SEDAN

We've had one built for you.

CUTLASS SUPREME BROUGHAM COUPE

2.5 GALLON FUEL TANK (GAS)
19 MPG (EPA)

STANDARD V6
28 Hwy Est. 19 EPA Est. mpg

INTERIOR

Diesel mileage estimates.

MODELS		Fuel Tank Cap.	Est. Hwy.	Est. Hwy. Range	EPA Est. MPG	Est. Range
Cutlass Supreme	(V6)	19.8	36	712	25	495
Cutlass Supreme	(V8)	19.8	34	673	23	455
Cutlass Cruiser	(V8)	18.2	34	618	23	418
Delta 88	(V8)	26.0	34	884	23	598
Ninety-Eight	(V8)	26.0	33	858	22	572
Custom Cruiser	(V8)	22.0	33	726	22	484
Toronado	(V8)	22.8	36	820	21	478

INTERIOR

82

$9857. **DELTA 88**

DELTA 88 ROYALE
$10,456.

88 DASH

CUSTOM CRUISER
WAGON
22 GAL. FUEL TANK
16 MPG (EPA)
$10,867.
(11,082. WITH 3RD SEAT)

Custom Cruiser facts, figures and features.

REAR-FACING 3RD SEAT OPT.

2.5 GALLON FUEL TANK
18 MPG (EPA)

$13,167.

98 DASH
252 CID V6,
307 CID V8
(150 HP) OR
350 CID DIES. V8

119" WB

NINETY-EIGHT REGENCY

COUPE
$12,990.

Oldsmobile

GRILLE

LS

15.7 GAL. GAS TANK
20/39 MPG

CUTLASS
CIERA LS SEDAN ←

24 MPG
EPA (4)
19 MPG
EPA (V6)

CUTLASS
CIERA ES

COUPE
AJ27

AJ19
$10,031.

104.9"
WB

$9842.

CUTLASS CIERA DASH

4 CYL. ENGINE
BY PONTIAC

V.I.N. = 1G3A
(J19)(E) XD (-) #

83

$10,524.

"SUPER
STOCK"
WHEEL
DESIGN

AM19 CUTLASS
CIERA BROUGHAM
(GRILLE LIKE L9)

151 CID
EFI 4
(92 HP)
181 CID V6
(110 HP)
263 CID DIESEL V6 (85 HP) 28/43 MPG
(16.4 GAL. FUEL TK. w. DIESEL)

P185/80R x 13 TIRES

BROUGHAM
INTERIOR

Brougham

Cutlass Ciera

Oldsmobile Diesel

AVAILABLE w. 19.8 GAL. FUEL TANK
(18.1 GAL. TANK w. GAS ENGINES)

Oldsmobile

CUTLASS SUPREME SEDAN

GR69

BUICK.
231 CID
V6
(110 HP)
263 CID
V6 DIESEL
(85 HP)
307 CID V8s
(155 OR
180 HP)
350 CID
DIESEL V8
(105 HP)

83

$10,354.
10,201.

GR47 CUTLASS SUPREME COUPE

GM47 ↗
CUTLASS SUPREME BROUGHAM

(GM 69
SEDAN
AVAIL
AT
10970)

$10,840.

← CALAIS INSTRUMENT GROUP

WRAP-OVER TAIL LIGHTS

108.1" WB

P195/
75R x 14
TIRES

17/37
MPG
(DEPENDING
ON TYPE OF
ENGINE)

CUTLASS CALAIS

GK47

$10,599.

T-BAR
ROOF
OPTIONAL

CALAIS HAS SAME
OUTSWEPT GRILLE AS
CUTL. SUPR. BROUGHAM.

215

21/30 MPG (V6)   17/24 MPG (V8)

CUTLASS CRUISER
$10,632.
GH35

23/35 MPG (DIESEL V8)

Oldsmobile

18.2 GAL. FUEL TANK (GAS OR DIESEL)

STOW-AWAY COMPARTMENT IN REAR SECTION OF CRUISER

BL69

DELTA 88 $10,396.

DELTA 88 DASH

231 CID V6 BUICK-BUILT; 307 CID V8 and DIESEL 350 CID V8 and DIESEL 262½ CID V6 are OLDSMOBILE-BUILT.

NINETY-EIGHT REGENCY COUPE

IN "98", 252 CID V6 IS BUICK-BUILT. 307 CID V8 and 350 CID DIESEL V8 are OLDSMOBILE-BUILT.

DELTA 88 ROYALE BROUGHAM COUPE

BY37
$10,983.

25 GAL. GAS TANK (28 GAL. DIESEL)

83

17/27 MPG (V6, V8)
22/37 MPG (DIESEL V8)

CX37
$13,793.

CRUISE-CONTROL STALK

16/26 MPG (V8)
22/38 (DIESEL V8)

GRILLE and DASH = 98 REGENCY

22 GAL. FUEL TANK (GAS OR DIES.)

BP35

CUSTOM CRUISER

$11,395. UP
(11,615. W. 3RD SEAT)

Oldsmobile

AVAILABLE ELECTRONIC INSTRUMENT PANEL

ON-BOARD COMPUTER CHECKS VARIOUS ENGINE FUNCTIONS CONTINUOUSLY.

AJ19

$10,347. LS

Cutlass Ciera.

AM19 CUTLASS CIERA BROUGHAM 4 DR. SEDAN

$10,865. ↗

AVAIL. 181 CID V6 ENGINE (110 HP)

MPG:
43 HWY., 28 EPA w.
263 CID (85 HP)
V6 DIESEL.
39 HWY., 25 EPA w.
151 CID (92 HP)
4 CYL. GAS ENG.

V.I.N. = 1G3A (C35P) — E — #

84

new Cutlass Cruiser.

$10,695. ⊛

Introducing the first mid-size, front-wheel-drive Olds wagon ever—the new Cutlass Cruiser.

Cutlass Ciera Holiday Coupe.

CUTLASS CIERA HAS 104.9" WB

V6 diesel

AVAIL. WITH "TRAVELING PACKAGE" (AM/FM STEREO RADIO, WIRE WHEEL DISCS, POWER DOOR LOCKS and CRUISE CONTROL OR REAR WINDOW DEFOGGER)

CUTLASS CRUISER WAGON IS NOW A PART OF CIERA SERIES. ⊛BASE PRICE RAISED TO $10945. DURING 1985.

J35E

$10,910. (WITH 3RD SEAT)

Room for 8

Limited Edition Hurst/Olds

reintroduced from 1968. ↩

307 CID V8 (180 HP)

"MUSCLE CAR!"

There is a special feel in an

Oldsmobile

217

Oldsmobile

$11,271. $10,632.

W/O VINYL ROOF

Cutlass Supreme

108.1" WB

$11,401.

$11,368.

MPG : 31 HWY, 21 EPA (STD. 231 CID, 110 HP V6) 41 HWY, 25 EPA (AVAIL. 263 CID, 85 HP DIESEL V6)

84

Delta 88

Let's get it together... buckle up.

AVAIL. 350 CID DIESEL V8 (105 HP)   116" WB
35 HWY, 23 EPA
OR STD. 231 CID V6 (110 HP) OR 307 CID V8

$11,816.
(BELOW)

DELTA 88 LS 4 DR. SED. INT.

Delta 88 LS

Ninety-Eight Regency.

119" WB

252 CID V6 (125 HP),
307 CID V8 (140 HP),
OR 350 CID
V8
DIESEL
(105 HP)

$15,876.

218

CALAIS COUPES ONLY,
IN FIRST (1985)
MODEL YR.

Oldsmobile

CALAIS IS NOW A SEPARATE, SMALLER SERIES, NO LONGER A COUPE IN THE CUTLASS SERIES.

Calais

NF27U
COUPE
$9824.
SUPREME CPE.
$10,239. NT27U

109 MPH

New

Calais

103.4" WHEELBASE

DASH

13.6 GALLON
FUEL TANK

P/85/80R
×13 TIRES

2.84
GEAR
RATIO

INDIANAPOLIS 500 PACE CAR

4 CYL. OR V6
(151 CID   (183 CID
92 HP)   120 HP)

OFFICIAL PACE CAR

(CUSTOM BUILT
ONLY)

CALAIS 500

V.I.N. =
IG3 (AJ19E)
— F — #

85

CUTLASS CRUISER WAGON IS A PART OF CUTLASS CIERA SERIES.

AJ35E
CUTLASS CRUISER
$11,337. ↓

OPTIONAL
V6 →

CALAIS
INTERIOR

CUTLASS
CRUISER
WAGON

CALAIS
REAR

CUTLASS
CRUISER

Cutlass Cruiser

**There is a special feel
in an** *Oldsmobile*

219

Oldsmobile

TRUNK-TOP LUGGAGE RACK OPTIONAL

CIERA DASH

ELECTRONIC DASH

Electronic instrument cluster, available. Offers easy-to-understand digital speedometer, bar graph fuel level and engine temperature gages, low-fuel warning indicator, trip odometer, English/metric conversion switch and turn signal indicators.

CONSOLE

CUTLASS CIERA BROUGHAM COUPE

AM27E

$11,266.

85

(CIERA PRICES START AT $10786. FOR AJ27E "LS" CPE.)
4, V6 or DIESEL V6

A = DELUXE DISCS ; B = WIRE WH. DISCS;
C = SUPER STOCK WHEELS (BODY COLOR);
D = DELUXE STYLED DISCS (STD. ON ES);
E = ALUMINUM-STYLED

CUTLASS CIERA HOLIDAY COUPE

ES 4

GT PKG. (BELOW) AVAIL. LATE IN SEASON, ALSO IN 1986 and 1987.

HOLIDAY COUPE INTERIOR

(AVAIL. IN CIERA, new DIGITAL AUTO CALCU-LATOR

COMPUTES M.P.G., DRIVING TIME, OTHER TRIP INFO.)

THERE IS A SPECIAL FEEL IN AN OLDSMOBILE

Cutlass Ciera GT.

Cutlass Ciera GT

CUTLASS SUPREME

Oldsmobile

CUTLASS SUPREME

$10,941. AND UP

BROUGHAM SEDAN $11,746.

COUPES ONLY HAVE THE OUTSWEPT GRILLE.

Rallye gage cluster available. Gages galore help you to stay informed.

85

CUSTOM SPORT STEERING WHEEL

OPT.

NEW

Cutlass 442.

CUTLASS SUPR. BROUGHAM CPE. has SIMILAR FRONT

4-4-2 HAS A 5.0-LITER V8

442 Oldsmobile

Delta 88.

CUSTOM CRUISER $12,832.

Custom Cruiser

88 FROM $11,801. (WITH 231 cud V6)

$16,539. 98 REGENCY BROUGHAM

Ninety-Eight Regency

OPT. **V6 diesel**

CRUISE CONTROL III

221

ES

1986 V.I.N. = 1G3 (AJ19W)
— G — #

Oldsmobile

NF27U
CALAIS
COUPE
$10,763.

CALAIS COUPE

(GT
RESEMBLES
ES)

There is a special feel
in an *Oldsmobile*

Olds **CALAIS**

CALAIS SEDAN

CALAIS SEDAN
(DETAILS)

4-DOOR CALAIS IS
New

86

NF69U
$10,958.

151 CID 4

(V6 ALSO AVAIL.)

NT27U
CALAIS
SUPREME
COUPE (RT.)

$11,148.

CALAIS SUPREME COUPE

New

CALAIS SUPREME
SEDAN
$11,343.
NT69U

California Calais

LIMITED EDITION (300 CARS)
FOR CALIF.   CUSTOM PAINT,
FUEL-INJECTED V6
CUSTOM AIR SCOOPS, ALLOY WHEELS
(HAS SPECIAL MEDALLION)

Oldsmobile

CUTLASS CIERAS FROM **$11,927.** AJ27W (L COUPE)

W. CIERA ES PACKAGE

SL COUPE **$12,945.** AM37W

111 MPH

CUTLASS CIERA

SED. **$12,036.** GR69A

$12,715.

CUTLASS SUPREME BROUGHAM SEDAN GM69A

CUTLASS SUPREME COUPE AND SEDAN

CUTLASS SUPREME

$11,862. GR47A CPE.

86

DELTA 88 BROUGHAM COUPE WHEEL

CUTLASS SALON AND CUTLASS 442

REAR DETAILS

DELTA 88 ROYALE COUPE

DELTA 88 ROYALE COUPE (HN37L) **$13,235.**

111 MPH

DELTA 88

DELTA 88

110.8" WB

$17,727. CW11B

NINETY-EIGHT REGENCY BROUGHAM COUPE

WHEEL STYLE

ABOVE: HY69L DELTA 88 ROYAL BRGHM. SEDAN **$13936.**

Ninety-Eight REGENCY

GRILLE

BROUGHAM SEDAN **$17,654.** CW69B

223

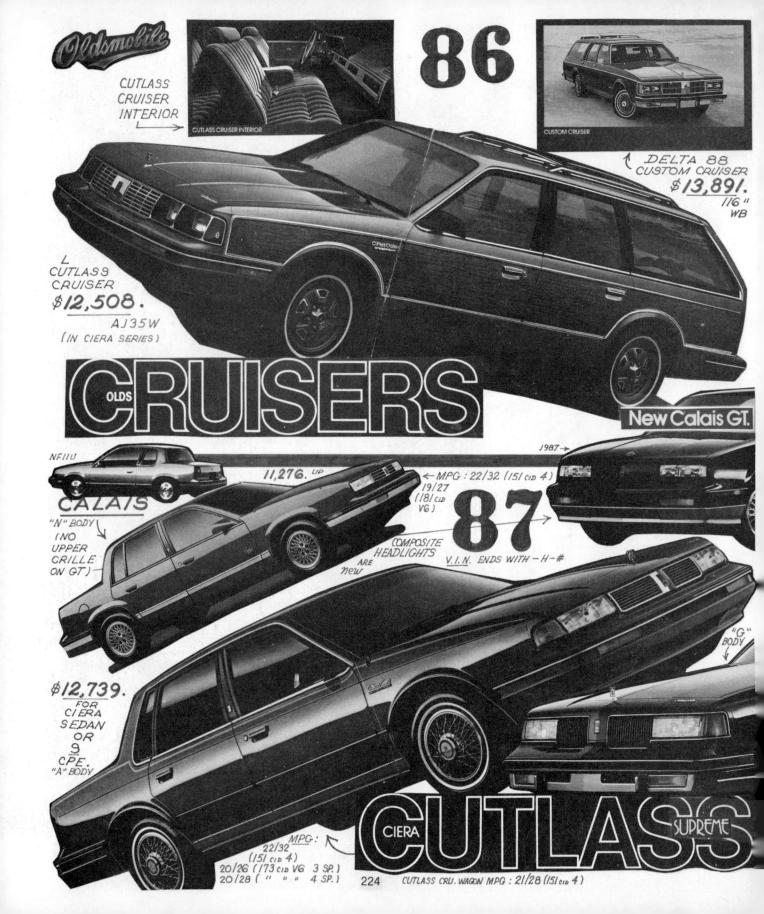

Oldsmobile

86

CUTLASS CRUISER INTERIOR →

CUTLASS CRUISER INTERIOR

↖ DELTA 88 CUSTOM CRUISER
$13,891.
116" WB

CUSTOM CRUISER

L CUTLASS CRUISER
$12,508.
AJ35W
(IN CIERA SERIES)

OLDS CRUISERS

New Calais GT.

1987 →

NF11U

CALA1S

"N" BODY
(NO UPPER GRILLE ON GT)

11,276. UP

← MPG : 22/32 (151 CID 4)
19/27 (181 CID V6)

COMPOSITE HEADLIGHTS

are new

87 →

V.I.N. ENDS WITH – H – #

"G" BODY

$12,739.
FOR CIERA SEDAN OR 9 CPE.
"A" BODY

CIERA CUTLASS SUPREME

MPG :
22/32 (151 4)
20/26 (173 CID V6 3 SP.)
20/28 (" " " 4 SP.)

224

CUTLASS CRU. WAGON MPG : 21/28 (151 CID 4)

DELTA 88 ROYALE BROUGHAM SEDAN

(CUTLASS SUPREME, SALON, and SUPREME BROUGHAM CONT'D. IN 12,728 — 13,886. PRICE RANGE. 3.8 L V6 OR 5.0 L V8)

Oldsmobile

$15,001.

MPG:
19/24 (231 cid V6)
18/25 (307 cid V8 4SP.)
17/23 " " " 3 SP.)

note WHEEL COVER VARIATION

ROYALE COUPE

"H" BODY ON DELTA 88

new GRILLE WITH ALL-VERTICAL PCS.

$14,114.

ROYALE SEDAN

3.8 L V6 STD. (88/98)
CUSTOM CRUISER WAGON ("B" BODY)

DELTA 88

87

98 TOURING SED.

GM 6.60

new
GM 6.60

CW113

98 REGENCY BROUGHAM CPE. $19,460.

new GRILLE WITH WIDER-SPACED PCS.

CX513

98 REGENCY 4-DR. SEDAN

$18,568.

"C" BODY

INTRODUCING THE TOURING SEDAN.

The limited edition 1987 Oldsmobile Touring Sedan.

NINETY-EIGHT

$24,607.
(OLDSMOBILE'S MOST EXPENSIVE '87 MODEL.) 225

Oldsmobile
Oldsmobile Quality. Feel it.

Oldsmobile

$11885. and up (SED. OR COUPÉ)

103.4" WB

INT'L. COUPE

CUTLASS CALAIS.

4 or V6 (3.0 L) (2.3 or 2.5L)

w. 150 HP "QUAD 4" ENG. (3.0 L V6 AVAIL. ALSO)

CUTLASS CALAIS

NK//D INT'L. COUPE TOP $14585.

CUTLASS CIERA INTERNATIONAL SERIES

$16995. AS513

CIERA INTERNATIONAL COUPE $16,165. (AS113)

104.9" WB

SYMBOL OF INTERNATIONAL SERIES

CUTLASS CIERA.

OLDSMOBILE QUALITY. FEEL IT.

88

V.I.N. = 1G3 (AJ113) — J — #

$13601. UP (SEDANS)

CIERA has 2.5 L 4 or 2.8 or 3.8 L V6.

CIERA SERIES INCLUDES THE **CUTLASS CRUISER** $14265. AJ813

AM813

CUTLASS SUPR. CLASSIC COUPE (GR11Y) $14,368.

BROUGHAM CPE. (GM11Y) 15,200.

5.0 L V8 108.1" WB

$14940. BROUGHAM CRUISER

GRAINED   UNGRAINED

$16074.

CUTLASS SUPREME CLASSIC.

226   **New** CUTLASS SUPREME INTERNATIONAL COUPE (WR11W)

2.8 L V6 ENG.   107½" WB

OLDSMOBILE

Oldsmobile DELTA 88

110.8" WB

NEW OPT. DRIVER'S-SIDE AIRBAG

"The new 3.8 SFI 3800 V6, built at GM's powertrain facility in Flint, Michigan, offers impressive performance. But not at the expense of fuel efficiency."

DRIVER'S AIRBAG OPTIONAL ON DELTA 88.

88

new

NEW 3.8 SFI 3800 V6 PROVIDES PREMIUM PERFORMANCE FOR DELTA 88, NINETY-EIGHT AND TORONADO!

BELOW:
98 TOURING SEDAN
$ 24,995. CY5IC

Ninety Eight Regency

NINETY-EIGHT REGENCY

"Seating areas are leather. Front buckets adjust 14 ways—not only for comfort, but also for front, side, and lumbar support."

"During hard braking, brake pressure corrects as conditions require, providing smooth, anti-lock braking power."

CX5IC SEDAN $19,192.
BRGH. SED. $20,268.
CW5IC

* CUST. CRUISER WAGON IN DELTA 88 LINE, BUT HAS 116" WB and 5.0L V8.

BP8IY CUSTOM CRUISER

OLDSMOBILE QUALITY. FEEL IT.

Limited Edition Touring Sedan

Oldsmobile

$13,443.
SL NT14U

STD. ENG.
2.5 L
4-CYL.
FUEL-
INJ.
"TECH
IV"
(33 HWY,
23 CITY)

23/35 MPG
(4)
20/27 MPG
(V6)

150 HP

16-valve Quad 4 engine

S, SL AVAILABLE WITH THE new 3300 V6, OR

CALAIS ADVERTISED SPECIAL PRICES OF $9995. UP

Cutlass Calais

S ↗
NF14U $12,294.

NK14D INT'L. COUPE $15,310.

(CALAIS SEDANS ALSO AVAILABLE)

V.I.N. ENDS WITH -K-#

89

(CRUISER WAGON AJ81W, $15,218; SL CRUISER WAGON AM81N, $16,645.)

A851N INTERNATIONAL SEDAN $17,245.

Cutlass Ciera

4 CYL., 2.8 OR 3.3 L V6 ENGINES

MODIFIED GRILLE ↓

new TAIL-LIGHTS, REAR WINDOW

23/30 MPG (4)
20/29 MPG (V6)

228

Oldsmobile

Cutlass Supreme

18/30 MPG

DISC BRAKES

Custom Cutlass Supreme
Limited Edition

Available only in the Western U.S., only for a limited time.
• Front and rear air dams
• Rear spoiler
• Side skirts
• 15' wheels with color-keyed covers
• Special numbered dash plaque
• Many more custom features

89

STD. ENGINE: 173 CID (2.8 L) V6 (130 HP @ 4500 RPM) 2.33 TO 1 GEAR RATIO

WR14W INTERNATIONAL COUPE $18,065.

WS14W SL COUPE $15,650.

(WH14W COUPE $14,750.)

107½" WB 4-SP. AUTO. TRANSAXLE P195/75R14 TIRES *

CUTLASS Supreme

INTERIOR →

AVIS

229

* WITH EXCEPTIONS

Oldsmobile

19/28 MPG

Eighty-Eight

3800 V6 ENGINE

ROYALE SED. $15,800.

HN51C

ROYALE COUPE HN11C $15,700.
ROYALE BROUGH. COUPE HY11C $16,800.

CHROME GRILLE ↑ OF THIS DESIGN ON CUSTOM CRUISER WAGON (V8) BP81Y $19,793.

89

new
98 REGENCY GRILLE RESEMBLES TOURING SEDAN GRILLE, BUT CHROMED.

18/28 MPG

CV54C

TOUR. SED. $26,545.

98 REGENCY

CX51C SEDAN $21,566.
CW51C BROUGHAM 22,535.

Ninety-Eight
Touring Sedan

new GRILLE

230

Oldsmobile CUTLASS CALAIS

W. QUAD 4-4-2 PKG.

$11680.
(SAME PRICE FOR STD. NL14U CPE.)

NL54U
STD. CALAIS SEDAN

90

151 OR 140 CID 4
(110, 160 OR 180 HP)
AVAIL. 204 CID V6
(160 HP @ 5200 RPM)

DASH (INT'L)
w. COMPACT DISC PLAYER OPTIONAL

The New Generation of OLDSMOBILE
A 1990 Option

SL COUPE NT14D
$14340.

$12680.

20/33 MPG
(VARIES ACCORD.
TO TYPE OF
POWERTRAIN)

V.I.N. = 1G3 (AJ14N)
— L-#

NF54U S SEDAN (SAME PRICE FOR NF14U S CPE.)

13.6 GALLON
FUEL TANK
103.4" WB
P185/75R14
TIRES

Cutlass Calais SL

Quad 4

NK54A
INTERNATIONAL
SEDAN SL
$15960.

NEW "SILHOUETTE" USED MINIVAN AVAIL.
191 CID V6 $17695.

THESE WHEELS STD. OR OPT. ON VARIOUS
CUTLASS SERIES (DETAILS AT LOWER LEFT)

WHEELS :

1 – ALUM. 16" (CUT. SP. INTL.)
2 – ALUM. 15" (CUTLASS SUPREME)
3 – DLX. 14" DISC " "
4 – ALUM. 14" (CUTLASS CIERA)
5 – SIMULATED WIRE 14" (CIERA, CRUIS.)
6 – DLX. 14" DISC (" , ")
7 – ALUM. 16" (CUTLASS CALAIS INT'L.)
8 – ALUM. 14" (CUTL. CALAIS SL)
9 – " " (" " S)
10 – 5 SPOKE CAST ALUMINUM 14"
      (CUTL. CALAIS S w. QUAD 4 PKG.)
11 – SPT. WHEEL w. STAINLESS STEEL
      TRIM RINGS, 14" (CALAIS S)
12 – DLX. DISC 14" (CUTL. CALAIS)

CUTLASS **CIERA**

Oldsmobile

CIERA DASH, GRILLE

$14,360.
S
CPE.
AJ113

CIERA MPG 23/31 (4) 20/29 (V6)

151 CID 4 (110 HP @ 5200 RPM) OR 204 CID V6 (160 HP @ 5200)

CUTLASS CRUISER

WAGON (ENTIRE TAILGATE CAN BE SWUNG UP)

FROM $15,360.

21/27 MPG (4)

20/29 MPG (V6)

The New Generation of **OLDSMOBILE**

CUTLASS SUPREME

SEDAN

191 CID V6 (135 HP) 140 CID QUAD 4 160 HP (HO 180 HP)

INTERNATIONAL SERIES DASH

16½ GAL. FUEL TK.
V6 19/32 MPG 22/29 " (4)
WS11W SL CPE. $16,550.

4 DR. **NEW 90**

107½" WB

SAFETY ROLL BAR

FRONT END DETAILS

New
CUTLASS SUPREME WT14T CONVERTIBLE

w. 135 HP 3.1L V6

CUSTOM CRUISER (w. 5.0 L V8)

Oldsmobile

REAR

88 ROYALE

88 ROYALE

NEW GRILLE (88 ROYALE)

REMOTE CONTROL KEY RING

88 ROYALE

18/27 MPG (88 and 98 SERIES)

90

98 REG.

98 REGENCY DASH

98 REGENCY GRILLE CLOSE-UP

88 and 98 have 3800 cc V6 (165 HP @ 4800 RPM) 18-GAL. FUEL TANK

TOURING SEDAN INSTRUMENT PANEL

98 TOURING SEDAN

Oldsmobile

FIRENZA *(1982-1988)*

NEW 82

101.2" WB
4 CYL.
(112 OR 121 CID)

SX HATCHBACK $9509.

Introducing Firenza.

P175/80R13 TIRES

INTERIOR

OTHER MODELS
4-DR. SEDAN $8978.
S COUPE 8943.
LX SED. (4 DR.) 9430.

Firenza SX Hatchback
The newest, smallest Oldsmobile.
Front-wheel drive
A 4-cylinder engine
Oldsmobile Firenza.

V.I.N.= 1G3A C69 G0C (-) 000001 UP

110 CID 4 BLT. BY GM OF BRAZIL!
121 CID 4 BLT. BY CHEVROLET (USA)

SUNROOF OPT.

WHEELS
A - SUPER STOCK
B - SIMULATED WIRE DISC
C - RALLYE
D - DELUXE WHEEL DISC, STD.

NEW FIRENZA CRUISER

WAGON $8903. ($9256. FOR CRUISER BROUGHAM)

25/46 MPG

LX SEDAN

INTERIOR

23/43 MPG (WAGON)

PADDED CUSTOM SPT. STEER. WH. and RALLYE INSTRUMENTS STD. on SX CPE.

FROM $8596. ("S" CPE.)

83

DASH

14 GAL. FUEL TANK

V.I.N. = 1G3A C69 (-) XD (-) 000001 UP

234

Olds Firenza

84

SEDAN	$8900.
S COUPE	8813.
LX SEDAN	9248.
SX COUPE	9352.
CRUISER WAGON	9120.
LX CRUIS. "	9468.

V.I.N.
1G3A (C69)
PXE (-)
000001 UP

WITH **GT.** PKG.

ES PKG.
INTERIOR

85

V.I.N.
1G3JC69PXF UP

ES PKG. $700.
(GT PKG. $1360.)

FROM $9038.
(S COUPE)

$9352. → Cruiser

FROM 9477.('86) 10301.('87)

MPG: 25/31 (122 CID 4)
1987
"J" BODY

COUPE, SEDAN, S HATCHBACK CPE.

86-87

JC27P COUPE ('86)

1986 EXAMPLES ILLUSTR.

1986 V.I.N. ENDS
with -G-#
1987 w. -H-#

"BLACKOUT" TRIM, 1987

FIRENZA CRUISER WAGON ('86)

LC and FINAL LX MODELS

1987 LC COUPE WHEEL

new
GT (JD77W)
HATCHBACK
COUPE (V6)
$11,254.
$12569.('87) JD21W
(NO 1988 GT)

JC511 SEDAN
$11075.
(CPE. SAME PRICE)

REDUCED TO 1 BASIC SERIES

JC111 CPE.

V.I.N.= 1G3 (JC111)
—J-#

RECLINING BUCKET SEATS →

88

$11775.
JC811 FIRENZA CRUISER WAGON

new GRILLE and new COMPOSITE HEADLIGHTS

(DISCONT'D. 1988)

(1973-1984)

REAR DETAIL

$7750. and up

STANDARD L4
Equipped with
Automatic Trans.
23 **33**
EPA Est. Hwy. Est.
mpg

81

new GRILLE
(STD. / BRGHM.)

V.I.N. = IG3AB37 UP (STD.)
IG3AE37 UP (BROUGH.)

BROUGHAM COUPE (VINYL-COVERED REAR QTRS.)

$8107.

ES-2500

DASH

VARIOUS WHEEL TYPES =

A - POLYCAST
B - WIRE (SIMULATED)
C - DELUXE WITH BODY COLOR
D - RALLYE
E - DELUXE CHROME
F - BRIGHT WHEEL WITH TRIM RING

SX

105" WHEELBASE

151 CID 4	90 HP
173 CID V6	115 HP
P185 / 80 R 13 TIRES	

SPORT OMEGA

sportOmega

Front-wheel-dr.

Oldsmobile
We've had one built for you.

OMEGA

14 GALLON FUEL TANK

Standard 4-Cyl. Engine
41 Hwy. Est | **26** EPA Est 'mpg

OMEGA

4-DR. $9000.

2-DR. $8814.

SEDAN ("ES") $10,338.

V.I.N. =
1G3AB37ROC UP (STD.)
1GAE37RXOC UP (BR.)

(BLACKED-OUT SIDE-PILLARS) ON ES

82

("ES" PKG. PART OF BROUGHAM SER.)

"ES" HAS OWN GRILLE

BROUGHAM SEDAN DETAIL

OPT. SUNROOF
"VISTA VENT"

$9317.

To you we present
OMEGA ES

OMEGA BROUGHAM SEDAN

$9148.

OMEGA BROUGHAM COUPE

237

Olds Omega

V.I.N. (1983) = IG3AB69 UP (STD.)
IG3AE69 UP (BROUGHAM)
(1984) = IG3AB69 ZXE UP (STD.)
IG3AE69 ZXE UP (BROUGHAM)

DASH ('83)

PRICED FROM
$8998. ('83)
9159. ('84)

FUEL TANK
14.6 GAL. (4)
15.1 GAL. (V6)

OMEGA COUPE & SEDAN →

ES 2800.

$1046.
EXTRA FOR '83 "ES" PKG.

SEDAN

COUPE

(1983 EXAMPLES ILLUSTRATED)

ON 1984 STD./BROUGHAM, EACH HALF OF GRILLE HAS THIS DESIGN. (1984 "E9" IS LITTLE CHANGED.)

151 CID PONTIAC 4 (24/42 MPG) OR 173 CID CHEVROLET V6 (21/34 MPG)

new GRILLES (EXCEPT ES)

83-84

WHEEL STYLES
A B C D

BROUGHAM ('83)

ALL '84s BUT E9 have HOOD ORNAMENT.

BROUGHAM
PRICED FROM
$9287. ('83)
9448. ('84)

1984 IS FINAL OMEGA.

Oldsmobile TORONADO

We've had one built for you.

(SINCE 1966)

Have a Toronado built for you. For you alone.

(ALL TORONADOS HAVE FEATURED FRONT-WHEEL-DRIVE, STARTING WITH THEIR VERY FIRST 1966 MODEL.)

$ 12,995

ALL 1981 MODELS ARE COUPES.

LONG "TORONADO" NAME ABOVE GRILLE.

EXTRA CONTROLS BUILT INTO ARM REST

DASH

V.I.N.
1G3AZ5740B(-)10000I UP

"XSC" HAS XSC DESIGNATION ON REAR QUARTER PANEL.

81

3Z 57 SERIES

AVAILABLE DIESEL V8 ENGINE (5.7-LITER) 350 CID (105 HP)

4 WHEEL TYPES
A — STANDARD WHEEL DISC
B — XSC PAINTED DISC
C — LOCKING SIMULATED WIRE DISCS
D — ALUMINUM SPORT WHEEL

AVAIL. LEATHER AND DOESKIN UPHOLST.

114" W.B.
252 CID V6

OR

307 CID V8
(150 HP)

P 205/75R
×15 TIRES
(P225/70R×15
ON "XSC")

15.2 CU. FT. TRUNK IS LINED AND CARPETED.

239

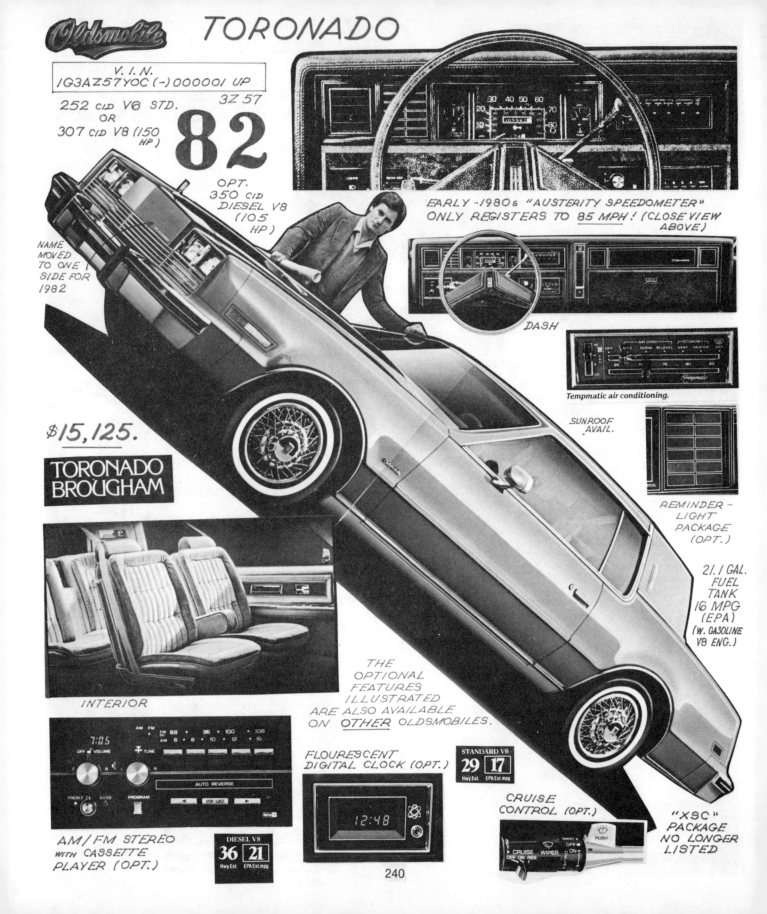

Oldsmobile TORONADO

V. I. N.
1G3AZ57YOC(-)000001 UP

3Z 57

252 CID V6 STD.
OR
307 CID V8 (150 HP)

82

OPT.
350 CID
DIESEL V8
(105 HP)

NAME MOVED TO ONE SIDE FOR 1982

EARLY-1980s "AUSTERITY SPEEDOMETER" ONLY REGISTERS TO 85 MPH! (CLOSE VIEW ABOVE)

DASH

Tempmatic air conditioning.

SUNROOF AVAIL.

REMINDER - LIGHT PACKAGE (OPT.)

$15,125.

TORONADO BROUGHAM

21.1 GAL. FUEL TANK 16 MPG (EPA) (W. GASOLINE V8 ENG.)

INTERIOR

THE OPTIONAL FEATURES ILLUSTRATED ARE ALSO AVAILABLE ON **OTHER** OLDSMOBILES.

FLOURESCENT DIGITAL CLOCK (OPT.)

STANDARD V6	
29 Hwy. Est.	17 EPA Est. mpg

CRUISE CONTROL (OPT.)

"XSC" PACKAGE NO LONGER LISTED

AM/FM STEREO WITH CASSETTE PLAYER (OPT.)

DIESEL V8	
36 Hwy. Est.	21 EPA Est. mpg

Oldsmobile **TORONADO**

V.I.N.= IG3A 257 YXD (-) 000001 UP

EZ 57
NO HOOD ORNAMENT IN 1983

83

EMBLEM ON HOOD (new).

DASH

"TORONADO" NAME NOW MOVED DOWN, ONTO GRILLE

BUICK-BUILT V6 STD. (252 CID, 125 HP) 17/29 MPG

16/27 MPG (V8)

OLDSMOBILE 307 CID V8 AVAIL. (140 HP) OLDSMOBILE (350 CID, 105 HP DIESEL V8 ALSO AVAIL.) 22/38 MPG

POWER CONTROLS IN DOOR

A B

A = STD. WHEEL DISC B= AVAIL. WIRE WHEEL DISC WITH LOCK.

15.2 CU. FT. LINED and CARPETED TRUNK

OPTIONAL ELECTRIC SLIDING ASTRO ROOF

$15,827. **BROUGHAM COUPE** →

WITH OPT.

V.I.N.= IG3AZ57 YXE (-) 000001 UP

new GRILLE. HOOD ORNAMENT RETURNS.

Caliente

PACKAGE

84

EZ 57

ELECTRONIC SYNTHESIZED VOICE INFORMATION SYSTEM AVAIL., or REMINDER LIGHTS.

Let's get it together... buckle up

$16,832. UP (BROUGHAM has LOWER ROCKER PANEL TRIM, PLUS A SEPARATE RUB STRIP FURTHER UP.)

There is a special feel in an *Oldsmobile*

INTERIOR

Oldsmobile TORONADO

110 MPH

SHOWN WITH OPT. **CALIENTE** PACKAGE (WITH HEAVY BRIGHTWK. UPPER BORDER OF GRILLE, PADDED TOP, ETC.)

new *EZ57Y*
LOWER SIDE TRIM

85

GRILLE MODIFIED

ELECTRONIC VOICE INFORMATION SYSTEM STILL OPTIONAL

There is a special feel in an *Oldsmobile*

FINAL 114"-WB MODEL

BROUGHAM COUPE $17,353.

V.I.N.=1G3-EZ57YXFX00000/ up

V.I.N.=1G3 EZ57B -G-#

ELECTRONIC INSTRUMENT PANEL

GM

INTERIOR

"20TH ANNIVERSARY PACKAGE" OPTIONAL

CLOSE DETAIL OF NEW BUILT-ON SIDE MIRROR

EZ57B

86

TOTALLY RESTYLED AND DOWNSIZED

new 108" WB

BUICK-BASED 231 CID V6 (140 HP @ 4400 RPM) 4 SP. AT 2.97 GEAR RATIO

P215/60R15 TIRES

BROUGHAM COUPE $19,918.

new FRONT PROFILE DETAIL

CONCEALED HEADLIGHTS RETURN

There is a special feel in an *Oldsmobile*

18 GAL. FUEL TANK

V.I.N. ENDS WITH —H—#

Oldsmobile
Oldsmobile Quality. Feel it.

TORONADO
"E" BODY

EZ113
87
DETAILS of CONCEALED
HEADLTS., CORNER LTS.

BROUGHAM
$20438.

TROFEO
$22433.

INTRODUCING TORONADO TROFÉO. New

EZ11C COUPE $21,363.

STD. TORONADO WHEEL
(NOT AVAIL. ON TROFEO)

88

new 3.8-LITRE SFI 3800 V6 ENGINE

TEVES ELECTRONIC ANTI-LOCK BRAKING SYSTEM OPTIONAL

OLDSMOBILE QUALITY. FEEL IT.

REAR DETAILS

Toronado Troféo

EV11C TROFÉO $23220. V.I.N. ENDS WITH —J—#

The New Generation of OLDSMOBILE

TROFÉO

89

V.I.N. = 1G3
EV (OR EZ) 11 C–K–#

WHEEL DETAIL
215/60R15 TIRES

EZ11C COUPE $23,132.

EV11C TROFÉO $25,545.

19/28 MPG

← note MINUTE VARIATIONS IN 1987~1989 LOWER LTS.

Oldsmobile TORONADO

INTERIOR, WITH OPTIONAL
CELLULAR TELEPHONE.

CD PLAYER
AVAIL.

90

LONGER
BODY

108" WB

18 GAL.
FUEL TANK
17/26
MPG

3.8L 231 CID
(3800) V6 ENG.
has 165 HP
@ 5200 RPM

$25545.
TROFÉO
EV14C

TORONADO
new 215/60.R 16 TIRES

VISUAL INFO. CENTER (OPT.)

V.I.N.
ENDS WITH
— L — #

EZ14C
$23284.
(STD. TORONADO)

244

PLYMOUTH and NEW RELIANT-K

99.6" WHEELBASE 4 CYLS. (135 OR 156 CID)

$5880* is the surprising price of the base model Reliant K Coupe.

($7552., WEST COAST)

K59 SE WAGON $8736.

STD., CUSTOM, and "SE" MODELS, TO $8736.

FRONT-WHEEL-DRIVE PLYMOUTH RELIANT-K AMERICA'S HIGHEST GASOLINE MILEAGE SIX-PASSENGER CAR.

FRONT-WHEEL-DRIVE AND HIGH MILEAGE

25	41
CITY	HWY

(CUSTOM WAGON K49 $8203.)

V.I.N. = 1P3B ( ) (-) OB (-) 000001/ UP

SEDAN

81 new

RELIANT IS

4-DRS. $100. MORE THAN CPES.

The Chrysler 2.2 litre "Trans 4" with Electronic Fuel Control. A significant step forward in automotive engineering.

SIMILAR TO new DODGE ARIES K-CAR.

SLOGAN: "THE AMERICAN WAY TO BEAT THE PUMP."

P175/75 R13 TIRES

$6865.

245

($8610. R27 GRAN FURY IS AVAIL. = SEE 1982 PAGE)

Plymouth

The New Chrysler Corporation

STD. DASH W. 2-SPOKE STEER. WH.

Reliant's standard instrument panel and two-spoke luxury steering.

PLYMOUTH

$7831.

P26 **RELIANT FOUR-DOOR**

front-wheel-drive
41 EST. HWY / 26 EPA EST. MPG

RELIANT CUSTOM 2-DR.

WITH CABRIOLET ROOF OPT.

P41 CUSTOM **$8520.**

RELIANT TWO-DOOR COUPE

AVAIL. CONSOLE SHIFT

13 GAL. FUEL TANK 26 MPG (EPA)

P59

RELIANT WAGONS P49 CUSTOM **$8956.**

SE (GRAINED) **$9528.**

40 EST. HWY / 26 EPA EST. MPG

V.I.N.= 1P3B ( )
(-) OC (-) 000001 UP

82

B26 **GRAN FURY**

(AVAIL. ONLY AS A 4-DR.)
WT. LIGHTENED TO 3364 LBS. FOR 1982.

GRAN FURY REAR

$8880.

WB SHORTENED FROM 118½ TO 112.7"

Premium Turbine Wheel Covers.

SIDE DETAILS

9:28 Chronometer
HRS · MIN

Electronic Digital Clock.

Tilt Steering Column.

Rear Window Defroster.

18 GAL. FUEL TANK 18 MPG (EPA)

225 CID 6 (90 HP) or 318 CID V8 (140 HP)

246

1982 PLYMOUTH . . . THE AMERICAN WAY TO GET YOUR MONEY'S WORTH.

IP3B

P49

CUSTOM WAGON
$9391.
(REG. PRICE)

PLYMOUTH
The American way to get your money's worth

RELIANT S.E. WAGON
$8,756*
(equipped as shown)

Plymouth Reliant Wagon $7,636* 41 est. hwy. `28` EPA est.MPG²

(P59 SE WAGON = $9727.)

New

83

Plymouth Scamp GT $7,255* 47 est. hwy. `26` EPA est.MPG²

GRAN FURY
18 MPG (6)
16 MPG (V8)
EPA AVERAGES

Plymouth Reliant K Sedan $6,718*
41 est. hwy. `29` EPA est. MPG¹

V.I.N. =
IP3B (M18B)
—D—#

Introducing the SCAMP

Reliant STD., CUSTOM (WAGON) OR SE SERIES

PICKUP CAR (ABOVE)
LISTED ONLY FOR
1983 MODEL YR.
M44 — $7517.
M64 GT—8006.
104.2" WB
135 CID 4
P175/75R13 TIRES
(P195/60R14 = GT)

GRAN FURY
ENGINES =
225 CID 6 (90 HP)
OR 318 CID V8
(140 HP)

GRAN FURY

B26 4-DR.
$9449.

P195/75R15 TIRES

P21C COUPE
$8743.
P41C SE
COUPE
$9256.

5/50 Plymouth Reliant K. Match it! (If you can.)

P49C CUSTOM
WAGON
$9529.

P59C
SE WAGON $9769.

84

V.I.N. = IP3B (P26)
CXE — #

112" WB

29/41
EPA MPG

RELIANT K

NEW
GRILLE WITH CENTER
CHRYSLER CORP.
PENTASTAR
MEDALLION

NEW

Plymouth Voyager

135 OR 156 CID 4
(99 OR
101 HP)

The Magic Wagon

$10252.
UP
(STD.,
SE
OR
LE)

P46C SE SED.
$9382.
5/50

P26C SEDAN
$8855.

(GRAN
FURY =
$10447.)

A five-year or 50,000-mile
Protection Plan.

24/37 MPG, EPA

Plymouth-the best built, best backed American cars- 247

Plymouth. Best built, best backed American cars.†

Plymouth

KPH41

NEW GRILLE FOR RELIANT

85

Reliant Super K. LE $9597.

1985 PLYMOUTH
V.I.N.=(1 OR J)
P3B (A24K)
—F—#

B26P GRAN FURY CONT'D., AT $10,748.

CARAVELLE →
4 CYL.
135 CID, 99 HP
OR 158 CID
WITH FRONT WHEEL DRIVE, and
103.1" WB

EJH41 "SE" SEDAN $10,042

New Plymouth creates the 5/50 Caravelle.
Engineered to challenge Buick Century and Olds Ciera.

(LE) RELIANT DASH

RELIANT K $9597.
P26D SEDAN $9640.

P46C LE 4 DR.

1986 PLYMOUTH V.I.N.=(1 OR J) P3 B (A24K)—G—#

86

135 C.I.D. 4s

2.2-liter (135 CID) four-cylinder electronically fuel injected engine: 97 hp @ 5,200 rpm; 122 lb-ft torque @ 3,200 rpm.

High-Output 2.2-liter (135 CID) OHC engine: 110 hp @ 5,600 rpm; 129 lb-ft torque @ 3,600 rpm.[1]

2.5-liter four-cylinder electronically fuel injected balance shaft engine: 100 hp @ 4,800 rpm; 136 lb-ft torque @ 2,800 rpm.

V8

2.6-liter (155.9 CID) four-cylinder balance shaft engine: 104 hp @ 4,800 rpm; 142 lb-ft torque @ 2,800 rpm.

5.2-liter (318 CID) V-8 engine: 140 hp @ 3,600 rpm; 265 lb-ft torque @ 1,600 rpm.

Turbocharged 2.2-liter (135 CID) four-cylinder electronically fuel injected engine: 146 hp @ 5,200 rpm; 170 lb-ft torque @ 3,600 rpm.[1]

BLACK PILLAR GIVES LOOK OF A H/T. →

DETAILS OF AVAIL. PLY. ENGINES (ALL MODELS)

$9464.
LE 2 DR.
P41C

248

ENGINE	1.6-Liter	2.2-Liter	2.2-L EFI	2.2-L High-Output[1]	2.2-L EFI Turbo[1,2]	2.5-L Balance Shaft	2.6-L Balance Shaft	5.2-Liter
Voyager / Voyager LE / Voyager SE	NA	S	NA	NA	NA	NA	O	NA
Caravelle / Caravelle SE	NA	NA	S	NA	O	O	NA	NA
Reliant K	NA	NA	S	NA	NA	NA	NA	NA
Reliant K LE / Reliant K SE	NA	NA	S	NA	NA	O	NA	NA
Turismo	S	O	NA	NA	NA	NA	NA	NA
Turismo Duster	S	O	NA	NA	NA	NA	NA	NA
Turismo 2.2	NA	O[3]	NA	S	NA	NA	NA	NA
Horizon / Horizon SE	S	O	NA	NA	NA	NA	NA	NA
Gran Fury	NA	NA	NA	NA	NA	NA	NA	S

THE PRIDE IS BACK...BORN IN AMERICA.

P42D RELIANT
LE WAGON
$10,607.

P39D RELIANT SE WAGON
$10,476.

PLYMOUTH RELIANT

SE WAGON INTERIOR

LE

86

(NO WAGON IN STD. SERIES)

GRAINED BODY PANELS STD. ON LE WAGON, BUT COULD BE DEDUCTED FOR CREDIT.

CARAVELLE

Options → WIRE WHEEL COVER W. LOCK

Caravelle

68.0"

53.1"

103.3"
187.2"*

57.6"   57.2"

*Including optional bumper guards

A/C   RECIRC   TEMP   HI
PANEL   BI-LEV   FLOOR

AIR COND.

1986 MODELS INCLUDE THE NEW, MANDATORY HIGH 3RD BRAKE LT. AT REAR.

CARAVELLE...

J36D SEDAN
$10,424.

MPG: 22/27 (152 CID 4)*

GRAN FURY

B26P SALON SED.
$11,385.

MPG: 16/21 (318 CID V8)*

VERY FEW CHANGES IN GRAN FURY (DURING THE 1982 –1989 ERA.)

*1987 FIGURE (EPA)

PLYMOUTH

114 MPH (SUNDANCE TURBO)

S41D

4 OR TURBO 4

S46D "P" BODY

New SUNDANCE

97" WB

COUPE $9204.

$9404.

100.4" WB ON WAGON; 100.3" ON OTHER RELIANTS

MPG: 23/28 (135 CID 4) SUNDANCE OR RELIANT

Reliant $10,769.

P39D LE WAGON

LE WAGON WITH GRAINED TRIM OPT.

RELIANT LE INTERIOR

87 New

119" WB GRAND VOYAGER WAGON ADDED TO "LINE. (98 MPH) $14203.

"E" BODY CARAVELLE

J36D SE = J46D

REAR DETAILS

$11021. and up

new steer. wheel

RELIANT LE

P36D

K BODY 10325.

CARAVELLE DASH

770 (LIMITED WARRANTY)

"M" BODY GRAN FURY B26P

$11922.

"THE PRIDE IS BACK."

88

SUNDANCE DASH

SUNROOF OPT.

Sundance

LIFTBACK REAR DETAILS

4 OR TURBO 4

S41D LIFTBACK COUPE (ILLUSTR.) $9652.

PLYMOUTH

BUCKET SEATS (SUNDANCE)

SUNDANCE (CONT'D.)

$9852. S46D SED.

SUNDANCE INT. →

SUNDANCE DASH

America

$10282

LE

$9888. UP

RELIANT LE INTERIOR

Plymouth Reliant America
$6995

SPECIAL PRICE =

88

GRAN FURY STEREO and INTERIOR

note "V6" EMBLEM JUST BEHIND HDLTS. OF GRAND VOYAGER MITSUBISHI V6 ENG. STD. IN GRAND VOYAGER LE.

Grand Voyager, like all Voyagers, is designed for easy garageability and handling

1988½ GRAN FURY has DRIVER'S AIRBAG.

Voyager

Gran Fury

B16P SEDAN = $12622.
B26P SALON " = 12766.

PLYMOUTH
SATISFY THE CUSTOMER

1989 PLYMOUTH SUNDANCE

4 CYL. OR TURBO 4

BASE M.S.R.P.	$8,395*
OPTION PACKAGE	+ $791
	$9,186

(P28D LIFTBACK SED. REG. $10,250.)

P24D LIFTBACK CPE. REG. $10,050.

SUNROOF AVAIL.

Full instrumentation

"RS" PACKAGE OPTIONAL

5-speed overdrive

19/34 MPG

Sundance RS interior

PLYMOUTH SUNDANCE. STARTING AT $8,395.

4.9%‡ A.P.R. OR $600 FACTORY CASH BACK

89

FINAL YEAR FOR RELIANT AND GRAN FURY.

18/23 MPG (V6)
18/28 MPG (4)

112" OR 119" WB

PLYMOUTH ACCLAIM LX. $14,395. (6) A76U

A46K ACCLAIM = $11,656.
A56K " LE = 13,031.
(19/34 MPG)

NEW

103.3" WB
4, TURBO 4, OR 6

PLYMOUTH VOYAGER. $13,095. UP

The New Chrysler Corporation.

Plymouth

SAPORO (MADE IN JAPAN)

BUILT BY MITSUBISHI   IMPORTED ONLY FOR PLYMOUTH   Plymouth

(1978 – 1983)

MPG: 30 HWY, 20 EPA EST.

156 CID
4 CYL.
105 HP
P195/70
R14 TIRES

D - 43

81

LUX COUPE
$7249.

(NO OTHER BODY TYPE AVAIL.)

99" WB

DASH →

V.I.N.= 3P3BD437
(-) B 100001 UP
5 SP. TRANS.

Sapporo. From Mitsubishi, Master Car Builders of Japan.

82

V.I.N.= JP3BD437
(-) C (-) 000001

36 HWY, 24 EPA EST.
(SAME IN 1983, WITH 34 HWY and 22 EPA EST. IN CALIFORNIA.)

HP REDUCED TO 100, MPG INCREASED

$8036. UP

V.I.N.= JP3BD437 (-) D (-) 000001 UP

83

note "BLACKOUT" SIDE-PILLARS

new OPTIONAL "TECHNICA" ELECTRONIC INSTR. PANEL and VOICE ALERT SYSTEM

MCA-Jet engine, with a third valve in each cylinder.

$8323.
DODGE "CHALLEN-GER" IS SIMILAR.)

22 MPG EPA CALIFORNIA

all new

1981 PONTIAC
T1000

PONTIAC
(SINCE 1926)

2M08

3 DR.
$5793.
5 DR. 5939.

94.3" WB

98 CID 4

70 HP

2M68

155/80R × 13 B TIRES

81

T1000 interior featuring available cloth seating.

Sport wheel and available auto. trans

Cargo area with rear seat down.

More **P**ontiac KN-OW-HOW to the **G**allon

LE MANS $8076.

30 HWY. EST. / 21 EPA EST. MPG

2F69

$8540.

GRAND LE MANS

Le M., Gr. Le M.
w. 108.1" WB,
231 CID V6 (115 HP)
265 or 301 CID V8
(120 or 140 HP)
185/75R × 14 TIRES

$8763.
2F35

Wagon.

PLUS PONTIAC'S NEW EFFICIENCY SYSTEM, INCLUDING GM'S COMPUTER COMMAND CONTROL

PONTIAC'S '81 GRAND LE MANS SAFARI
(195/75R × 14 TIRES)

LE MANS DASH

new TAILLIGHTS

V-6

formal

30 HWY. EST. / 21 EPA EST. MPG

254

108.1" WB
231 c.i.d V6 (115 HP)
265 c.i.d V8 (120 HP)
(AVAIL.= 350 c.i.d
DIESEL V8)

$8462.=STD. (2J37) $8841.=LJ (2K37)
$9974.=BROUGHAM (2P37)

29 HWY. EST. / 20 EPA EST MPG

GRAND PRIX
(new BROUGHAM REPLACES SJ MODEL)

PONTIAC

GRAND PRIX DASH

GRAND PRIX
V.I.N.= 1G2AJ37A0B (-)
100001 UP
(ALL PONTIAC V.I.N.s BEGIN WITH 1G2A)

81

(THE FINAL CATALINA)

CATALINA 116" WB
2L69 SED.
$8620.

(2L37 COUPE $8516.)

28 HWY. EST. / 19 EPA EST MPG

V-6 BONNEVILLE 116" WB

$8798.
UP

2R37
BONVL. BRGH.
CPE.
$9729.

2L35

SAFARI

↑ $9730.
(new AUTO. O.D.
TRANS.; OPT. ON
BONNEVILLE)

**BONNEVILLE
SAFARI** 2N35

↑ GRAND LE MANS

255

'82 PONTIAC

L68C T1000
5 DR. SED.
$6478.

T 1000

T1000's sporty instrument panel and steering wheel.

12.5 GAL.
FUEL
TANK

26
MPG
(EPA)

J-2000 COUPES FROM
$8406.

T-1000 DASH
(ABOVE)

82

L08C CPE.
$6315.

J2000
is
New

101.2"
WB
112 CID
4
85 HP

14 GAL.
FUEL
TK.

THE NEW·J GENERATION

P175/
80R 13
TIRES

J 2000
PRICE
RANGE =
$8406.
TO
9306.

J2000
mpg rating

42 HWY.
26 EPA
(OR 30 EPA)

DASH

INTER.

NOW THE EXCITEMENT BEGINS

256

PONTIAC

15.9 GAL. FUEL TK. 26 MPG (EPA)

4 VERTICAL PCS. IN EA. 1/2 OF GRILLE (NOT VISIBLE IN PICTURE)

6000 DASH

$9803. UP

104.8" WB

PONTIAC 6000

40 | 25
Hwy. Est. | EPA Est. mpg
2.5 Litre L4

NEW

(DESIGNED LIKE QUALITY IMPORT CARS, TO MEET THE IMPORT COMPETITION)

GRAND PRIX

GRAND PRIX

108.1" WB

23/34 MPG EPA w. DIESEL V8

LJ

82

GRAND PRIX LJ $9961. (K37C)

CATALINA SERIES IS DISCONTINUED.

'82 BONNEVILLE MODEL G

$9700. N69C SEDAN

231 cid V6 (115 HP)

new SHORTER 108.1" WB

N35C WAGON $9867.

Coming or going, the Model G Wagon looks impressive.

OPT. 350 cid DIESEL V8 (105 HP) (R69C BROUGHAM $10,158.)

18.1 GAL. FUEL TANK 21 MPG (EPA) (23/34" w. V8 DIESEL)

BONNEVILLE REAR

257

PONTIAC 1000

(3-DR. L08
$6146.
98 CID 4
(70 HP)
94.3" WB

L68
5 DR.
$6349.
97.3" WB

1000 INSTR. PANEL

1000
27 MPG EPA
42 MPG EPA (DIESEL) MANUAL TR.

1000 INSTR. PANEL

2000
101.2" WB

28 MPG EPA

C67
2000 SUNBIRD CVT.

$12,614. **NEW**

Not since 1975 had Pontiac offered a ragtop.

2000 INSTR. PANEL

C27

109 CID 4 (85 HP)
122 CID 4 (90 HP)
P175/80R13 TIRES

P195/70R13 ON SE

C69
$8708.

2000 LE
4 DR. SEDAN

5-SPEED
83

2000 SE HATCHBACK

$9708. (D77)

G27

6000 AVAIL. W. EFI 151 CID 4 (90 HP), OR
173 CID V6 (108 HP), H.O. V6,
260 CID V6 DIESEL (85 HP)

P185/80R13 TIRES

6000 LE
$9976.
10,123.
G19

6000 STE
$14,711.
H19

6000
(DASH ILLUSTR. ON FOLLOWING PAGE)
104.8" WB

105 MPH

New

P195/70R14 TIRES (STE)

STE
SPECIAL TOURING EDITION

258

PONTIAC

1983

6000 STE

110 MPH

With a simple touch of your finger you can adjust the climate of your driver environment. It's easy and precise with the STE's new climate control center which uses advanced electronics and light-emitting diode locators.

6000
24 MPG (4)
22 MPG (V6)
28 MPG (DIESEL)
EPA AVG.

6000 DASH
(2 VIEWS)

WE BUILD EXCITEMENT

83

108.1" WB

EPA MPG
20 (V6)
18 (V8)
23 (DIESEL V8)

$9949.

231 CID V6 (115 HP) GAS V8 OR 350 CID DIESEL V8

GRAND PRIX

GRAND PRIX LJ

$10,417.
(T-BAR ROOF EXTRA)

New PARISIENNE

115.9" WB V6, V8 OR DIESEL V8
$10,921. UP

20, 18, 23 MPG EPA

BONNEVILLE
(INSTRUMENT PANEL SIMILAR TO GRAND PRIX, AT LEFT)
$10,150. UP
108.1" WB

$10,363.
BONNEVILLE WAGON

2000 WAGON

259

1000 DASH

PONTIAC

Pontiac 1000's instrument panel features optically soothing orange lighting and new graphics.

1000 HAS
1.6 L OHC
98 CID 4
65 HP

1000

V.I.N.
1G2A L08
CXE (-) 00000/ UP

84

$6184.
3 DR. L08E
5 DR. L68E $6384.

2000 DASH

All 2000 Sunbirds feature instrument panels with optically soothing orange lighting and distinctive graphics.

$13,069.
C67E

NEW

2000 Sunbird LE Convertible comes equipped with a power vinyl top

2000 SUNBIRD
V.I.N. STARTS w.
1G2AB69OXE (-)
(LE : C69OXE)
(TURBO SE :
D69OXE)

120 HP
TURBO
4

2000
SUNBIRD
TURBO

114 MPH

2000 SUNBIRD TURBO
D69E SED.

10,580.

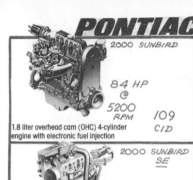

PONTIAC

2000 SUNBIRD

84 HP @ 5200 RPM — 109 CID

1.8 liter overhead cam (OHC) 4-cylinder engine with electronic fuel injection

2000 SUNBIRD SE

150 HP @ 5600 RPM — 109 CID

1.8 liter overhead cam turbocharged 4-cylinder engine with electronic multi-port fuel injection

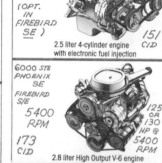

FIERO FIREBD. PHOENIX 6000 — 92 HP @ 4400 (OPT. IN FIREBIRD SE)

151 CID

2.5 liter 4-cylinder engine with electronic fuel injection

6000 STE PHOENIX SE FIREBIRD S/E — 5400 RPM — 125 OR 130 HP @ 5400 RPM — 173 CID

2.8 liter High Output V-6 engine

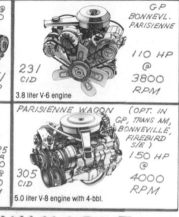

GP BONNEVL. PARISIENNE — 110 HP @ 3800 RPM — 231 CID

3.8 liter V-6 engine

PARISIENNE WAGON (OPT. IN GP, TRANS AM, BONNEVILLE, FIREBIRD S/E) — 150 HP @ 4000 RPM — 305 CID

5.0 liter V-8 engine with 4-bbl.

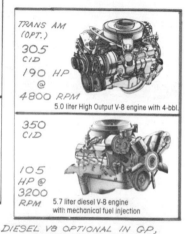

TRANS AM (OPT.) — 305 CID — 190 HP @ 4800 RPM

5.0 liter High Output V-8 engine with 4-bbl.

350 CID — 105 HP @ 3200 RPM

5.7 liter diesel V-8 engine with mechanical fuel injection

ENGINES AVAILABLE

DIESEL V8 OPTIONAL IN GP, BONNEVILLE, PARISIENNE

FUEL INJECTION

The 6000 STE's new fluorescent instrumentation reveals key operational functions in a manner that's easily seen and understood.

NEW!

104.9" WB

6000 STE

$14,851.

H19E

A digital speedometer and analog tachometer are new features on the STE's all-electronic instrument panel.

INFLATOR — ON — OFF

INFLATOR MOUNTED IN TRUNK, WORKING OFF AIR PRESSURE SYSTEM, FOR ELECT. RIDE CONTROL (STE)

84

6000 SERIES WAGONS ARE **New**

$10365. UP

STD. 6000 SERIES DASH

The Pontiac 6000's slim, easy-to-read instrument panel is bathed in an optically soothing orange light. A new tachometer and rally gages are available.

6000 STE has P195/70R x 14 TIRES (P185/75 x 14 ON OTHER 6000 SERIES MODELS)

New

The STE's new neutral-density taillight includes amber lens turn signals.

261

PONTIAC 6000

G27E

6000 LE CPE. $10,286.

84

PONTIAC

G19E
6000 LE SED. $10,436.

$10,401. UP (GP)

DASH (GP)

LE REPLACES LJ SERIES $10880.

108.1 WB
231 CID V6 (110 HP)
V8 (150 HP)
OR 350 CID DIESEL V8 (105 HP)
195/75R x14 TIRES

GRAND PRIX

CRUISE OFF ON R/A
WIPER
MIST
OFF
LO
HI
PUSH

The new electronic tri-mode cruise control, available on all Grand Prix models has accelerate, resume and tap-up/tap-down features.

BROUGHAM CONTINUES AS TOP OF LINE GRAND PRIX MODEL. $11555.

106 MPH

PARISIENNE L69E SED. $11,198.

T69E BROUGHAM $11,598.

10,387. UP

REAR DETAIL OF BONNEVILLE LE

BONNEVILLE

PARISIENNE

WE BU

PONTIAC WE BUILD EXCITEMENT

262

NEW PONTIAC 6000 SPORT WAGON

F35E

$10,365

SHOWN WITH
TAILGATE
LOWERED

PONTIAC

Parisienne's available gage package includes a trip odometer. temperature gage and fuel economy gage, all

NEW

PARISIENNE WAGON

$11,711. (8 PASS.)
L35E

1984

84

WAGON
V.I.N. ═══

1G2AL35HXE
(-) 000001 UP

115.9" WB
150 HP   V8
(350 CID, 105 HP
DIESEL V8 AVAIL.)

225/75 R x 15 TIRES
(205/75 R x 15 ON SEDANS)

PONTIAC SUNBIRD

WAGON
$8971.
UP

1985

TAIL-LIGHT
DETAIL (4-DR.
SEDAN)

LE 4-DR. C69F
$9249.

$11,160.

IN 1985, KNOWN
AS "SUNBIRD"
(INSTEAD OF
"SUNBIRD
2000")

$6130.
2 DR. **1000**

$6380.
4 DR.

PONTIAC 1000

1985

D77F 3 DR.
SE
TURBO

85

1000 INTERIOR

SUNBIRD TURBO 4 ENGINE

SUNBIRD
DASH

D69F
$10,850.

SUNBIRD
S/E TURBO

note
AIR SLOTS
ON
HOOD
(ARROW)

A

263

PONTIAC

GRAND AM MODEL RETURNS

(COUPES ONLY)

LE

AVAILABLE GRAND AM WHEELS

P185/80R13 TIRES

103.4" WB

GRAND AM

New

E27F STD.= $ **9390.**

LE = **9880.**

V27F

85

CONSOLE

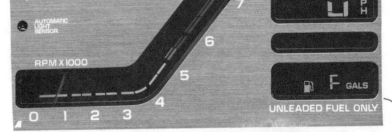

Drive Information
SYS CHK
PONTIAC
SYSTEMS OK

PONTIAC
AUTOMATIC LIGHT SENSOR
RPM X1000
0 1 2 3 4 5 6 7
0 MPH
F GALS
UNLEADED FUEL ONLY

CLOSER VIEW OF PANEL

AM/FM STEREO + CASSETTE CONTROLS

WE BUILD EXCITEMENT

ELECTRONIC INSTR. PANEL DETAILS

151 CID 4 (92 HP) OR 181 CID V6 (125 HP)

ADVERTISED SPECIAL PRICE $7995. UP
LE = $9158.

LIGHT SWITCHES (SEE ARROW AT LEFT SIDE OF DASH)

WIPER CONTROLS

PONTIAC 6000

104.8" WB
151 CID 4 (92 HP)
173 CID V6 (112 HP)

P185/75R14 TIRES

262 CID DIESEL V6 (85 HP) AVAIL.

With multi-port fuel injection. (New)

F19F SED. $10,223.
F27F COUPE 10,043.
F35F WAGON 10,579.
LE: G19F SED. 10,683.
G27F CPE. 10,529.
G35F WAGON 11,013.

6000 DASH

FUNCTION MONITOR
WASHER FLUID
LOW COOLANT
LOW FUEL
LAMP CHECK
HEAD HI BEAM
TURN SIGNAL
BRAKE TAIL
LIGHT

SERVICE REMINDER
CHANGE OIL
OIL FILTER
ROTATE TIRES
TUNE UP
MILES

6000 STE

H19F $15,243.

GRAND PRIX DASH

112 MPH

6000 STE

1985

P195/70R14 TIRES (STE)

GRAND PRIX

108.1" WB (GP OR BNVL.)

231 CID V6 (110 HP)
OR 305 CID V8 (150 HP)

G37A $10713. and up
GRAND PRIX, LE
and BROUGHAM AVAIL.
(GP37A)

GJ37A
GK37A (LE)

WITH REAR DETAILS

1985 V.I.N. ENDS WITH -F-#

PARISIENNE

116" WB
L69F SEDAN $11,600.

BONNEVILLE

4 DRS. ONLY

N69F STD.,
S69F LE, OR
R69F BROUGHAM

1985

new FENDER SKIRTS (Parisienne)

T69F BROUGHAM $12,330.

L35F PARISIENNE WAGON $12,150.

$10,693. UP

265

WE BUILD EXCITEMENT

$6684.

PONTIAC

TL 68C 5 DR. 1000
97.3" WB

86

V.I.N. =
1G2
(TL08C)
- G - #

$6464.

1000

TL 08C
3 DR. 1000
94.3" WB

1000 DASH

(3-DR. and 5-DR.
HATCHBACKS ONLY IN 1000
LINE.)

JD270 SUNBIRD SE COUPE $9201.

4 DR.
ROOFLINE
(SUNBIRD)

JB 350
WAGON ↑
$9611.

SUNBIRD
101.2" WB

STD., SE, new GT
MODELS (LE PKG.
AVAIL.)

TURBO GT CVT.
↓ $15879.
JU67J

JU77J TURBO GT 3-DR.
HATCHBACK
$11299.

1.8 L
OHC 4
(84 HP
@ 5200
RPM)

STD.
ENG.
IN
SUNBIRD

TURBO GT
FRONT
END
→

PONTIAC

STD. ENG. IN
SUNBIRD GT
110 CID (1.8 L)
OHC
TURBO 4
(150 HP @
5600 RPM)

(OPT.
IN OTHER
SUNB.
MODELS.
NOT AVAIL. IN WAGON)

NEW

266

PONTIAC

$10,229.

GRAND AM

NE69 U STD. 4 DR.,
NE27U " CPE.,
NV69 U LE 4 DR.,
NV27U LE CPE.

3.0 L V6
(125 HP @ 4900 RPM)

OPT.

New

4 DR. GRAND AM

6000

LE

STD., LE, SE or STE

GRILLE

TAIL LTS.

WITH T-BAR ROOF OPTION

NEW!

GRAND AM SE

CPE.
111 MPH

NW27L 181 CID V6

AVAILABLE 5.0 L V8 (150 TO 170 HP)

NW27L 2-DR. **$12,514.** (NW69L 4 DR., 12,764.)

GRAND PRIX

$11,423. UP

(STD., LE or BROUGHAM)

GRILLE

86

2.8 L V6 (130 TO 140 HP)

GN69A **$ 11,413.**
GS69A (LE) 11,693.
GR69A (BROUGHAM) 12,243.

BONNEVILLE

(FINAL YR. THAT BNVL. USES GM "G" BODY)

DASH LIKE 1985 GP DASH ILLUSTR.

6000 STE

AH19W
$16,363.

(FINAL PARISN.)

$13,174.

PARISIENNE

BROUGHAM SEDAN BT69Z

267

WE BUILD EXCITEMENT

BL35H

PARISIENNE WAGON **$13,004.**

305 CID V8 (5.0 L)

Limited-production Grand Prix 2+2, only 200 were built and sold only in the south.

PONTIAC

GM "T" BODY

1000 DASH

(1987 IS FINAL 1000 MODEL.)

87

1000
TL21C
3 DR. $6699.
TL61C 5 DR. 6839.

SUNBIRD
$17,029.

JU31M GT CVT.

SUNBIRD
new 122 CID
2.0 L 4
25/31 MPG
(96 HP)
SUNBIRDS $9561. UP

SUNBIRD S/E
AVAIL. W. TURBO 4

PONTIAC

GM "J" BODY

SUNBIRD MODELS
STD. OR GT
4 DR. SEDANS;
SE OR GT CPES.;
SE OR GT 3-DR. HTCHBKS.;
SE OR GT CONVERTIBLES (120 MPH, GT)

OHC 111

GRAND AM DASH

GRAND AM AUTOMATIC BELT SYSTEM STD. AFTER JAN. 1987.

PONTIAC

GRAND AM
20/27 MPG
22/32 "

NPM 724

GRAND AM

GRAND AM 4 DR. SED.	
$11,034. UP	
COUPE	$10,609.
LE SED. ⟹	11,734.
LE CPE. ⟹	11,534.
SE SED. ⟹	13,944.
SE CPE. ⟹	13,704.

(GM "N" BODY)

6000 DASH

PONTIAC 6000
22/32 MPG (151 CID 4)
FROM
$12,298.
(GM "A" BODY)

WAGON
AE81W SE
$14,238
21/28 MPG

New

LARGEST PONTIAC WAGON (FORMERLY PARISIENNE) IS NOW KNOWN AS **SAFARI** (NOT TO BE CONFUSED W. GMC "SAFARI" MINI-VAN.)

$14,434.

new 4.3 L V6 AVAIL. (GP)

PONTIAC

119 MPH

87

GRAND PRIX

GJIIA STD. $12,258.
GKIIA (LE) 12,988.
GPIIA (BRGM.) 13,708.
(GM "G" BODY)
19/24 MPG (V6)

BL81H (GM "B" BODY) 116" WB 5.0 L V8 (307 CID) 16/24 MPG

NEW PONTIAC BONNEVILLE →
WE BUILD EXCITEMENT

WITH FRONT-WHEEL DRIVE

3.8 L V6
110-120 MPH

BONNEVILLE TOTALLY RESTYLED

USES GM "H" BODY

new 110.8" WB

new AUTOMATIC SAFETY BELT SYSTEM FOR DRIVER AND RT. FRONT PASSENGER STD. ON BONNEVILLE AFTER. NOV., 1986 (AND ON GR. AM AFTER JAN., 1987)

HZ513

BONNEVILLE LE
$15,341.

AIR CONDITIONING IS STD. EQUIPMENT ON BONNEVILLE.

269

PONTIAC

GRAND AM = 16/36 MPG with
2.5 L 4 and
AUTO. TR.

4 DR.
$11,634.
NE51U

RETURN OF THE
LE MANS →
NOW
MFD. IN KOREA BY
DAEWOO.
(REPLACES
1000)

SEDAN
$8215.
TN516

AEROCOUPE TN116
$7615.

NW11M
$14,434.

GRAND AM SE

(SE HAS TURBO 4, POWER DOOR LOCKS,
P215/60R14 GOODYEAR EAGLE GT+4 TIRES)

(LE MANS
IS ONLY
FOREIGN-MADE MODEL OF
PONTIAC)

88

BRAND NEW

99.2" WB
98 CID 4
(74 HP @ 5200 RPM)
5 SP. TRANS.
(A/T AVAIL.)
13-GAL. FUEL TANK

(SUNBIRD, 6000, BONNEVILLE SERIES
AND SAFARI WAGON ALSO AVAIL.)

GRAND PRIX

(TOTALLY RESTYLED)
173 CID V6 (130 HP @ 4800 RPM)

WP11W
SE COUPE $15,679.
(ILLUSTRATED)

INTERIOR VIEWS

DASH

WJ11W
COUPE $13,744.

WK11W
LE COUPE
$14,444.

new 107.6" WB

P215/65R15
GOODYEAR TIRES
(EAGLE GT+4)

MOTOR TREND'S
CAR OF THE YEAR

We Build Excitement

PONTIAC

TR51K SE 4 DR.
$9744.

99.2" WB

LE MANS

1.6 L 4 (74 HP)
2.0 L 4 (95 HP)

SE

FRONT DETAILS

22/40 MPG

(LOWEST-PRICED MODEL IS TX216
"VALUE LEADER" 2 DR.
AEROCOUPE = $6714.)

STANDARD WHEELS:

$9464.

TS 21K
"AERO COUPE"
(FASTBACK)
LE MANS
GSE
New

GSE

89

LeMans' semi-independent rear suspension is simple, sturdy, and leaves a low load floor. The transverse beam "twists" to glide over bumps and through potholes, while the 18 mm stabilizer bar resists body roll.

SUNBIRD
20/36 MPG
SE

JB51K SED.
$11,072.
LE

JB11K LE CPE.

$10,972.

SUNBIRD LE

JD11K SE CPE.
$11,222.

FRONT
END
OF
GT
CVT.
JU 31M
$18,414.

271 SUNBIRD GT INTERIOR

Bonneville LE
HX51C

LE

PONTIAC

18/28 MPG

$15,334.

3.8 L "3800 SFI"
V6 (165 HP)

$17,704.

BONNEVILLE SERIES

SSE

(SSE INTRO.
IN 1988
MODEL YR.)

SE   HZ51C

Choose the available UT4 Delco sound system
and Pontiac reinvents the wheel. Not only are function
controls duplicated on the hub, but so are heating and
air conditioning adjustments.

HY51C

A gear-driven balance shaft in the
LE's 3800 SFI V6 rotates at crank
speed, but in the *opposite* direction
to help eliminate unbalance before it
happens. When it comes to engines,
there are no "good vibrations."

BONNEVILLE WHEELS

89

STANDARD AND AVAILABLE WHEELS:

BONNEVILLE SSE
AND
INTERIOR

ANTI-LOCK BRAKES STD. ON SSE

$23,404.

SAFARI
INTERIOR

STD. WHEEL
COVER (L.)
(WIRE
OPT.)

WAGON

BL 81 Y
(FINAL
PONTIAC
SAFARI
WAG.)

SAFARI
WAGON
17/24
MPG

"Understressed" is an understatement for Safari's
5.0L 4-bbl V8 and its 255 lbs-ft of torque. It makes cargo
a going proposition.

KEY TO BONNEVILLE WHLS.

(L to R):
Aero-Torque 14" wheel covers on 6"-wide wheels. Standard on LE.
Diamond-Spoke 15" x 6" aluminum sport wheels. Available on LE and SE.
Tri-Port 15" x 6" cast aluminum wheels. Standard on SE.
SSE Specific Aero-Lite 16" x 7" cast aluminum wheels. Standard on SSE.

$16,164.

273

LE SEDAN (FRONT END)

22/40 MPG (VARIES WITH POWERTRAIN USED)

PONTIAC
LE MANS

4 CYL (1.6 OR 2.0 L) 74 OR 96 HP

98 OR 121 CID

LE MANS DASH (OTHER GAUGE CHOICES AVAIL., BUT STD. DASHBOARDS SHOWN)

TN516

SUNBIRD DASH

LE MANS LE AEROCOUPE TN116 (ABOVE)

21/36 MPG

SUNBIRD

4 OR TURBO 4

SUNBIRD LE CONV'T. ALSO AVAIL. 21/33 MPG

SUNBIRD SE $11230.

NEW TRANS SPORT MINIVAN AVAIL. $16,300. UP

JD11K

SUNBIRD LE JB51K

$10825. ($15534., CONV'T.)

NV11U

GRAND AM LE NV11U

GRAND AM 3 DIFF. 4 CYL. ENGS. AVAIL.

GRAND AM LE $12229.

13.6 GAL. FUEL TANK 23/37 MPG (VARIES WITH POWERTRAIN USED)

$12229.

AEB1W

6000 DASH (OPT. GAUGES ABOVE)

6000 V6 SE

6000 LE $14064.

$18959.

AEB1W

AG51W 19/31 MPG

GRAND PRIX DASH

90

LIGHT-BAR GRILLE ON G.P. STE

GRAND PRIX LE SEDAN

GRAND PRIX SE V6

$15019.

NEW SPOILER REPL. LUGGAGE RACK ON 1990 BONNEVILLE SE

BONNEVILLE DASH

BONNEVILLE SSE $24499.

19649.

HZ513

BONNEVILLE

110.8" WB 18/27 MPG

274

3.8L 231 CID V6 (165 HP @ 5200 RPM)

HY513

SUNDANCE DASH

(RELIANT DISCONT'D.)
SUNDANCE.

$10585 COUPE

$10785. SEDAN

93, 100 OR 150 HP

PLYMOUTH
SATISFY THE CUSTOMER

XP28D

Sundance

135 OR 153 CID 4 OR 4 TURBO

20/32 MPG (EPA)

LASER with 92, 135 OR 190 HP. (107 OR 122 CID 4 OR TURB. 4)

4-CYL. LASER ENGINE

THE NEW 1990 PLYMOUTH LASER

AVAIL. WHEEL

LASERS
LIFTBACK CS34T $11309.
RS LIFTBK. CS44T $12354.
RS TURBO $14359. CS 44J

LASER IS MADE IN JAPAN BY MITSUBISHI

LASER DASH

90

LASER has 15.9 GAL. TANK, 97.2" WB 22/32 MPG (EPA)

IN CHRYSLER LINE FROM 1984 TO 1986 LASER RETURNS IN 1990 PLYMOUTH LINE.

ACCLAIM LX DASH

GRAND VOYAGER w. LONG 119" WB

UNEXPECTED PRICE:
The new Plymouth Laser.
$10,397 starting price.

PERFORMANCE:
Plymouth Laser RS Turbo.
16-valve intercooled turbo.
190 horsepower.
0-60 in 6.6 seconds.
$13,394 as shown.

VOYAGER 2WD 18/28 MPG EPA (4) 18/24 MPG EPA (V6)

(4-DR. ONLY)

ACCLAIM
STD. = $12,318.
LE = 13,626.
(4 CYL., TURBO 4, OR V6)
LX = $15,064. (V6)

21/32 MPG (EPA)

SE (K413) $15536.
LE (K513) 16862. (ILLUSTR.)
112" WB VOYAGER (4 OR V6)
AVAIL., FROM $13095.

PONTIAC FIERO *(1984-1988)*

TRUNK IS IN BACK OF MID-ENGINE CMPT.

"ENDURAFLEX" FIBERGLASS BODY PANELS ATTACHED TO STEEL FRAME

ALTERNATE WHEEL CHOICES

DISC BRAKES

POP-UP CONCEALED HEADLIGHTS

93.4" WHEELBASE

MID 4 CYL. ENGINE MOUNTED IN BACK OF FRONT SEAT.

151 CID
2.5 L

NEW 84 COUPES ONLY

V.I.N.= 1G2A --- RXE UP

10.2 GAL. FUEL TANK
MPG : 40 HWY, 26-27 CITY, EPA

E37 — $8431.
M37 SPORT— 9244.
F37 "SE"— $10,344.

INSTR. PANEL

EMBLEM

105 MPH

Fiero's mid-engine layout, the first for an American car.

PONTIAC FIERO

Fiero

SE DASH ('86)

SPORT COUPE $9740. ('85) PM37R

(ONLY CAR TO USE GM "P" BODY)

SE ('85)

GT IS **NEW** FOR 1985.

GT 125 MPH (1985) 123 " (1986)

('85)

GT EMBLEM

Fiero GT

PG379 $12,590. ('85)

GT SPOILER REAR ↘

V.I.N.
(1985)
1G2 ( )-F-#
(1986)
1G2 ( )-G-#
(1987)
1G2 ( )-H-#
(1988)
(1G or KL)2
( )-J-#
(INDIVIDUAL BODY MODEL NUMBERS APPEAR IN BLANK PARENTHESES)

85-88 GT

(LARGER 12-GAL. FUEL TANKS STD. IN 1987)

OTHER 1985 MODELS = PE37R CPE. $8927.
→ PM37R SPT. CPE.   9740.
→ PF37R SE CPE.   10,740.

INTERIOR VIEWS (GT, '85)

1986	PE37R CPE.	$9381.
	PM37R SPT. CPE	10,234.
	PF37R SE CPE.	11,380.
	PG979 GT CPE.	13,710.
1987	PE11R CPE.	9231.
	PM11R SPT. CPE.	10,799.
	PF11R SE CPE.	12,049.
	PG119 GT CPE.	14,299.
1988	PE11R CPE. (4)	9809.
	PE119 FORMULA CPE. (V6) (125 MPH)	11,809.
	PG119 GT CPE. (V6)	$14,809.

V6 ENGINE   ('85)

FIERO GT

$14,809. ('88)

WITH 2.8 L V6 HP INCREASED TO 135 FOR 1988.

FINAL 1988 MODEL ↘

An all-new suspension, a whole new feel for the road! ↘

(DISCONTINUED AUG., 1988)

Wide, light, rugged Diamond-Spoke cast aluminum wheels carry meaty 15" Eagle GT+4 radials. The rear rubber is even wider than the front.

5-SP. TRANS. AVAIL. 1987 and 1988

WE BUILD EXCITEMENT

(MECHANICALLY SIMILAR TO CHEVROLET CAMARO)

Pontiac

FIREBIRD

(SINCE 1967)

108.2" WB

81

V.I.N. STARTS WITH 1G2A, INCLUDES —0B (—)

2T87 **ESPRIT** (FINAL YEAR) $8657.

2V87 **FORMULA** $8867.

231 cid V6 (115 HP)

2987 STD. COUPE $8262.

OR 305 cid V8 (301, 265 cid AVAIL.) (120 -210 HP)

2W87 **TRANS AM** $9335.↓

INSTRUMENT PANEL

205 OR 225/70R × 15 TIRES

PONTIAC ▼ NOW THE EXCITEMENT REALLY BEGINS

W87 **TRANS AM** $10,906.

82 RESTYLED

new SHORTER 101" WB

15 MPG (EPA, CITY)

new HATCHBACK BODIES

new 4 CYL. (151 cid) ENG. AVAIL. ALSO.

REAR SPOILER

COWL

P205/70R 14 TIRES

278

S87 STD. COUPE
$9692.

PONTIAC
new 151 CID 4 OR
173 CID V6,
305 CID V8

FIREBIRD

LEATHER
SEATS
(W. VINYL
BOLSTERS)
AVAIL. →

New

One grip of the standard Formula steering wheel and you'll feel the excitement of Pontiac's new Trans Am for 1982. (Available Viscount seats shown.)

X87 **S/E** →
$11,196.

TRANS AM w. OPT.
T-BAR ROOF

24
MPG
(EPA)

14 GALLON
FUEL
TANK

82

V.I.N. INCLUDES
877 (-) C (-)

TRANS AM

4 CYL.
24 MPG
(EPA)

W87 **TRANS AM** $11,942.

DASH

V.I.N.
INCLUDES
-87 (-)
XD (-)-

REAR

EFI 151 CID 4
(90 HP)
173 CID V6 (105 HP)
(H.O. V6 AVAIL.)
305 CID V8
(105 HP IN
CFI VERSION)

RECARO SEATS AVAIL.
14 GAL. FUEL TANK

83

S87 STD. COUPE
$10,225.

X87 S/E COUPE
$11,768.

195/75R14 TIRES
(205/70R14, S/E, TA)

V8
15 MPG
(EPA)

PONTIAC FIREBIRD

When you're out making night moves, new orange lighted instrument graphics will help you keep track of your Firebird's vital statistics.

This sophisticated 2.8 liter High Output V-6 charges Firebird S/E with 125 eager horses.

(107 OR 125 HP 173 CID V6 ALSO AVAIL.)

WE BUILD EXCITEMENT

S87E STD.

$10,380. (V6)

($8795. ADV. PRICE W. 151 CID 4)

S/E X87E $12,200.

151 CID 4 HAS 92 HP.

84

V.I.N. INCLUDES -87HXE-

195/75 R 14 OR 205/70 R 14 TIRES

W87E TRANS AM $12,250.

5.0 L (305 CID) V8 (150 OR 190 HP)

280

W87 TRANS AM
$12,874.

TRANS AM HAS AVAIL.
P245/50 VR16
UNIDIRECTIONAL
TIRES.

987
STD. COUPE
$10,553.

135 MPH

TRANS AM

$12,874.

195/75R14, P205 70R14,
P215/65 R15 TIRES ALSO

85

S/E $12,618.
(X87)

FLOOR
CONSOLE

151 CID 4 (88 HP),
173 CID V6, 305 CID V8 (150 HP) (205 HP w. EFI)

V.I.N.=
1G2
(FS87S)
–F–#

TRANS AM

305 CID V8
(210 HP @
4400 RPM)

PANEL

WE BUILD EXCITEMENT

281

INTERIOR (TRANS AM)

PONTIAC FIREBIRD

FINAL S/E $13,624.
FX87S

STD. COUPE $11,258.
FS872

2.5 L "TECH 4" ENG. AVAIL. (88 or 92 HP)

190 HP V8

86
new HIGH-UP 3RD BRAKE LIGHT (see arrow)

ENGINES AVAIL.
2.5 L "TECH 4" (ILLUSTR.) 4 CYL. (88 HP @ 4400 RPM)
2.8 L V6 (130 - 140 HP)
5.0 L V8 (150 - 170 HP)
(ALSO "HO" HIGH OUTPUT VERSIONS of 5.0 L V8 with 190 HP @ 4400 or 205 @ 4200 RPM)

INTERIOR

FW87H
TRANS AM
14,024.

SHOWN WITH OPTIONAL (EXTRA COST) T-BAR ROOF

V.I.N. = 1G2 (FS872) - G - #

2 BASIC MODELS IN 1987. (S/E DISCONTINUED)

87
2.8 L V6 (135 HP)
5.0 L V8 (205 HP) or Corvette
5.7 L V8 (210 HP) (ALL WITH MULTI-PORT FUEL INJECTION)

FS2I9   STD. CPE.
$12,038.

FW21H
TRANS AM
$14,938.
(145-MPH GTA PKG. AVAIL.; ALSO 305 or 350 CID EFI V8s)

FORMULA RETURNS AS OPTION PKG.

note "FORMULA 350" on LOWER EDGE OF DOOR
134 MPH (GM "F" BODY)

205 HP EFI HI-OUTPUT V8

V.I.N. = 1G2 (FS2I9) - H - #

282

88-90

STD. CPE. (w. 2.8 L V6)   STD.
$12,798. ('88) FS2/S   INTERIOR →
$13,703. ('89) "
$13,079. ('90)
FS
23S

V.I.N. (1988) (IG or KL) 2 (FS2/S)-J-#
(1989) (IG2 or KL2)(FS2/S)-K-#
(1990)(IG or KL) 2 (FS23S)- L -#

FORMULA $13,798. ('88) FS21E
$14,878. ('89) "
FS23H
15564.
('90)

$17464. ('90)

TRANS AM
$15,798. ('88) FW21E
$16,928. ('89) "

5.0 L
V8
(IN
FORMULA,
TRANS AM)
AVAIL. WITH
170, 190, 215 OR
225 HP.

1989 EXAMPLES SHOWN, UNLESS OTHERWISE INDICATED.

STANDARD AND AVAILABLE WHEELS:

(L to R):
Diamond-Spoke 16" x 8" aluminum wheels. Standard on GTA. Available on Trans Am.
Deep-Dish 15" x 7" Hi-Tech Turbo aluminum wheels. Standard on Coupe and Trans Am.
Deep-Dish 16" x 8" Hi-Tech Turbo aluminum wheels. Standard on Formula.

2.8 L V6 ENG.
(18/27 MPG
EPA, 1990)

(16/26 MPG EPA, 1990
WITH V8)

DISC BRAKE DETAIL

('88)

TRANS AM GTA

$19,713. ('88)
FW21F

$20,778. ('89)

(w. 5.7 L V8,
225 HP)
$23,759. ('90)
FW23J

We Build Excitement

283

PONTIAC PHOENIX

ENGINEERED WITH FRONT-WHEEL DRIVE
Phoenix offers a choice of L4 or V-6

(1977 — 1984)

GM
MARK OF EXCELLENCE

SUNROOF OPT.

2Y37 COUPE $7714.

BUMPER GUARDS AVAIL.

2Y68 5-DR. SEDAN $7905.

STD. SERIES V.I.N. = 1G2AY3750B (-) 10000/ UP

104.9" WB

151 CID 4 (90 HP) OR 173 CID V6 (115 HP)

PLUS PONTIAC'S NEW EFFICIENCY SYSTEM, INCLUDING GM'S COMPUTER COMMAND CONTROL
A computer adjusts the air/fuel mixture in the carburetor

INTERIOR

81

MPG
More PONTIAC Know-How TO THE Gallon

LJ 2Z68 5-DR. SEDAN $8376. (2Z37 CPE. 8/85.)
LJ V.I.N.= 1G2AZ350B(-) 10000/ UP

ALL SEDANS ARE HATCH-BACKS.

SEDAN and COUPE WITH $449. "SJ" OPTION = (BLACKED-OUT SIDE-PILLARS, SPECIAL TRIM PKG., ETC.

AVAILABLE

P185/80R x 13 TIRES

32 HWY. EST. 22 EPA EST. MPG

284

PHOENIX: PONTIAC'S 1981 "X" CAR

V.I.N. (81D.) IG2AY37ROC (-) 000001 UP
(LJ) IG2AZ37ROC " "
(SJ) IG2AT37ROC " "

V6

PONTIAC PHOENIX

1982 PHOENIX SJ Pontiac puts some punch into front-wheel drive! A new High Output 2.8 liter V-6 with cold air induction and free-flow exhaust puts some real excitement into your driving! A standard four-on-the-floor keeps you on top of the action.

LJ
$9097.

PADDED REAR QUARTERS

26 MPG (EPA) 14 GAL. FUEL TK.
P185/80R13 TIRES (STD., LJ)

4 CYL. and V6 AS IN '81

82

Phoenix Hatchback is ready to play when you are!

$8793. (ABOVE)

Available luxury notchback seats (standard on Phoenix LJ) add an extra touch of richness that helps make Phoenix as comfortable as it is beautiful.

STD.	Y37C COUPE	$8585
	Y68C HATCHBACK	8793
LJ	Z37C COUPE	9097
	Z68C HATCHBACK	9279
SJ	T37C COUPE	10,148
	T68C HATCHBACK	10,309

DASH

BLACK WINDOW TRIM, 2-TONE PAINT ON SJ →

SJ

PHOENIX SJ

SJ
$10,148.

2 VIEWS OF SJ COUPE ↙

SJ DASH and SPORT* STEERING WHEEL
205/70R13 TIRES ON SJ
* FORMULA

High output excitement characterizes this road-ready street machine! With an available rear deck spoiler to complete the SJ Coupe scene!

Slick up your Phoenix with available Delco-GM AM/FM stereo radio and cassette tape, electric rear window defogger and rally gages (standard on Phoenix SJ).

PONTIAC **NOW THE EXCITEMENT BEGINS**

285

To personalize your Phoenix, order available rally gages with tach, Delco-GM AM/FM stereo cassette and air conditioning, all operating out of the racy instrument panel.

151 CID EFI 4 (90 HP)
OR 173 CID V6
(115 HP; H.O.
135 HP)

PONTIAC

PHOENIX

Z37 LJ CPE.
$9219.
(STD.,
$8672.)

1983 PHOENIX LJ

SJ and WHEEL

83

new GRILLE

SJ CPE.
$10,381.

V.I.N.
(STD.) 1G2AY37
(-) XD (-) 000001 UP
(LJ) 1G2AZ37 (-) XD (-) 000001 UP
(SJ) 1G2AT37 " " "

| 27 MPG EPA (4) |
| 22 MPG EPA (V6) |

Z68 LJ HTCHBK.
$9428.

PONTIAC • **WE BUILD EXCITEMENT**

(STD. CPE. FROM $8830.) (LE REPLACES LJ)

FORMULA STEER. WHEEL (OPT.) →

LE $9556.

151 CID 4
(92 HP)
OR
173 CID V6
(112 OR
130 HP)

new INTERIOR TRIM, SEATS and HEADRESTS

V.I.N. FROM =
1G2AY37ZXE (STD.)
1G2AZ37ZE (LE)

1G2AT37ZE (SE)

84

FINAL YEAR

After dark, the Phoenix instrument panel glows bright with new optically soothing orange lighting.

SE
(REPLACES SJ)

2.8 L
H.O.
V6

(DISCONTINUED AFTER 1984)

286